FLORIDA STATE
UNIVERSITY LIBRARIES

JUN 0 1 2001

TALLAHASSEE, FLORIDA

IRAQ – PRIMUS INTER PARIAHS

Also by Geoff Simons

* from the same publishers

Iraq – Primus Inter Pariahs

A Crisis Chronology, 1997–98

Geoff Simons

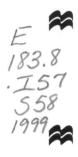

First published in Great Britain 1999 by
MACMILLAN PRESS LTD
Houndmills, Basingstoke, Hampshire RG21 6XS and London
Companies and representatives throughout the world

A catalogue record for this book is available from the British Library.

ISBN 0–333–74114–5

First published in the United States of America 1999 by
ST. MARTIN'S PRESS, INC.,
Scholarly and Reference Division,
175 Fifth Avenue, New York, N.Y. 10010

ISBN 0–312–22341–2

Library of Congress Cataloging-in-Publication Data
Simons, G. L. (Geoffrey Leslie), 1939–
Iraq – primus inter pariahs : a crisis chronology, 1997–98 / Geoff
Simons.
   p.   cm.
Includes bibliographical references and index.
ISBN 0–312–22341–2 (cloth)
1. United States—Foreign relations—Iraq—Chronology.   2. Iraq–
–Foreign relations—United States—Chronology.   3. Disarmament–
–Iraq—Chronology.   I. Title.
E183.8.I57S58   1999
327.730567—dc21   99–17487
                                                              CIP

© Geoff Simons 1999

All rights reserved. No reproduction, copy or transmission of this publication may be made without written permission.

No paragraph of this publication may be reproduced, copied or transmitted save with written permission or in accordance with the provisions of the Copyright, Designs and Patents Act 1988, or under the terms of any licence permitting limited copying issued by the Copyright Licensing Agency, 90 Tottenham Court Road, London W1P 9HE.

Any person who does any unauthorised act in relation to this publication may be liable to criminal prosecution and civil claims for damages.

The author has asserted his right to be identified as the author of this work in accordance with the Copyright, Designs and Patents Act 1988.

This book is printed on paper suitable for recycling and made from fully managed and sustained forest sources.

10   9   8   7   6   5   4   3   2   1
08   07   06   05   04   03   02   01   00   99

Printed and bound in Great Britain by
Antony Rowe Ltd, Chippenham, Wiltshire

To Natasha

Contents

List of Tables

List of Figures

Preface

In writing and researching this book, I have become increasingly aware of aspects of the 1997/8 US/Iraq crisis that deserve particular attention. We need to remember that the disputes over UN weapons inspections have occurred in the context of an Iraq that is being subjected to a merciless genocide.

By 1998, about one million Iraqi children, for example, had died through starvation and disease directly attributable to the US-led sanctions regime. The posture of the Iraq government through the period of the crisis can only be understood in this context.

On 18 March 1998 Martin Thomas, a nursing student at Chelmsford's Anglia Polytechnic University in England, was arrested and questioned for four hours in London for attempting to take children's antibiotics to Iraq. He faced the possibility of five years' imprisonment. In April Felicity Arbuthnot, journalist and Middle East expert, took medicine to Iraq for a dying surgeon. Later she planned to take braille books for blind Iraqis. She too faced the possibility of five years in jail.

In the United States the aid worker Kathy Kelly, of the charity Voices in the Wilderness, has been informed by the US Treasury Department that if she collected medicines and toys in America, and conveyed them to Iraq for dying children, she would face a fine of up to $1 million and 12 years in jail.

This is the point that the United States and Britain have reached – murderous weapons are shipped to tyrannical regimes (such as Indonesia and Saudi Arabia) to aid torture, repression and massacre; while courageous aid workers are harassed, threatened with fines and imprisonment, for attempting to relieve the suffering of dying Iraqi children.

The present book should be read with these facts in mind.

GEOFF SIMONS

Acknowledgements

Various people, either through deliberate contribution or unknowingly, provided information for this book. I am particularly grateful to two who supplied invaluable newspapers, reports, UN resolutions and other documentation: Felicity Arbuthnot, journalist and Middle East expert; and Alexandra McLeod, Librarian at the United Nations Information Centre, London.

I am grateful also to Amnesty International for supplying reports that bear directly on the human-rights situation in the United States; and to the many journalists who, sometimes in danger or in harrowing circumstances, have worked to inform people about the conditions afflicting the civilian population of Iraq.

I applaud the many people who are striving, against pressures from Washington and London, to relieve the suffering of the helpless men, women and children of Iraq, today despairing under comprehensive siege by a superpower. The stalwart activists in this field include: Felicity Arbuthnot, George Galloway, MP, Hugh Stephens, Ramsey Clark, Sabah Al-Mukhtar, Kathy Kelly and many others.

Christine Simons helped with research and in many other ways.

GEOFF SIMONS
September 1998

Acknowledgements

Introduction

The 1997/8 Iraq crisis, when a new war was averted at the last minute, was not essentially a crisis between Iraq and the United Nations but between Iraq and the United States. Washington exploited its vast propaganda resources in a vain attempt to demonstrate that the so-called 'international community' supported the American countdown to war. It was easy to show that the Iraqi authorities were in technical breach of Security Council Resolution 687 (1991) in their objection to the composition of the UNSCOM teams and in blocking UNSCOM inspection of 'sensitive sites' in Iraq.

At the same time there was ample evidence to demonstrate that UNSCOM staff were often needlessly provocative, that the Iraqi authorities had shown a substantial degree of co-operation over seven years, and that *the Americans, having orchestrated terrorist plots against the Iraqi leadership and having launched unilateral bombing strikes against Iraq, had an enduring espionage interest in crawling over as many sensitive Iraqi sites as possible.* Throughout the 1997/8 crisis many countries urged Baghdad to comply with all the terms of Resolution 687; none, apart from a predictably supine Britain, shared the American enthusiasm for Gulf War II as a response to the relatively minor Iraqi derelictions.

It was plain also that there was growing international awareness of the appalling effects of the US-led economic siege of the helpless Iraqi people. By 1998 around one million Iraqi children had perished through starvation and preventable disease as a direct result of the embargo. Saddam Hussein was being routinely condemned by Western propagandists for starting the 1980–8 Iran–Iraq War (when Saddam was funded by Kuwait and Saudi Arabia, armed by Russia and the West, and supported by the US as an active belligerent in the Gulf), for invading Kuwait in 1990 (which the United States had encouraged[1]), and for killing *thousands* of his own people in the infamous chemical attack on Halabja. At the same time the United States was knowingly causing *millions* of casualties among the innocent civilian population of Iraq. The obvious brutalities of Saddam Hussein are rightly deplored as gross violations of human rights. How ironic that the morally posturing United States has caused vastly more suffering among the helpless men, women and children of Iraq than Saddam ever managed to accomplish.

This book is intended in part to encourage a candid appraisal of the ethical status of the United States during the 1997/8 crisis. What are Washington's moral credentials for acting as judge, jury and executioner? Is the United States ethically fit to brand this, that or the other country a

'pariah state'? *Quis iudicabit ipsos iudices?* (Who is to judge the judges?).
Chapter 1 poses the question as to whether the United States, militarily
unassailable, is morally equipped to define the ethical categories from which
the political schemes with global consequences so naturally flow. Our
response to such considerations should be allowed to inform our interpretation of the 1997/8 crisis that threatened a new and devastating war, with
untold consequences.

We do well to remember details of the historical record. Over decades the
American Central Intelligence Agency (CIA) developed as a torture and
assassination bureau, active in dozens of countries around the world.[2] It
helped to mount a *coup d'état* in Iraq in 1963, which in turn helped to launch
the career of Saddam Hussein; in Vietnam, via the horrors of the Phoenix
Program, it arranged the torture and murder of thousands of innocent peasants; it provided espionage information to the South African authorities
which led to the 27-year-long incarceration of Nelson Mandela; and in 1990s
Iraq it strived, so far in vain, to accomplish the assassination of the Iraqi
leadership. Saddam's abuses are properly advertised in the West but less
attention is given to the crimes committed by Christian democracies. Thus,
as one example, US troops massacred more than one thousand men, women
and children in Somalia in 1993,[3] a crime for which no American soldier was
disciplined. US staff have been used to train the torturers of Latin America,
as revealed by Penny Lernoux, Noam Chomsky and many others.[4] At the
same time Washington works to disguise the crimes of its allies, proxy states
and those countries where there is perceived commercial advantage to the
United States. Thus Washington bitterly opposed the publicity given to the
Israeli massacre of Lebanese civilians in the Qana refugee camp in 1996,[5]
could not support a UN human-rights resolution on China in 1998,[6] and continues to consort with the Taliban abusers and torturers in Afghanistan.[7]

The 1997/8 crisis was supposedly linked to Iraq's failure to observe the
demands of international law (as enshrined in particular in Resolution 687).
Yet Washington habitually regards the strictures and constraints of international law with cavalier disdain.[8] The United States routinely ignores the
resounding annual votes in the UN General Assembly condemning the US
economic blockade of Cuba, just as it ignores any rulings of the International
Court of Justice at The Hague (the World Court) which Washington finds
uncongenial. It ignored the World Court judgement that it should pay compensation for its 1980s terrorism against Nicaragua; just as in 1998 it ignored
the World Court ruling that the 1971 Montreal Convention should be
observed in the Lockerbie case; and the World Court ruling that it would be
illegal to execute Angel Francisco Bread, a Paraguayan, in the state of
Virginia.[9]

Chapter 2 profiles aspects of the American human-rights record, both
domestically and internationally. Such considerations are important in any

assessment of American judgements about other states, of American policies in general, and of the 1997/8 crisis in particular.

It is important also to appreciate that the United States and Britain have no *principled* difficulty with the character and opportunism of Saddam Hussein (just as other brutal dictators – Marcos, Noriega, Mobutu, Rhee, Batista, Somoza *inter alia* – have served Western strategic interests over decades). Saddam helped the CIA in his early days, and was a darling of the West, supported as a tool for taming the Iranian ayatollahs, through the 1980s. Chapter 3 profiles the evolution of Saddam Hussein from 'darling' to 'demon', presents aspects of the weapons question, and outlines the sanctions situation.

Much of the 1997/8 crisis derived from America's proclaimed enthusiasm for detecting and destroying Iraq's so-called 'weapons of mass destruction' – as if the West had not been responsible for Saddam's weapons potential and would in no way, as a matter of ethical judgement, carry out comparable weapons development and production. There is no doubt that the UNSCOM inspectors have often been harassed and obstructed by Iraqi officials – hardly surprising in view of the fact that a proud Arab people were being forced to suffer gross erosions of their national sovereignty while at the same time the United Nations, under US/UK prompting, was orchestrating a sanctions-caused genocide of the Iraqi people. At the same time, US officials, in unguarded moments, were prepared to comment that any Iraqi weapons posed no danger to neighbouring states.[10]

The background context to the crisis should be appreciated also. For example, it is useful to recall:

- that the West (among others) supplied Iraq with weapons expertise, equipment, chemicals, biological cultures, etc.;[11]

- that the United States probably used biological weapons in Korea,[12] and used chemical weapons in Vietnam;

- that 'American scientists tested humans with mustard gas, other chemical agents, exposed others to radiation tests, and still others to a variety of pathogens without the subjects' knowledge or consent.'[13]

The United States and Britain thus stand condemned for perpetrating many of the practices that have contributed to the demonisation of Saddam Hussein. Consider, for example, that in the United States retarded boys have been used in radiation experiments,[14] that US tests on unsuspecting citizens have been conducted over a period of years,[15] that the British Ministry of Defence has admitted 40 years of human radiation tests,[16] that Britain carried out secret biological warfare tests off Caribbean islands and told officials to lie,[17] that similar tests were carried out in London,[18] and that the

United States and Britain carried out secret mustard gas experiments on about 2000 Australian servicemen.[19] Such examples, which could easily be extended, suggest that current US/UK indignation at Iraqi behaviour is strategically contrived rather than a matter of principled objection. Of course, Washington and London did not invade Kuwait (only Korea, Vietnam, China, Honduras, Guatemala, the Dominican Republic, El Salvador, Nicaragua, Panama, Grenada, Cuba, Lebanon, Libya, Somalia, Haiti, etc.), so perhaps the comparisons do not stand.

It is important also to remember that behind all the fabricated indignation of unprincipled Western pundits and politicians the genocidal sanctions remain in place, achieving their dreadful daily, monthly, yearly toll of despair, disease and death. I cannot do better than quote from the Preface of an impressively researched book, clearly written with a burning sense of outrage:

> The US-contrived economic siege of Iraq has now lasted well over seven years ... with, according to all the estimates, millions of casualties – perhaps 2,000,000 dead through starvation and disease, more than half of them children, and many millions more emaciated, traumatised, sick, dying ...

> The United States is the conscious architect of this years-long genocide. Knowingly, with a cruel and cynical resolve, US officials work hard to withhold relief from a starving and diseased people ...

> Procrastination or veto in the Sanctions Committee, harassment of aid workers, threat (of up to $1 million fines and 12 years in jail) to American citizens taking medicines and toys to dying infants – these are some of the tools sanctioned by an American government committed to the slow extermination of a people ... [20]

Any attempt to evaluate the behaviour of Iraq through the period of the 1997/8 crisis should take fully into account what the civilian population is being forced to endure, how *'The old and the sick, emaciated pregnant women, the kwashiorkor children, grossly under-weight babies with no chance of survival, the desperately weak and vulnerable ... are those most directly targeted for extinction by Washington.'*[21] Would the officials of any nation always act with courtesy and polite forbearance when forced to deal with the knowing murderers of their people?

Part II profiles the chronology of the 1997/8 crisis, with focus on the principal players in the unfolding drama, emphasising the constant US threat of war (in gross violation of Article 2(4) of the UN Charter) and how American 'diplomacy' was no more than the transparent attempt to dragoon erstwhile allies into support for the launching of Gulf War II.

In Part III the circumstances and character of the deal negotiated between Iraq and the UN Secretary-General Kofi Annan are described. Perhaps there is reason for hope in the remarkable circumstance that a single softly-spoken United Nations official, formerly viewed with suspicion by many as 'Washington's man', was able to arrest the vast momentum of the US military Establishment. But the story is not over. The sanctions are still in place; the UNSCOM prevarications continue as before; the children are still dying by the thousand; and in the United States, that unsullied land of Christian virtue, there are powerful men who will not sleep easy until Iraq is bombed again.

Afterword

The last sentence of the Introduction (above) was written in September 1998. Three months later, on 16 December, the United States and Britain began the most massive bombing campaign on Iraq since the 1991 Gulf War. For four nights of terror – screaming children, thousands of civilians suffering trauma, mutilation and death – the whole of a largely defenceless country came under comprehensive military attack. The US Navy launched more than 325 cruise missiles, the US Air Force nearly a hundred – twice as many cruise missiles as were launched during the whole of the 1991 Gulf War; in addition, American and British bombers flew 650 sorties, with the RAF Tornados dropping some fifty 2000lb bombs.

Few details of the munitions have yet become available but it is likely that depleted-uranium ordnance, known to leave a widespread radioactive residue, was again used. The soaring leukaemia and other cancer rates in Iraq, caused by US and British forces, would again be boosted. The celebrated journalist Maggie O'Kane has reported (*The Guardian*, 21 December 1998) the three-fold increase in the number of deformities in babies born to Iraqi mothers after the 1991 war: missing ears, missing fingers, stump-limbs, head-sized tumours and no heads at all (Dr Zenad Mohammed reported from a teaching hospital in Basra: 'August – we had three babies born with no heads ... in September we had six with no heads ... In October, one with no head, four with big heads and four with deformed limbs or other types of deformities').

After the four-night bombing onslaught the Western propagandists were keen to describe their successes. It was claimed that most of the targets were military and that the campaign had achieved its objectives. At the same time many reports of failures leaked through the propaganda shield. Thus after two nights of bombing only a tenth of 80 targets had been destroyed; of 27 anti-aircraft missile sites hit, only three were damaged; of five airfields attacked, none was destroyed. General Henry Shelton, chairman of the US Joint Chiefs of Staff, commented: 'We in fact have had some very good success with our strikes, but not all of them have gone exactly as planned' (*The Observer*, 20 December 1998). Some observers were asking how weapons-of-mass-destruction (WMD) sites could be targeted since even the UN weapons inspectors did not know whether they existed. And little attention was given to the total absence of UN Security Council authorisation for the bombing raids (three Permanent Members opposed) or to the fact that the crucial UN Resolution 687 allows Iraq to retain a military capacity (for example, Clause C 8(b) of 687 permits Iraq to retain missiles of less than 150 kilometre-range). Thus the United States and Britain were acting in comprehensive violation not only of the UN Charter in general but of the specific Security Council resolution that they were constantly quoting in justification.

Nor was much attention given to the wide range of *non*-military targets that had been hit either by accident or design. These included:

- the Hail Adel residential area (outskirts of Baghdad);
- the Baghdad Teaching Hospital;
- the main grain silo in Tikrit;
- the Basra oil refinery;
- the house of Saddam's daughter Hala in Baghdad;
- the Baath Baghdad Academic Institute;
- the Baghdad Museum of Natural History;
- the Tikrit Teaching Hospital;
- the Baghdad Ministry of Labour and Social Affairs (responsible for the distribution of food rations).

The US Pentagon had already predicted that 'as a medium-case scenario' 10,000 Iraqi civilians would be killed. In Saadoun Street, Baghdad, massed coffins described by Western journalists gave some indication of the accumulating civilian casualties. Tariq Aziz, the Iraqi deputy premier, subsequently reported fewer than a hundred military fatalities, with civilian casualties 'much, much higher'; after the bombing, Iraqi doctors in Baghdad were reporting hundreds of civilian casualties; and Nizar Hamdoon, the Iraqi UN ambassador, spoke on CNN's *Late Edition* (20 December 1998) of 'thousands' of civilian casualties throughout Iraq.

The US/UK pretext for this further bout of mass destruction and mass murder was the report prepared in early December by Richard Butler, head of the UN Special Commission (the UNSCOM inspectors). Butler was despised by many United Nations staff for his partisan truculence, had been criticised by UN Secretary-General Kofi Annan for his provocative behaviour, and had been dubbed a 'congenital liar' by a still-serving senior UN official in Iraq (in conversation with British Member of Parliament George Galloway). It was also known that Butler was conspiring with the Mossad secret service of Israel, dedicated to the overthrow of the Iraqi regime, and that he habitually leaked information to Washington before communicating with the UN Security Council.

The thin (10-page) Butler Report in fact covered some 300 site inspections with access hampered in only five cases. On the strength of this and other trivial items Washington, denying the UN Security Council its legitimate right to discuss the report before any action was undertaken, was now determined to wage war against a helpless people in circumstances where there would be no threat to US military personnel. The reasons, nothing to do with imaginary weapons of mass destruction, were obvious: munitions had to be expended to keep the arms factories working; missile, communications and other newly-developed systems needed to be tested 'in the field'; an impeachment debate had to be stymied, if at all possible; and it was useful to demonstrate yet again American military hegemony in the world.

On 11 December (*The Independent on Sunday*, 20 December 1998), or 13 December according to national security adviser Sandy Berger (*The Guardian*, 17 December 1998), details of the forthcoming Butler Report, nominally prepared for the UN authorities, were leaked to the White House to facilitate an American initiative before the Security Council would have any chance to respond. A US official was happy to record American intentions ('It was agreed that we'll set the timing, not the United Nations'); few observers doubted that UNSCOM was acting as a US agent. Thus when Kofi Annan attached a letter to the Butler Report, urging that Iraq should be given more time, the American response was immediate. Peter Burleigh, the US ambassador to the United Nations, described what happened to the letter of the UN Secretary-General: 'We tore it up' (*The Observer*, 20 December 1998). The bombing onslaught, denounced by three of the five Permanent Members of the UN Security Council, began a short time later.

The reaction throughout the world to the US/UK aggression was almost universal outrage. Sergei Lavrov, the Russian ambassador to the United Nations, declared that the crisis had been 'created artificially by the irresponsible acts of Richard Butler'; Qin Huasan of China judged that Butler had played a dishonourable role. President Yeltsin denounced the aggression as 'an act of state terrorism': 'The United States and Britain have crudely violated the UN Charter and generally accepted principles of international law'; Yevgeny Primakov, the Russian prime minister, described the raids as 'outrageous', and the Russian ambassadors were withdrawn from Washington and London. With some European states offering token support to Britain, France distanced itself from the aggression, and Italy urged an end to the bombing (observers noted that Prime Minister Blair, knowing of the planned attacks, had failed to inform his EU partners at the Vienna Summit, and that this grave omission had eroded British influence in Europe).

The Arab countries were either silent or hostile to the US/UK aggression. Ismat Abdel Meguid, secretary-general of the Arab League, denounced the raids as 'aggression' and condemned Richard Butler; a statement on behalf of Sheikh Zayed bin Sultan al-Nahyan, the ruler of the United Arab Emirates, referred to the 'terrible operation' as 'beyond comprehension and ... unacceptable'; Syria denounced the United States and Britain as guilty of 'flagrant aggression'; in Damascus thousands of demonstrators attacked the American embassy and a British cultural centre, with US guards firing tear gas at Syrians who scaled the embassy walls and tore down and burned the American flag while chanting 'All of us support you, our brothers in Iraq' and 'Aggression against Iraq is an aggression against Syria'; President Hosni Mubarak of Egypt demanded an end to the bombing raids, while 4000 students burned American and Israeli flags at Banha University, north of Cairo; some 3000 Palestinians, defying a ban from their leadership, demonstrated in support of Iraq; and in Beirut members of the Lebanese parliament joined hundreds of students demonstrating against the US/UK aggression. Even Kuwait, having allowed Tornado bombing flights from its territory, began to respond to the universal sense of outrage in the Arab world: after the aggression there was talk of a diplomatic row between Britain and Kuwait, with the possibility that the Tornados would be evicted from their Kuwaiti bases (*The Daily Telegraph*, 23 December 1998).

The US-led aggression had been condemned throughout the world (a British official admitted that the Tornados had been under American command), and even by leading observers nominally sympathetic to anti-Iraq policies. Thus General Sir Peter de la Billière, who had commanded British forces in the 1991 Gulf War, declared that the assault had strengthened Saddam and united the Islamic world against the West; and in the same vein Lord Healey, a former Labour defence secretary, affirmed that Britain's influence had been weakened throughout the world and that the air attacks were clearly unlawful: 'It is illegal to attack with bombs targets in a sovereign country without direct authorisation from the Security Council.'

In retrospect, the December aggression against Iraq may be seen as a watershed: if the United States and its British poodle can so flagrantly ignore the Security Council in order to wage war against a defenceless country, other states – Russia, China, France, the Islamic world, etc. – may have little compunction in ignoring the UN resolutions that nominally demand the maintenance of a genocidal sanctions regime *in perpetuity*. The United States routinely abuses, suborns and undermines the authority of the United Nations. Perhaps the main advantage of the cruel December aggression will be that the vast majority of the world's nations – opposed as they are to merciless sanctions – will find the humanity and the will to save the Iraqi people from yet more years of starvation and disease inflicted by the malign and arrogant strategists of the United States.

GEOFF SIMONS
24 December 1998

Part I
Pariah Politics

1 Who is to Judge?

In March 1998 evidence emerged that the United States regarded Iraq's alleged 'weapons of mass destruction' as *very ineffective*. Jim Larocco, the US ambassador to Kuwait, reportedly declared at an embassy meeting in early February that, considering the possibility of an Iraqi attack on Kuwait, there was no requirement for gas masks: 'No one at the American embassy has gas masks and the American embassy does not recommend any.' A principal reason for this attitude was that Iraq's 'biological and chemical warheads are very ineffective' – a judgement suggesting, according to Dr Julian Perry-Robinson, a senior fellow at the Science Policy Research Unit and an expert on Iraqi weapons, that the United States did not believe that Iraq was in a position to deliver its weapons.[1]

To anyone who was aware of the parlous state of Iraq's industry and social infrastructure, following the 1991 war and the long years of punitive economic sanctions, the Larocco revelation was unremarkable. In early 1998 Iraq was still being denied the opportunity to rebuild its industry, its population was starving and diseased, and no-one denied that the UN inspectors – though frequently obstructed by Iraqi officials – had succeeded in locating and destroying masses of military hardware. What *was* remarkable was that, while the United States knew that Iraqi weapons posed no significant threat to the Middle East and beyond, Western leaders were working hard to convey exactly the opposite message. Iraq, declared President Bill Clinton, Prime Minister Tony Blair, British Foreign Secretary Robin Cook *inter alia*, posed a threat to its neighbours and the region, indeed *to the entire world*. Cook, for instance, keen equally to proclaim his ethical sensitivities and to underwrite American war plans, repeatedly urged people to believe that the threat posed by Iraqi weapons was 'terrifyingly real'.

The contrast between the real world and political hyperbole is widely appreciated. Put simply, most politicians are well prepared to lie to credulous publics in order to further strategic plans. For their part the various publics, while proud of their worldliness in knowing that *politicians cannot be trusted*, nonetheless absorb enough propaganda to discourage any impulse to independent thought. In the case of Iraq there is now abundant evidence, for those who care to notice it, of the lies and distortions that provide spurious justification for the continuing US/UK punishment of the civilian population.[2] In this context it is important to note that the contrived propaganda has both particular and general features. In addition to the awesome power of Iraqi

3

weapons – able, we are told, to kill *every man, woman and child on earth* – we are constantly assured that Iraq, under the present regime, is a 'pariah state', a 'rogue state', a 'terrorist state'. It is useful to glance at why the United States deems it helpful to indulge in this particular form of political propaganda.

PARIAH POLITICS

One of the main roles of the *pariah*, as implicitly or explicitly assigned by others, is to reinforce the wider community's sense of its own virtue. To dub a person, a class, a race or a nation a 'pariah' necessarily assumes the relative perfidy of the labelled minority. Thus any attempt to understand the concept of the pariah (the individual or wider grouping) must address the broad judgemental context in which the labelling takes place.

The original usage of the term *pariah* was descriptive rather than pejorative, though the description implied substantial obligations of social role and status. In the Tamil country of Southern India the term *paraiyar* (plural of *paraiyan*) signals 'hereditary drummer' or 'those of the drum' (*parai*). Since drum skins are impure the *paraiyar* belong to the class of Untouchables, who traditionally supplied most of the domestics in European service, and had a monopoly of village bands.[3] English speakers in India wrongly came to regard *pariah* as synonymous with *Untouchable* (a much broader grouping) and, through the pressures of race and class, to invest the term with its pejorative content.

Individuals can be assigned pariah status to reinforce the communal sense of virtue and to provide a hedge against social anxiety. Thus the 'scab' worker, having betrayed group solidarity, can be 'sent to Coventry' in an industrial environment; just as the delinquent in Amish society can be subjected to a protracted 'shunning' until the time of proper repentance. Lepers and plague victims, stirring social anxieties, may be dubbed *pariahs*; as may released paedophiles and the mentally ill suddenly injected into an unsuspecting and resentful community. Castes, as with the *paraiyar* and other Untouchable groups, may be assigned a *de facto* and *de jure* social status; just as Jewish communities have traditionally been assigned a pariah image for race, religion, class and scapegoating reasons throughout history.[4]

In all these cases it is significant that the labelled pariah is in a relatively weak social and political position. The pariah does not choose to adopt the label: it is assigned by a broader community, a more powerful caste, a stronger nation. This implies that the assigning of pariah status to individual, group or nation has much more to do with the prevailing power relations – with all the social and political vested interest that this implies – than with any transparently obvious ethical propriety. In short, the pariah may or may not deserve the label. Who is to say? The 'pariah individual' and the 'pariah state' may be wrongly, hypocritically or maliciously labelled. Who is to judge?

WHO IS TO JUDGE?

It is easy to think of pariahs who were unjustly labelled by their communities. Today we recall the hapless woman branded *witch*, a species of pariah, and dragged to the pyre as a victim, not as a diabolical consort rightly burned. The community, exhorted by a bigoted church, had no doubt about its self-appointed role as judge and executioner but we have learned that majorities are often less than virtuous. How are we to estimate the credentials of the judge? And what does that tell us about whether the advertised pariahs deserve their labels? The Juvenal tag *quis custodiet ipsos custodes*? ('Who will guard the guardians?') can be recast to address the problem of pariah politics –

Quis iudicabit ipsos iudices? ('Who will judge the judges?')

If, in the context of the present book, a particular regime or country is dubbed a *pariah state*, it is essential to consider the political circumstances in which this occurs. Is the judge self-appointed? What is the political agenda, overt or covert? If the judge is itself ethically derelict does the branded state thereby escape the pariah label?

DOES THE UNITED STATES QUALIFY?

The branding of Iraq as a 'pariah' or 'rogue' state is largely the work of the United States. Throughout the 1980s Baghdad and Washington were allied in the substantial Coalition against Iran, but with the Iraqi invasion of Kuwait on 2 August 1990 representing a perceived threat to American interests the United States was quick to cast Iraq in the pariah role. It seemed an easy matter to sustain the charge. Iraq, a repressive state, had committed an unambiguous aggression in violation of the UN Charter and international law. Now Iraq was to be allowed no voice, its social and industrial infrastructure was to be destroyed, and its innocent civilians slaughtered by the hundreds of thousands in one of the most comprehensive cullings since the Second World War.

The moral climate for the US-led mass killing – through the 1991 war and the long years of deliberately induced starvation and disease that followed – was shaped in large part by Washington's branding of Iraq as a 'pariah state', a potent way of depersonalising a national people. The *pariah* – shunned, feared and hated – has no rights, deserves no protection in law and common decency; the *pariah* may be abused, tortured and exterminated – the dismal fate of individual and group pariahs over the ages. Under its newly assigned role of 'pariah', 'rogue' and 'terrorist' state, Iraq – specifically the Iraqi civilian population – has been mercilessly punished through the entire decade of the 1990s.[5] It is important to consider the international moral framework, particularly the ethical posture of the United States, within which this punishment has been inflicted.

We may ask whether the United States embodies what may be considered the indispensable condition (*sine qua non*) of ethical propriety without which any branding of other countries as 'pariah' or 'terrorist' states is no more than tactical *realpolitik* and self-serving propaganda. Put simply, is the United States, viewed in both domestic and international terms, morally fit to determine whether this or that state should be consigned a pariah status in the global community? Does the United States qualify as *judge*, let alone as *executioner*? In this context it is impossible to assess the moral status of Iraq, and to attempt a political analysis of the Iraq Question, without considering the role and posture of the United States.

SUMMARY

Through the 1990s (but not in the 1980s when the nature of the Iraqi regime was the same) the United States has worked hard to characterise Iraq as a 'pariah', 'rogue' or 'terrorist' state. To the extent that this characterisation was successful, Washington gained a *de facto* and (to a lesser extent) *de jure* right to inflict both continuous and sporadic forms of punishment on the Iraqi people. Other states, stagmatised by Washington in the same way, were routinely abused and punished by American power, though posing less of a threat to perceived US interests, to a lesser degree.[6]

Any judgement as to whether, if ever, pariah status is properly assigned to a state cannot be evaluated by considering only the character of the state in question. For particular reasons, mainly the assumed Iraqi threat to the American control of cheap energy sources, Washington came to perceive Iraq as the quite unambiguous *primus inter pariahs** – from which flowed all the copious propaganda, demonisation and slaughter. Before describing the chronology and circumstances of the 1997/8 crisis, and the late diplomatic solution achieved by UN Secretary-General Kofi Annan, it is useful to consider the moral credentials of the United States as a hegemonic nation with unassailable military power. If Washington is not ethically equipped to assign pariah status to other regimes and nations, then all the events outlined in this book should be interpreted accordingly.

---

* The first, not among equals (*primus inter pares*) but among pariahs.

2 US – The Arrogance of Hegemony

PREAMBLE

The United States comes to the matter of foreign policy from a position of *power* – which means that Washington is often able to ignore the burdensome constraint of morality. This state-of-affairs, viewed in a historical context, is unremarkable: powerful individuals, regimes and nations – keen to achieve their own objectives – have generally been well prepared to ignore or circumvent the ethical appeals made by the weak to keep the strong in check. This is an important consideration in assessing Washington's dealings with other states. In supporting what American leaders laughably call 'diplomacy' by the threat of military action, Washington is in almost constant violation of Article 2(4) of the UN Charter. This is one dereliction among many but should be remembered in considering how the United States is able to shape the image and behaviour of Iraq and other countries around the globe.

NEW WORLD HEGEMONY

There is now abundant evidence that Washington manipulated the UN Security Council in imposing punitive sanctions resolutions on Iraq, Libya and other states; that it systematically betrayed UN resolutions on Indonesia, Israel, Turkey and South Africa; that it achieved an unjust UN 'tilt' in favour of US proxies in Angola and El Salvador; that it treats the World Court with contempt when – as with decisions on Nicaragua and Libya – the court rules against Washington; that it uses its dominant position in the UN-linked financial institutions to further the interests of American capital; that it fails to pay its obligatory UN dues, while exhorting other states to observe the requirements of the Charter; that it exploits UN-gathered intelligence for its own strategic purposes – to the point that a UN Secretary-General is forced to issue a rebuke; and that it often frustrates the best efforts of various UN bodies (UNICEF, WFP, FAO and others) by pushing policies designed to further a self-serving American agenda.[1] The problem with American power, as with all substantial power, is that it cannot be trusted.[2]

Washington's abuse of American power is sometimes acknowledged in unexpected places. Thus *Time* (4 August 1997) can ask whether the United States is 'in danger of becoming a global bully?' In the same issue James

Walsh, in a Special Report headed 'AMERICA THE BRAZEN', notes the 'mounting umbrage at American "arrogance" abroad'; and gives examples of Washington's crass and self-interested behaviour, not least subjecting world leaders at the Denver economic summit 'to humiliation and braggadocio in equal measure'.[3] It is easy to see how the 1991 collapse of the Soviet Union, a seismic event in world affairs, encouraged the already-imperialist United States to assume a fresh arrogance buttressed by unassailable military power. Comparisons have been made between the current position of the United States and the great empires known to history. Thus Rome never extended much beyond the compass of the Mediterranean, Napoleon was defeated in the Russian vastness, and even at the height of *Pax Britannica* there was always serious contention with other imperial powers. Today, in contrast to the greatest empires known to history, the United States has undisputed global reach. Its military technology, prodigiously funded, is the most advanced in the world; huge armies, enjoying massive logistical support, can be conveyed over oceanic distances.[4] In such circumstances the 'imperial temptation'[5] is seductive and irresistible.

The collapse of the Soviet Union encouraged Washington to perpetrate a prompt violation of the UN Charter by allowing the Russian Federation to assume the former-Soviet permanent seat in the Security Council. Article 23 of the Charter defines the composition of the Security Council, with Article 108 prohibiting any amendment without a *two-thirds majority vote* in the General Assembly (no such vote was ever made). The US calculation was that an aid-seeking Russia would be sufficiently grateful not to veto Washington-sponsored resolutions in the Council. The ploy worked for a time. Russia supported the crucial Gulf War cease-fire/disarmament Resolution 687 (3 April 1991), though in 1998 it was plain that the Yeltsin regime was developing a more independent posture.

Through the period of the 1990/1 Iraq crisis, with no real prospect of a Soviet or Russian veto in the Security Council, the United States succeeded in suborning the so-called 'international community' into underwriting American international objectives. There was talk of an 'American Caesar' and reference also to the dollar-bill's traditional Latin phrase *novus ordo seclorum* (a new order for the ages).[6] At the same time political radicals were quick to highlight the features of the new imperialism. Thus the dissident Noam Chomsky drew attention to a view expressed in a national security review during the period of the Bush Administration: 'In cases where the US confronts much weaker enemies, our challenge will be not simply to defeat them, but to defeat them decisively and rapidly.' Chomsky was clear what this meant: '... a "much weaker" opponent must not merely be defeated but pulverised if the central lesson of World Order is to be learned: we are the masters and you shine our shoes'.[7] The new imperialism, devoted primarily to safeguarding and extending American capitalism, could tolerate no dissent:

All we, as people, are allowed to do is listen to the statements, then believe, agree and obey. Anyone who disagrees or disobeys will be shunned, treated with suspicion, condemned, and punished accordingly.[8]

In the heady aftermath of the Gulf War the United States seemed 'set to police the planet',[9] though the metaphor was unfortunate: any properly constituted police force is accountable to a higher legal authority – and to whom would the United States be accountable now? The Soviet counterweight in the UN Security Council was no more, and Washington was newly placed to bully or bribe the other members of the Council as circumstances required.[10] In fact Washington was not acting as a policeman, but as a gangster or mercenary, keen to protect vested interest but largely indifferent to inconvenient legal constraint.

In 1992 we learned that the Pentagon was drawing up plans to target selected Third World countries, the 'pariah' or 'rogue' states, with nuclear missiles. It was now plain, with the Cold War over, that Washington was reluctant to let its vast nuclear arsenal run to waste. The possible targets for American nuclear weapons included Libya, Pakistan, China, India, Iran and Syria; and just as the United States conducts espionage against its allies and so-called 'friendly' countries, even states like Israel might be targeted for a nuclear strike when circumstances demanded such a response.[11] Russia and Eastern Europe, formerly offering some 12,000 targets, was still considered a potentially threatening region but one that no longer warranted the focused attention of the American nuclear arsenal.

The secret report, drawn up by the Pentagon and handed to General Lee Butler, head of the Strategic Air Command, included targeting recommendations for presidential consideration. One option being discussed was that the US president could have an automated 'dial a nuke' facility to hit a preselected target anywhere in the world. One anonymous Pentagon source was prepared to admit that such a scheme was politically problematic: 'Once you get into pre-planned options for Third World countries, then you are in danger of a diplomatic disaster.'[12] Today, in the absence of unambiguous information in the public domain, we may assume that the American military planners have drawn up a comprehensive list of targets for nuclear strikes and that Iraq is high on the agenda.*

---

* There is evidence that America had drawn up plans for the use of nuclear bombs in the 1991 Gulf War. Major Johan Persson, a liaison officer at a Swedish army field hospital, declared that he had seen US guidelines for the use of chemical and nuclear weapons (*The Guardian*, 28 September 1991): 'There was such an order. I saw it. I had it in my hand. It was the real thing.' The authoritative writer Mohamed Heikal observed that US Secretary of State James Baker had suggested that nuclear weapons would be used in certain circumstances (*Illusions of Triumph: An Arab View of the Gulf War* (London: Harper Collins, 1992, p. 289).

The United States, keen to deny particular countries access to 'weapons of mass destruction', is heavily committed to the development of its own nuclear arsenal – with a scale of funding beyond that at the height of the Gulf War. (This selective approach to the weapons of other countries is a violation of Article 2(1) of the UN Charter, which specifies the 'sovereign equality' of all UN Members.) In August 1997 it emerged that the United States was engaged in a massive programme for the development of a new generation of nuclear weapons. A 300-page document, the *Stockpile Stewardship and Management Plan* compiled by the US Energy Department, was obtained by the Washington-based arms control monitoring group, the Natural Resources Defense Council, involved in legal action against the US government for breach of the test ban treaty. The Council's Matthew McKinzie, formerly a physicist at the Los Alamos nuclear laboratory, noted that the nuclear programme, envisaging growth of $4 billion a year, was bigger than during the Cold War. Robert Bell, the director of arms control at the National Security Council, had earlier commented that the effect of the test ban was 'to rule out opportunities to create new weapons'; but the Energy Department report talked about 'the development of advanced new types of nuclear weapons' and revealed that 'laboratories are currently working on programs to provide new or modified designs' to nuclear weapons. Clearly the United States was breaching the spirit of the test ban treaty in 1997 and continues to breach it today.*

In late 1997 President Bill Clinton reaffirmed the importance of America's nuclear arsenal. A 'presidential decision directive' confirmed the US right of first use of nuclear weapons to defend American forces or those of its allies; allowed the use of nuclear weapons against both military and civilian targets in Russia, despite the end of the Cold War; and allowed missiles to be aimed at China. At the same time officials were confirming that the directive required plans for nuclear strikes against specifically listed 'rogue' states (including Iraq) with 'prospective access' to nuclear, chemical and biological weapons. In the American journal *Medicine, Conflict and Survival* the US consultant William Arkin reported that there may be early deployment of

---

* The United States, while deploring Iraq's weapons arsenal, was well prepared to use illegal weapons and weapons of mass destruction in the 1991 Gulf War. Thus UN General Assembly Resolution 32/84 (12 December 1977) condemns 'radioactive material weapons ... and any weapons ... which might have characteristics comparable in destructive effect to those of the atomic bomb ...'. US tanks alone fired some 5000 depleted uranium rounds, leaving 50,000lb of radioactive material on the battlefield (enough, in one estimate, to cause 500,000 deaths); and fuel–air explosives were detonated, 'designed to produce nuclear-like levels of destruction without arousing popular revulsion' (*The Guardian*, 21 June 1991).

newly developed acoustic weapons that burn human flesh, rupture bodily organs and create fatal cavities in human tissue. The new generation of nuclear weapons, the fuel–air explosives (designed to produce massive fireballs) and the new generation of acoustic devices (designed to cause 'instantaneous blastwave-type trauma') may be regarded as supplementing the 'earthquake' bombs, Rockeye cluster bombs (each containing 247 'anti-personnel' grenades that individually explode into 2000 razor-sharp fragments that effectively 'mince' people), 'improved' napalm (designed to cause deep burning, thrombosis, heatstroke, oxygen starvation), phosphorus incendiaries (producing fragments that can burn deep in human flesh for hours), the depleted-uranium ordnance (producing widespread radioactive contamination) and other weapons of mass destruction. *This is the obscene paraphernalia, already used to appalling effect in many countries around the world, that in the last resort is designed to secure US military hegemony.* Even Newt Gingrich, Speaker of the US House of Representatives, while deploring any challenge to American arrogance, was forced to admit that the United States was in danger of looking 'like an isolated bully using very sophisticated weapons ... '.[13]

The United States also protects its hegemonic power by controlling the world's financial institutions. It is significant that the headquarters of both the International Bank for Reconstruction and Development (the World Bank) and the International Monetary Fund (IMF) are sited close to each other in Washington; and that the political character of the World Bank/IMF system has long been apparent. Governments are offered loans only in the context of US-friendly terms designed to weaken organised labour, to reduce the funding of state-run public services, and to expose national economies to penetration by US capital. Thus in Chile the socialist government of Salvador Allende was allowed no significant support from the international financial institutions whereas the successor regime of the fascist General Pinochet, having seized power through a CIA-aided *coup*, was quickly offered substantial loans. Vietnam, punished for more than two decades for defeating American imperialism, was denied international finance; whereas South Africa, after crushing the Soweto uprising in 1976, was offered IMF support; as was the El Salvador regime, waging a genocidal war against its own people to protect American business interests, and the Somoza faction defeated in 1979 by the anti-fascist struggle of the Nicaraguan people.

The 1990/1 Coalition against Iraq was constructed in part by American manipulation of international financial institutions. Loans were offered to China, the Soviet Union, Ethiopia, Turkey, Iran, Zimbabwe and other countries; with Egypt, Zaire and others promised debt forgiveness. When Yemen voted against Resolution 678 (that provided spurious justification for the use of force in 1991) the United States moved promptly to block projected IMF and World Bank loans.

In the same fashion international financial support to Russia, since the collapse of the Soviet Union, and to such countries as South Korea and Indonesia, through the 1997/8 economic crisis, has been conditional upon the introduction of privatisation programmes and fresh opportunities for American investment. In South Korea and elsewhere commentators and political activists alike have protested at what they see as the furtherance of American foreign policy thinly disguised as financial aid. In this context it is also significant that American dominance of the G7 group of nations, the most powerful economies in the world, is used to further extend US influence around the globe. Thus in 1993 Michel Camdessus, the IMF head, was able to portray the US-dominated G7 nations as *the world's steering committee*, committed to the solution of 'global problems ranging from the Gulf War to exchange rate crises'.[14] In such a candid appraisal there is clear acknowledgement that the G7 powers work to achieve global political goals; in particular, to make the world economy safe for capitalism, of which the United States remains the principal exponent. Typically, as with a $3 billion loan in July 1993 to facilitate the privatisation of Russian industry, the G7 group was expected to approve the IMF financial package; just as 'structural adjustment' and 'stabilisation' policies, without which struggling national economies have been denied access to world finance, are designed to strengthen the global posture of the United States and the other wealthy countries. Such policies are almost invariably pursued at the expense of local peoples, with Washington continually striving to erode any state provisions for health, education and other social services,[15] while the relatively small plutocratic élites continue to accumulate wealth.[16]

The hegemonic arrogance of the United States, fortified by unrivalled military and economic power, is demonstrated in many ways: for example, by the passing of domestic American laws intended to have a global impact (so-called 'extraterritorial' legislation), by the constant flouting of international laws and treaties,[17] and by the continuous involvement of the United States in local and regional political disputes all around the world. Extraterritorial legislation designed to punish countries, even nominal US allies, for trading with such states as Libya, Iran and Cuba has infuriated countries with extensive commercial interests. The European Union had hoped to appeal to the free-trade World Trade Organisation (WTO) to declare punitive US sanctions illegal, but US dominance of the WTO brought new problems: countries struggling to protect vulnerable national economies are confronted with unsympathetic US-devised WTO demands, while the United States picks and chooses which free-trade provisions it will observe. The journalist Martin Walker, writing in August 1996, summarised the prevailing situation:

International law is now in danger of becoming whatever Washington says it should be. Since the days of the Monroe Doctrine, when the US declared the western hemisphere off limits to any other power, the US has not been shy of legislating on behalf of others. The difference now is that it has the untrammelled power to enforce its will.[18]

In May 1997 President Bill Clinton reaffirmed the American intention 'to lead the world'. On the eve of a three-day European tour he used the Memorial Day celebrations to lay a wreath at the Tomb of the Unknowns at Arlington National Cemetery and to emphasise the principle that American world leadership was as necessary now as it was in the aftermath of the Second World War. In the same spirit, Secretary of State Madeleine Albright was later to declare on more than one occasion that the United States was the one 'indispensable' country. The rest of the world was not consulted on such matters; no polls were taken; there was no referendum in the United Nations. It was enough that American leaders, conscious of the unrivalled US military and economic power, judged it appropriate that the United States should work to shape not only international events but the domestic affairs of sovereign states.

It was still thought necessary to advertise the existence of 'pariah' or 'rogue' states (typically those states apt to perpetate 'state-sponsored terrorism'); and to publicise a most wanted list of specific terrorist organisations. (A list of some thirty terror groups published by the Clinton Administration in October 1997 omitted to mention the Irish Republican Army or any other Irish Republican faction – explained on the ground that a ceasefire was in place at the time.) No reference was made to any US-friendly terrorist groups or to the well-documented fact that the United States itself is a principal sponsor of terrorism (see pp. 33–8). It is thought necessary also to indicate the Pentagon's long reach with suitable practical demonstrations. Thus in September 1997 some five hundred US paratroopers dropped onto the steppes of the former Soviet Republic of Kazakhstan in the heart of Central Asia as part of a multinational military exercise involving troops from Kazakhstan, Uzbekistan, Kyrgyzstan and the United States. The US troops had flown for nineteen hours from North Carolina, an operation that required three in-flight refuellings. The US Marine Corps General John Sheehan explained a main purpose of the operation: '*I would like to leave the message that there is no nation on the face of the Earth that we cannot get to.*'[19]

At the same time the United States is a lead participant in disputes and conflicts in countless countries around the world, not least in what is risibly called the 'peace process' of the Middle East. Here, while ignoring Israeli aggressions and acts of terrorism, the CIA instructs Yasser Arafat on which Palestinians should be held in jail. An agreement concluded in December 1997 between Palestinian, Israeli and American security officials required the Palestinian Authority to hand over to the CIA the names of detainees who were to be released. The CIA would then pass on the names to the Israelis, who would be allowed to voice objections. Thus while maintaining the absurd pretence of impartiality the United States was supervising the imprisonment of Palestinians while ignoring Israeli terrorism and Israeli violations of international law (including UN Security Council resolutions). The case is typical: Washington calculates its strategic interests and then acts accordingly. This leaves weaker nations the choice of opting for the arduous and punishing route of political independence (inviting 'pariah' or 'rogue' branding, CIA-staged *coups*, economic sanctions and other penalties) or obvious acquiescence in American strategic aims (and tolerance or reward, according to US needs). The Tory politician William Waldegrave is candid about how he perceives the British interest: *'Britain needs international order. Only America has the will or the means to ensure international order. Ergo, Britain should support the United States.'*[20] It is scarcely necessary to point out that there is *no* international order; or that, even if there were, any successful tyranny could be given support in the same cynical terms.

It is important to realise that American hegemony, however unassailable in terms of military or economic power, is not unqualified. There are endemic commercial tensions between the (often corrupt) defence contractors seeking orders, military planners frequently disagree among themselves, a Democratic US president is often at odds with a Republican Congress, and today (mid-1998) many states are showing a growing reluctance to tolerate American political arrogance. In December 1997 a 94-page report, *Transforming Defense*, published by the influential United States National Defense Panel commented that the Pentagon was hampered by 'a far-flung infrastructure that is ponderous, bureaucratic and unaffordable'; and that its $260 billion annual income should be spent to better meet the needs of the twenty-first century. Pentagon planners should acknowledge the end of 'the certainties of the cold war'; and between $5 billion and $10 billion a year should be spent on developing new weapons and new fighting concepts. The report criticised the old strategic principle that the United States should be prepared to fight two major wars simultaneously.

Such debates bear little on the central circumstances of American power. The military option is always open to the Washington planners; and US economic power gives America a dominant influence in the allocation of global financial support. Today, following the 1997/8 economic crisis in Asia, the International Monetary Fund is increasingly seen as a mechanism for softening up national economies for US domination, no more than an agent for American interests. Thus Martin Khor, head of the Third World Network in Malaysia, has commented: 'What the rich couldn't do through bilateral or multilateral pressures, they are now extracting by using the IMF loans as leverage.' The 37,000 American troops stationed in South Korea have been seen as a mechanism for pressurising the government into observing the terms of US-friendly IMF agreements. Thus in November 1997 President Clinton gave the then South Korean president Kim Young Sam a two-day deadline to conclude an IMF deal: with the thousands of US troops stationed in the country, 'Kim took the deadline seriously.'[21] In the circumstances of the Asian crisis it was plain that the United States would be the main beneficiary. With the Asian nations now increasingly unable to trade with each other, they needed to sell goods to the United States more than ever: '... to the chagrin of China and champions of Asian solidarity, the US will not be confined to the Pacific shore of California. Now more influential across the Pacific than at any time since the end of the Vietnam War, *it umpires Asia's military and economic fate*' (my italics).[22]

In this fashion the United States exploits its domination of such international bodies as the IMF, the World Bank, the G7 group and the World Trade Organisation to enlarge its control over national economies around the world. At the same time international agreements are being drawn up to restrict the power of national governments to regulate the encroachments of the transnational corporations, the largest number of which are American. Thus a specific international accord, the Multilateral Agreement on Investment (MAI), debated for three years in conditions of almost total secrecy, was reaching a final draft form in 1998. In February, representatives from the world's 29 richest countries met in Paris with the aim of giving the largest companies unprecedented power. The planned MAI would allow the transnationals to sue any national government for profits lost through restrictive laws. The Agreement, if eventually enshrined in law, would threaten international UN treaties on climate change and over-fishing, threaten environmental and worker-protection legislation, and in general establish the principle that corporate capital has more power over domestic social and industrial environments than national and local governments.

The Multilateral Agreement on Investment was developed by the Organisation for Economic Cooperation and Development (OECD) and was designed to supplement the regulations imposed by the World Trade Organisation (WTO) and the North American Free Trade Agreement (NAFTA). Renato Ruggerio, the WTO director-general, commented on the MAI: 'We are writing the constitution of a single global economy.' Figure 2.1 shows a few of the many national laws that would be threatened by the MAI.

The significance of such developments (G7, WTO, MAI, etc.) is that the power of US-led world capitalism is being constantly enlarged at the expense of worker organisations, public services and the democratic controls exercised by accountable national governments. The coercive power of an unassailable military might is self-evident but the economic underpinning of all

Australia Requires foreign investors taking a substantial stake in an existing Australian business worth A$5 million, or establishing a new one worth A$10 million, to submit to a screening based upon a 'national interest' test. **Taiwan** Forbids foreign investment in 'highly polluting industries'. **US** Some states restrict non-residents' use of public land for grazing and for mineral, oil and gas extraction. **Mexico** Bars foreign ownership of development-banking institutions and credit unions. **Canada** Requires a 'benefits plan' to encourage the employment of Canadians, and offer opportunities for Canadian contractors, before approving foreign investment in the oil and gas sectors.	**Venezuela** Limits the number of foreign employees in companies with more than 10 workers to 10 per cent, with a 20 per cent payroll limit for foreign employees. **Colombia** Bars foreign investment in the processing or disposal of toxic or radioactive waste not produced in Colombia. **New Zealand** Requires approval for foreign direct investment that results in control of 'significant' assets, such as businesses worth more than NZ$10 million. **Chile** Bars the repatriation of capital until one year after a foreign investment is made.

Figure 2.1   Some national laws threatened by MAI

the American weapons of mass destruction is equally essential to a sustainable hegemony. Moreover, massive economic power is itself a weapon of mass destruction: control of the world's national economies – to the point that entire domestic populations can be denied food, clean water and medical facilities – represents one of the ultimate coercive capabilities, as shown by the years-long genocidal sanctions on Iraq (see pp. 53–60).

The 'indispensable' United States, wielding vast military and economic power, is proud to boast of its hegemonic status in the world. As a corollary it assumes without question a Divine Right to brand this or that state 'pariah', 'rogue' or 'terrorist' – from which all types of punishment, including genocide, can flow. It is useful to look at the human-rights credentials of the one country that sets itself up – at least for purposes of public-relations hyperbole – as the moral arbiter of the world's affairs.

HUMAN RIGHTS – US

The human-rights nature of the United States derives from the two heavily intertwined phenomena of quasi-democracy and plutocracy. We may consider the obvious requirements of true democracy, and then note that they are largely absent in the American polity. For example, if we assume that a democratically empowered government acts under the substantial mandate of a majority of the adult citizens of the state it is obvious that the United States falls far short. We find that no more than two out of every ten nominally eligible American adults supported Bill Clinton's re-election as President in November 1996. Around one-third of Americans entitled to suffrage were not in fact registered to vote – which thus excluded them from the electoral process. Of the remainder, less than half (perhaps 45 per cent) took the trouble to vote; and, despite Clinton's seemingly overwhelming victory, he received only around 50 per cent of the popular vote. The sum is a simple one: convert 66 × 45 × 50 into a percentage and we find that a mere 15 per cent of nominally eligible American adults provided the Clinton Administration with a mandate to continue governing the most powerful nation on earth.

The desultory pro-Clinton vote relates in large measure to the fact that a majority of American citizens do not identify with the US political regime – for the simple reason that it is wealth and wealth alone that provides access to political power. With the bulk of American wealth enshrined either directly or indirectly in corporate America, no politician unwilling to protect the corporate interest *above everything* can expect to attract the funding that alone can guarantee the winning of political power. One estimate suggested that the cost of the 1996 presidential campaigns amounted to around $1.5 billion: at a time when, for example, substantial cuts in public-service expenditure were being contemplated. This situation has immense implications for human rights. In early June 1996 nearly a quarter of a million people demonstrated in Washington in support of poor children and to expose the political developments that were harming them further. Marian Wright Edelman, head of the Children's Defense Fund, which helped to organise the demonstration, commented on the situation in modern America: 'In the richest nation in history, a child dies from poverty every 53 minutes.'[23] That a fifth of all American children live in poverty, with the number living in 'extreme poverty' (family income less than half the official poverty level) having doubled since 1975, is – or should be – a massive human-rights issue, particularly when set against the small but growing number of multibillionaires protected by private armies and indifferent to the scale of destitution in the society from which they derive their wealth.

There is a sense in which the plutocracy of the modern United States accords well with the insight and vision of the Founding Fathers: the

American Constitution, with all its much-hyped 'checks and balances', made no provision for the taming of private wealth in the interest of democracy – quite the reverse. Thomas Jefferson was well prepared to acknowledge that money, 'not morality, is the principle of commercial nations'; John Jay, a Chief Justice of the United States, urged that 'the people who own the country ought to govern it'; and President John Adams believed that the 'great functions of state' should be reserved to 'the rich, the well-born and the able'. The virtuous writers of the American Constitution, mostly representatives of the comfortable merchants of the North, 'had it in mind to make their world safe for commerce'.[24] For *commerce* read *capitalism*; and for *capitalism* read *graft, corruption, inequality* and *exploitation*. Woodrow Wilson acknowledged the 'heartless' character of the American economic system; while Henry Adams noted the grim inevitability of how the 'monied interest can't help winning and running the country'. In modern America while some three million homeless men, women and children live in 'spider-hole' caves in California, in subway stairwells, in the tunnels under New York streets, and under railway arches, some American wives spend $20,000 a week on flowers, incidental porcelain and luxury limousines and organise $300,000 wedding receptions in Manhattan.[25]

Such matters are not deemed relevant to human rights by the American pundits and politicians most keen to pontificate about the 'pariah status' of other nations. In this context the principal goal of the American political Establishment is to consolidate and extend the power, privilege and wealth of the minority plutocratic élite: 'Instead of attempting a more equitable division of the nation's wealth, the oligarchy seeks its greater concentration in monopolies always more narrowly held and implacably defended.'[26] The 'ferocious élites ... often criminal ... with the force and arrogance of capitalism intimidate the world's parliaments' as did ancient military commanders who bullied the Roman Senate; and maintain their complicity 'in the well-financed banditry at large in the world',[27] while cynically diverting the public's attention with trivial accounts of Hillary Clinton's astrologer and her husband's sexual habits. There is no sign that a plutocratic élite, copiously equipped with mercenary propagandists and politicians, has any interest in human rights at home or abroad. There are consequences in this situation, not only for such obvious social issues as housing, health provision, education and family poverty, but also in such areas as policing, judicial process and racial persecution.

For many years a number of human-rights groups have worked to expose the nature of human-rights abuses in the United States. For example, Amnesty International published a (December 1990) document describing allegations that the police in Chicago tortured or otherwise ill-treated suspected criminals between 1972 and 1984. The document includes copies of a letter (16 February 1990) to the Attorney General of Illinois and his reply.[28]

One of the best-documented cases of torture involved Andrew Wilson, arrested on 14 February 1982 and charged with the murder of two police officers. He was beaten and kicked in the eye; a plastic bag was placed over his head causing near suffocation; alligator clips were attached to his ears, nostrils and fingers, and he was given electric shocks from a device resembling a small generator; during the electric shock torture he was handcuffed over a hot radiator until his chest, thigh, face and chin sustained burns; a cattle prod was applied to his leg and groin; and a gun was placed in his mouth and the trigger pulled. After some 13 hours in police custody Andrew Wilson signed a confession. Whilst in transit to jail he was hit over the head with a revolver and was sexually abused. After a protracted (two-year) enquiry a Police Department Office of Professional Standards (OPS) investigation ruled that Wilson's complaints were 'not sustained'.

The torture of Andrew Wilson was not an isolated case. Attorneys located more than 20 other people who were tortured by police officers from Chicago's Area 2 police station between 1972 and 1984. The victims' claims included being hit by guns, being given electric shocks, being subjected to near suffocation, and being threatened with death. Darryl Canon, for example, awarded damages in 1988, was driven to a remote area; officers played 'Russian Roulette' with him, pointing a gun at his head and pulling the trigger; he was given electric shocks to his mouth and testicles. Another victim, Gregory Banks, was beaten, threatened with death, and almost suffocated. The various OPS investigations failed to identify the police officers responsible.[29]

A later (June 1992) Amnesty report revealed many cases of police brutality in Los Angeles. One man was blinded in one eye after being beaten by three police officers; another man – unarmed, handcuffed and mentally disturbed – died after being 'subdued' by some twenty officers who repeatedly beat him and repeatedly gave him electric shocks with a 'taser' gun; after a car chase a 21-year-old driver was shot dead; and a police dog was allowed to maul two bystanders located at different places.[30] Despite such common incidents it was only the Rodney King case that promoted serious discussion about the incidence of police brutality in Los Angeles. King was struck with a 'taser' gun, subjected to 56 baton blows, and then – suffering facial lacerations (that required 20 stitches), a broken cheek-bone, a broken ankle and a fractured skull – was 'hogtied' (handcuffed and bound) and left at the side of the road until an ambulance arrived.

A March 1991 report revealed more than one hundred cases between 1986 and 1989 in which settlements of more than $15,000 had been awarded to victims of police brutality in Los Angeles.[31] The cases involved assaults, shootings and deaths. The Amnesty report (June 1992) reveals many cases of abuse – involving electric shocks, beatings, burst eardrums, broken limbs, fractured skulls, contusions, kicking (of men and women) in the face and head, bruising, broken noses, a scarred eye retina, nerve damage, lacerations, internal haemorrhaging, a fractured testicle (requiring surgical removal), a damaged liver, a punctured lung and other injuries. Amnesty also highlights shootings of unarmed men, including cases of repeated shootings at men already disabled by gunshot wounds, some of which incidents resulted in the deaths of unarmed men. The guidelines for official investigations of police shootings were 'not followed' and the procedures were 'flawed'.[32]

Various human-rights groups have criticised the working of the death penalty in the United States, judicial and police discrimination against racial minorities, and the character of trials in political cases; the treatment of Haitian and Cuban asylum seekers has also been criticised. In such areas Amnesty International has found frequent American violations of international covenants, including the International Covenant on Civil and Political Rights and the Convention Against Torture, both ratified by the United States.*

Amnesty and other bodies have found that the imposition of the death penalty is in practice both unfair and discriminatory: *'The evidence suggests that factors such as class, race, politics and location of crime can play a far more decisive role in who receives the death penalty than the crime itself; that it is imposed disproportionately on the poor, minorities, the mentally ill or retarded and those without adequate legal counsel.'*[33] It has also been noted that the United States remains one of the few states to execute children. In the decade following 1985 nine juvenile offenders were executed, with 37 juveniles under sentence of death in 12 states at the end of 1994. Between 1990 and 1995 only four countries worldwide were reported to have executed juveniles: one was executed in Saudi Arabia, one in Pakistan, one in Yemen, and six in the United States. In the period the US led the world in the execution of children.

The legal representation available to capital defendants is often appallingly inadequate. Many prisoners subsequently executed were represented by inexperienced lawyers untrained in capital punishment law or even

---

* The United States ratified the UN Convention Against Torture and Other Cruel, Inhuman or Degrading Treatment or Punishment in October 1994. It is worth noting that when the US ratified the International Covenant on Civil and Political Rights in June 1992 it included reservations to the following non-derogable Articles: Article 6 on the right to life, where the US government reserved the right of US states to execute juvenile offenders; Article 7, prohibiting torture and other cruel, inhuman or degrading treatment, where the US considered itself bound only to the extent that cruel, inhuman or degrading treatment met the definition of 'cruel and unusual punishment' prohibited under the US Constitution; and Article 15(1), prohibiting retroactive penal legislation. The US also made a reservation to the Convention Against Torture similar to its reservation under Article 7 of the ICCPR.

with no experience of any aspect of criminal law. In some states no funding is provided for appeals beyond a certain stage and prisoners have to rely on 'volunteer' lawyers working without a fee. In early 1995 many of the 400 prisoners on death row were without legal representation. Where there is a large death row population, as in Texas, prisoners are more likely to be denied the option of legal representation for subsequent appeals. In one celebrated case, George McFarland was sentenced to death after his lawyer had slept through the entire trial.[34]

In June 1996 Amnesty published reports on police brutality in New York[35] and on the use of electro-shock stun belts.[36] The cases included people beaten with fists or batons, deaths in custody, and shootings in violation of official guidelines. The victims included men, women and children from various social, racial and ethnic backgrounds; but most of the victims were from racial minorities, particularly African-Americans and people of Latin American or Asian descent; in cases involving deaths in custody and questionable shootings there was a strong racial element. The cases concerning police brutality in New York involved beatings (sometimes fatal), smashing a victim's head through a plate glass window, a crushed spinal cord resulting in permanent paralysis from the neck down, punching in the face to the degree that plastic surgery was required, bruisings, back injuries, cerebral concussion, loss of hearing, lacerations to mouth, nerve damage, repeated hits to heads with pistols and nightsticks, dragging along the ground, a broken jaw, broken ribs, head lacerations, dragging a woman from a car by her hair, repeatedly beating an epileptic about the head, and other injuries.

Deaths in custody have resulted from the use of the pepper-spray Oleoresin Capsicum (OC), apt to cause an extreme burning sensation of the skin, an involuntary closing of the eyes, and inflammation of the mucous membrane, oesophagus and upper respiratory tract. The American Civil Liberties Union (ACLU) reviewed 26 cases where people had died in California after having been sprayed. Mohammed Assassa, aged 55, reportedly went into cardiac arrest after struggling with officers on 7 December 1995. It was later revealed that the hyoid bone, near the voice box, had been broken, suggesting severe compression of the neck. The 29-year-old Anthony Baez, a sufferer from chronic asthma, was placed in a choke hold while officers knelt on his back. He was left in a prone position on the ground before being dragged to a police car. No attempt was made to resuscitate him and he was pronounced dead in hospital an hour later. Other fatalities involved Richard Butler, having suffered 'multiple blunt impacts' to his head and body delivered by police officers; the epileptic Johnnie Cromartie, having suffered 'multiple blunt impacts preceding restraint, with subsequent postural compromise of respiration'; Dane Kemp, who was 'asphyxiated as the result of compression of his chest and neck ... '; Frederico Pereira, having suffered traumatic asphyxia associated with compression of the neck (the autopsy also noted multiple blunt force injuries, a laceration above the eye, abrasions to the head, contusions, etc.). The New York Police Department patrol guide states that *'The primary duty of all members of the service is to preserve human life.'*

Police shootings have involved woundings and fatalities, often of unarmed men in circumstances that were not properly investigated and where no officers were found to be culpable. Thus the unarmed Luis Allende, sitting in his car, was surrounded by police and shot in the head; the unarmed Frankie Arzuega was shot in his car as he tried to drive away; the unarmed Lydia Ferraro was shot dead in her car; the 16-year-old Yong Xin Huang was shot dead at close range by a police officer who claimed that his gun went off accidentally (a witness claimed that the officer had also smashed Huang's head into a glass door – a charge consistent with autopsy); the unarmed Mary Mitchell was shot dead in her Bronx apartment in the presence of at least eight police officers; and so on. In these and many other similar cases there are desultory police enquiries, if at all, occasional Grand Jury investigations, but rarely any strong action taken against the responsible officers.[37]

In June 1996 Amnesty International published its report on the use of electro-shock stun belts, remote-controlled devices introduced for use on prisoners in chain gangs, judicial hearings and transportation. At the push of a button such devices can inflict severe pain and incapacitate a prisoner: the 50,000-volt shocks last about eight seconds at a time and may result in long-term physical and mental injuries. Amnesty judges that such devices appear designed to degrade and humiliate prisoners; and that they could constitute a violation of international human-rights standards which prohibit cruel, inhuman or degrading treatment of prisoners.

In May 1996 the Wisconsin State Senate endorsed a vote in the State Assembly to introduce 12-person chain gangs for medium-security prisoners. The Senate ruling followed a declaration by the Wisconsin Department of Corrections that 'inmates will not be chained to one another, but will be restrained by the use of stun belts and individual leg restraints. At least one of the 2 correctional officers supervising the 12 inmate work crew will be armed in order to provide an extra degree of security.' The company that provides the stun belt was pushing for the widespread use of such devices: Stun Tech Inc. of Cleveland, Ohio, was urging their use in the chain gang programmes in Alabama, Florida and Louisiana. At the same time the US Federal Bureau of Prison was using remote-controlled stun belts on prisoners being transported and making court appearances.

Amnesty has highlighted some of the effects of these devices.[38] In November 1993 Edward Valdez was subjected to a stun-belt shock in front of waiting jurors in a San Diego courtroom: *'He screamed and crashed into the wall and fell down, and was out for about a minute ... It was very effective'* (according to the prosecutor). On 16 December 1994 the defendant Bruce

Sons was reported to be accidentally incapacitated by a stun belt while talking to his defence attorney. A subsequent photograph showed the welt marks caused by the electric shocks. In April 1995 the defendant James Oswald was forced to wear a stun belt despite being shackled in a wheelchair throughout the trial. His defence lawyer commented that the belt was *'part of a multiphase effort to torture this guy'*. Oswald claimed that he had been stunned twice; the judge agreed that Oswald had been accidentally stunned once. Stun Tech have admitted that no strictly independent medical tests have been carried out on the belt, but have quoted a Nebraska doctor who has experimented with anaesthetised pigs (he claimed that the belts were safe to use on people *'under circumstances of proper usage'*, but gave no explanation of what this meant). The US Bureau of Prisons and the company manual warn that the belts should not be used on pregnant women, persons with heart disease, multiple sclerosis, muscular dystrophy or epilepsy. The Bureau has admitted that not all prisoners are medically examined before being fitted with a stun belt, and that some are examined only after incapacitation. Research published by the UK Home Office Forensic Science Service showed that stun guns can cause extreme pain, whole-body incapacity and death.[39] American companies have been keen to sell electric-shock weapons to many countries with a well-documented history of torture.

Reports have also described the ill-treatment of prisoners in American jails.[40] In March 1996, for example, the paraplegic Richard Post was placed in an isolation cell for a protracted period with no access to medical attention. When he eventually protested he was dragged from his wheelchair and strapped in a four-point restraint chair, his legs clamped in metal shackles and his arms padlocked near his ankles. Straps strained his shoulders backwards and he was threatened with a stun gun. The ill-treatment given to Post at one of the Maricopa County jails in Arizona resulted in severe decubitus ulcers around the anus, compression of the spine, nerve damage to the spine and neck, and significant loss of upper body mobility. In July 1998 it was revealed that inmates at the Concoran jail in California were being subjected to mass beatings, guard-organised rapes and arbitrary executions. In one case a frail inmate was put into a cell with a 17-stone sexual predator and repeatedly raped; the guards rewarded the rapist with new shoes and extra food (see reports in *The Guardian* and *The Daily Telegraph*, London, both 30 July 1998).

In summary, the many reports (those of Amnesty and other organisations) provide copious evidence of serious human-rights abuses in the United States. Such abuses occur in a society where private financial gain – necessarily encouraging corruption, crime, exploitation and totally inadequate social provision – is the overwhelmingly dominant cultural principle. Apart from the many sociological reports that reveal widespread destitution, obscenely vast private fortunes, inadequate social housing, abysmal public health provision, etc., the reports exposing the *commission* of human-rights abuses (as opposed to the *omission* of human-rights protection)[41] reveal such derelictions as:

- widespread torture in jails (humiliation, beatings, burnings, use of electric shocks, denial of medical attention, near suffocation, etc.);

- shootings (often fatal) of unarmed suspects;

- excessive use (if *any* use is justified) of electro-shock stun guns;

- inadequate (sometimes totally absent) legal representation of defendants (even those facing possible execution);

- execution of innocent defendants;

- execution of juveniles;

- execution of the mentally retarded;

- brutal execution methods (one man in the electric chair caught fire while he was conscious; another was electrocuted over a period of 45 minutes before being pronounced dead);

- the complicity of medical professionals in torture and brutal executions;

- discriminatory sentencing on the basis of race, class and religion.

This well-documented list of ethical and social dereliction is far from exhaustive but it shows the character of a brutal state keen to publicise the moral failings of other nations that are unwilling to acquiesce in the presumptions and arrogance of American hegemony.

The persistent racist element in American society, evident in both popular sentiment and official attitudes, is of particular significance for a central theme of the present book: the labelling of Arab Iraq as a 'pariah state' characterised by a range of ethical shortcomings that Christian white America would not tolerate. Brief reference has been made to the incidence of racism as one cause of discrimination in judicial and penal practice in the United States. I have outlined elsewhere the incidence of American racism as it has affected Filipinos, Chinese, Japanese, Koreans, Vietnamese, Negroes, Arabs and others,[42] but in the context of this book it is useful to emphasise again the scale of anti-Arab racism in the United States.

American racist attitudes to Arabs, like those directed at Asians and Negroes, are well documented.[43] There was a sudden surge in anti-Arab bigotry immediately after the 1990 Iraqi invasion of Kuwait, with a growing number of threats made against American-Arab individuals and groups who spoke publicly against prejudice and related issues. The media were then encouraging the growth of racist attitudes: 'Inflammatory and bigoted remarks on talk shows and call-in radio programs are helping to create a climate of opinion conducive to anti-Arab racism and violence.'[44] The American-Arab Anti-Discrimination Committee (ADC), based in Washington, noted the rapid growth in the number of 'hate crimes' that followed the Iraqi invasion. The ADC office received more than 4 dozen reports of such crimes: ' ... from threats to actual incidents to the destruction of persons or property... Some include hate mail or phone threats ... vandalism, arson, physical assaults ... shootings.' Telephone calls were made to 'Arab pigs', a Star of David was sprayed on an Arab-American's car, Arab-American stores were fire-bombed, and death threats (including threats to children) were made.[45] In the Chronology publication the ADC lists 6 pages of racist abuse and attacks (verbal and physical) made against Arab-Americans. These included threats to destroy property, the planting of incendiary devices, obscene phone calls, physical assaults, terminations of employment (because Arab-Americans 'might do something'), the bombing of a grocery store, and shootings (in one case by men in combat fatigues).

In a period of a little over a year at least seven mosques were burned down or seriously vandalised: for example, in Springfield, Illinois; High Point, North Carolina; and Huntsville, Alabama. On 25 August 1995 the ADC filed a request with the US Department of Justice asking for a Department investigation under Title 18 of the United States Code following attacks on three mosques. In Atlanta, when a mosque was desecrated by satanic symbols and vandalised the DeKalb County police made no effort to visit the site until local organisations publicised the incident. The ADC has found that local authorities only rarely bring prosecutions against the perpetrators of hate crimes. Moreover, the police often use the occasion of such a crime to investigate the victims rather than the perpetrators (*The New York Times*, 28 April 1995). Thus worshippers at a vandalised mosque have been interrogated about their beliefs by FBI agents.

In Northern Virginia an Indian family mistaken for Arabs was vandalised. The satanic '666' symbol was spray-painted on the family's front door, and '*Fuck you Arab*' painted onto their driveway. No police investigation was carried out. The ADC Campus Chapters at Metro State College in Aurora, Colorado, received a threatening phone call and threatening letters when trying to organise an 'Arab Awareness Week'. The Chapter President was later assaulted. Cases of police abuse of Arab-Americans include the shouting of profanities, beating with nightsticks, and prolonged harassment. The ADC has collected copious examples of employment discrimination against Arab-Americans, including arbitrary dismissal, other forms of disparate treatment, racist abuse and ridicule, a pejorative computer simulation at Rockwell International (the company later apologised to the ADC), and clear management-orchestrated humiliation of Arab-Americans in the presence of other workers. In response to all such forms of racist discrimination the courts seemingly have difficulty in recognising the incidents for what they are. One lawyer, quoted by the ADC, has commented that because of anti-Arab attitudes it is almost impossible for Arabs and Muslims to obtain a fair trial in the United States. In a Special Report the ADC concludes: *'The findings of this report indicate that anti-Arab racism continues to be a problem of considerable proportions for the Arab-American community and becomes more conspicuous in times of crisis. Indeed, one of the trends that has emerged from this study is the high correlation between crisis situations and anti-Arab hate crimes or discrimination, as evident in the upsurge of incidents in the wake of the Oklahoma City bombing. This finding itself demonstrates the need for continued vigilance and renewed efforts aimed at confronting anti-Arab racism.'*[46]

This section has highlighted various human-rights abuses in the United States. Most of these are essentially domestic, though they can often be seen to have substantial international ramifications. This is particularly the case with the prevailing incidence of anti-Arab racism – a phenomenon that facilitates the continued American abuse of such countries as Iraq, Libya, and Sudan. Before considering the Iraq Question in more detail it is useful to outline the general international posture of the United States. The branding of Iraq as a 'pariah state' derives in large part from an American global arrogance underwritten by racist assumption, a fortuitous command of world resources, and the physical power of the inveterate bully.

INTERNATIONAL SCENE

The international positioning of the United States has been outlined (see 'New World Hegemony', above). Here it is sufficient to give a few examples of policy issues – to illustrate the American impact on other countries as a human-rights matter. The domestic derelictions of the United States have many global counterparts. The six selected cases are illustrative, a fraction of the many examples that could be given to demonstrate US indifference to human rights around the world.

China

The appalling human-rights record of China is not in question: political and other dissidents are imprisoned and tortured; the various freedoms to publish, discuss and assemble are massively curtailed; the legal representation of defendants is often wholly inadequate; the use of capital punishment is excessive, arbitrary and brutal. There have long been suggestions that men and women have been executed as a means of supplying bodily organs to wealthy purchasers at home and abroad. Thus the investigative journalist Olga Craig presents 'hard evidence of China's role in this most horrific trade'.[47] We learn that criminals on death row are 'matched' to prospective organ recipients, that execution dates are brought forward to meet the demand, how the condemned are given anti-coagulation and muscle relaxant drugs to aid prompt organ removal, how some victims with removed kidneys are left to die, and how prospective organ purchasers queue up to offer cash during executions at the Guangzhou Military Medical University.[48]

The United States has decided that such matters are of no concern when set against the prospects of American financial gain from the vast Chinese market. In March 1998 Washington decided to abandon its support for an annual United Nations resolution condemning China's record on human rights. Since the 1989 Tiananmen Square massacre the annual resolution, routinely opposed by China, has done much to focus attention on human-rights derelictions that continue despite sustained international opposition. The American position – following that of Britain with its 'ethical' foreign policy – has been defended by a US State Department spokesman: 'Fundamentally, we feel there's been enough progress to warrant an approach that is somewhat different this year. That does not mean that we consider the human rights situation in China to be satisfactory, and we still have serious concerns, but we feel there are other ways to address them this year'. In London *The Daily Telegraph* (16 March 1998) voiced concerns that are shared by many human-rights workers: '*Has the [Chinese] Communist Party done anything to repudiate that brutal [Tiananmen] crushing of the democracy movement? The answer is no ... there is no good reason to relax pressure on Beijing over human rights. The rape of Tibet, the lao gai labour camps, the trading in organs of executed criminals, the one-child-per-family policy: all are evidence of an egregious dictatorship. ... Western policy on human rights in China, corrupted by greed, has become miserably myopic.*'

Libya

The genocidal use of economic sanctions by the United States against recalcitrant states is well documented, though rarely explored in detail in the Western media.[49] This US policy represents a multifaceted abuse of human rights in unambiguous violation of international law designed to protect them. This is manifestly the case with Iraq (see Chapter 3), Cuba (see below) and Libya. The example of Libya was given cursory exposure following a World Court ruling in February 1998 that the Court was entitled to consider the relevance of the 1971 Montreal Convention to the matter of the 1988 Lockerbie bombing outrage.

The Convention, specifically designed to address acts of terrorism against civil aircraft, protects (in Article 8(2)) the right of Libya, in the absence of an extradition treaty, *not* to hand over the two Libyan suspects for trial in the United States or Britain. It was the fact that Libya was honouring international law as enshrined in the Convention that forced Washington to intimidate the UN Security Council into passing the sanctions resolutions (Resolutions 748 and 883). The significance of the 1998 World Court ruling is that it undermines the ground for continued sanctions against Libya. The United States (and Britain), indifferent to such considerations, is insisting that the sanctions be maintained, seemingly in perpetuity, with all the adverse human-rights consequences that this policy implies. (A UN report, 15 January 1998, noted the drastic effects of sanctions on health, social services, agriculture and transportation in Libya. Poverty had increased throughout the country, and patients were dying while being deprived of urgently needed medication – see report S/1998/20.) The London-based Libyan news agency was quick to point out the significance of the World Court ruling: 'After the ruling of the International Court of Justice that it has jurisdiction over the Lockerbie case all members of the Security Council with the exception of the two concerned states [the United States and Britain] agreed on the need to lift the sanctions imposed on Libya.'[50]

The ploy of the United States in choosing to ignore the jurisdiction of the World Court is not unprecedented. Washington was quick to ignore the 1986 Court ruling that the United States had committed terrorist acts against Nicaragua and that in consequence reparations should be made. Both the 1971 Montreal Convention and the 1998 World Court ruling are directly relevant to the Lockerbie issue. Washington's indifference to international law here and elsewhere give the United States the 'rogue' status so frequently cited in American propaganda about other countries.

Saudi Arabia

While the United States is keen to criticise the well-documented human-rights abuses in Iraq, minimal exposure is given to official derelictions in Saudi Arabia and other client and friendly states. Saudi Arabia is marked by endemic corruption, religious persecution, the torture of dissidents, public mutilation, the almost total absence of any civilised legal process, sexual suppression, an incidence of slavery that has both *de facto* and *de jure* support, and (in one account[51]) the plucking of children off the streets to steal their bodily organs.[52]

The United States directly aids Saudi repression by supplying weapons, surveillance support and training for security personnel. When an American citizen was tortured during a 39-day detention he tried to seek compensation by suing the Saudi government in the US courts, but all his efforts were blocked by the Foreign Sovereign Immunities Act.[53] Washington's failure to address the appalling human-rights record in Saudi Arabia – for fear of disturbing the US grip on cheap-energy sources and a lucrative arms market – should be borne in mind whenever American spokespersons express concern for human rights and the need to protect the citizen from the power of dictatorial states.

Turkey

Turkey – like many other US allies and the United States itself – practises institutionalised torture, oppresses organised labour, and frequently resorts to aggression against other states. To illustrate the character of Turkish penal philosophy we need cite only the case of Ilhan Karatepe, a left-wing journalist sentenced to 18 years in a Turkish prison on a trumped-up charge.[54]

When Karatepe was arrested in 1995 he was tortured at the headquarters of the Turkish CRC, the equivalent of the UK Special Branch, in Ankara. Firstly he was blind-folded, then hung on a cross, his legs dangling down; electrodes were attached to his penis and one of his toes, and water thrown over his body to heighten the pain caused by the electric shocks. Then he was thrown into a lightless *oubliette*, a hole so small that he could not lie down. Then Karatepe was crucified again before being returned to the hole, a procedure that was repeated many times until he was incarcerated in jail. The case is not untypical. 'Paula', a 26-year-old Kurdish woman, was stripped, electrocuted, beaten and sexually abused. At one stage, after she had been forced to undress, her hands were tied behind her back to a stick and then she was hoisted off the floor (so-called 'Palestinian hanging'), doused with water, given electric shocks, and sexually abused. She was tortured for seven hours on the first night and periodically for days afterwards.[55]

The United States has frequently declared that sanctions will remain on Iraq until UN Security Council Resolution 688, designed to protect Iraqi citizens from persecution, is fully implemented. Where are the US-sponsored resolutions urging an end to torture in Turkish prisons? Why is the Council resolution condemning the Turkish invasion of Cyprus not enforced? Where are the resolutions condemning the frequent Turkish invasions of Iraqi territory? On 5 December 1997 some 20,000 Turkish troops launched an invasion of northern Iraq, using US-supplied military equipment – one aggression among many. In August 1997 the Iraqi government issued a letter to the UN Secretary-General claiming that Turkey had launched 19 military invasions of Iraqi territory between 20 June and 12 August 1997: '... Turkey is persisting in its attacks on Iraq's territory and is threatening the safety and security of Iraq's people.'[56] A statement from a spokesman for the Secretary-General was issued on 1 October 1997: '*The Secretary-General is following the situation in northern Iraq with growing concern. As he has made clear in the past, Iraqi sovereignty and territorial integrity must be respected. He therefore urges Turkey to withdraw its troops as soon as possible.'*

American indifference to Turkish torture and aggression is closely analogous to its unwillingness to address torture and aggression perpetrated by Indonesia, Syria, Israel and other states. For example, Security Council Resolutions 384 (22 December 1975) and 389 (22 April 1976), calling upon Indonesia to withdraw from East Timor, have been ignored by Washington for commercial and strategic reasons. All such ethical and political derelictions have immense consequences for human rights.

Israel

Israel, a key US ally, practises torture on a systematic basis and remains in violation of international law in this and many other respects. Again there is copious documentation of the Israeli willingness to resort to torture as a practical device to aid the consolidation and expansion of the Jewish grip on Arab land.[57] The Israelis have refused to allow the Red Cross to visit Khiam prison, a notorious Israeli-supervised torture centre in southern Lebanon. The many testimonies of victims include details of stripping, beatings, incarceration in a cell the size of a dog kennel and electrocution. In 1995 the Israeli authorities gave torture a legal status, though ostensibly outlawing such practice. The draft bill, entitled *Prohibition of Torture*, was condemned by Amnesty International as 'an outrage which violates Israel's treaty obligations'. The legislation defines torture as 'severe pain or suffering, whether physical or mental, *except for pain or suffering inherent in interrogation procedures or punishment according to the law'* (my italics). It has been noted by Amnesty and other human-rights groups, including Israeli organisations, that Palestinians have been subjected to hooding, sleep deprivation, beating, violent shaking, deprivation of food and drink for lengthy periods, incarceration in freezing cells, and confinement in tiny box-like compartments.[58] Israel, while denying the existence of systematised torture, has nonetheless conceded the use of unpleasant interrogation methods: 'The main duty of the government is to protect its citizens and therefore we have to resort to methods that are not so nice. In other circumstances we would not do it, but we are faced with a very dangerous enemy, and it is the enemy not only of Israel but of the free world.'[59]

The acknowledged use of torture by Israel violates the UN Torture Convention and compounds Israel's abuse of international law. Security Council Resolution 242, requiring the withdrawal of Israeli armed forces from occupied Arab territory, has never been observed or enforced, just as the other resolutions subsequent to 1967 have also been ignored. Resolution 338 (1973) calls for observance of 242; Resolution 465 (1980) condemns Israel's illegal changes to the status of Arab land; Resolution 476 (1980) condemns again the prolonged occupation of Arab lands; Resolution 478 (1980) condemns Israel's violation of international law over Jerusalem; and Resolutions 672 and 673 (both 1990) make further serious criticisms of Israeli behaviour in the region. Many of the Security Council resolutions record Israel's violation of the Geneva Convention.

The issue of Israel's weapons of mass destruction, highly relevant to the Iraq Question, has long been considered by analysts of Middle East tensions.[60] Brian Masters, a correspondent in *The Daily Telegraph* (6 February 1998), highlights what are essentially the gross double standards applied by the United States in the Middle East: 'Israel has weapons of mass destruction. Will the US government demand that inspectors be allowed to see them, and arrange for their removal? And will Israel agree to being inspected and having its weapons removed? ... Does the US government intend to bomb Israel in order to force compliance [with UN resolutions]? Israel has demonstrated its political instability and belligerence by invading four neighbouring countries. Will the US government now seek to punish the invader?' The point can be emphasised by recalling part of the preamble to UN Resolution 687, the ceasefire resolution intended to ensure the destruction of Iraq's weapons of mass destruction. The 1991 resolution includes the words:

Recalling the objective of the establishment of a nuclear-weapons-free zone in the region of the Middle East,

Conscious of the threat which all weapons of mass destruction pose to peace and security in the area and of the need to work towards the establishment in the Middle East of a zone free of such weapons.

This suggests that the authority of the much-hyped Resolution 687, the key resolution in the 1997/8 US/Iraq crisis (see Parts II and III), can be used to demand that Israel allow UN inspectors to locate and destroy all its weapons of mass destruction. Furthermore, if, according to 687, no such weapons are to be allowed in the Middle East, what does this say about the prodigious American military presence in the waters of the Gulf and at bases in Turkey, Kuwait, Saudi Arabia and elsewhere in the region? Resolution 687, like all pieces of international law that contain 'inconvenient' items, is selectively interpreted by the United States. The issue of Israel and 'double standards' is a further indication that Washington, indifferent to law and human rights, is motivated primarily by the cynical calculation of commercial and strategic advantage.

Cuba

The United States had been running a unilateral economic blockade on Cuba for the best part of four decades, begun soon after Fidel Castro deposed the US-backed dictator Fulgencio Batista in 1959. For most of the period Cuba received support from the Soviet Union, until its collapse in 1991. Since that time Washington has worked to strengthen the embargo, primarily through domestic legislation (the 1992 Cuban Democracy Act and the 1996 Helms-Burton Act) designed to strengthen American restrictions on contact with Cuba and to intimidate other countries into adopting similar policies. The United States has not been able to achieve UN sanctions on Cuba; and in fact the UN General Assembly (GA) has shown massive and increasing opposition in recent years to American policy (Figure 2.2 shows the mounting GA hostility to the American blockade).

The majority United Nations view on the American embargo is a virtual consensus that carries enormous moral weight. It is also the case that US policy on Cuba violates many trading conventions and agreements, not least the laboriously achieved terms of the General Agreement on Tariffs and Trade (GATT) and the associated World Trade Organisation (WTO), both eagerly cited by Washington when it judges that US interests are at stake.

The American policies on such countries as Iraq and Cuba breed remarkable degrees of hypocrisy and double standards. Thus Professor Robert Goldman, an American specialist in international law, was able to argue that Somali 'war lords' could be tried by any government for violation of international law prohibiting the use of starvation against humanity[61] – when this is precisely what the United States is attempting to accomplish against Iraq (see Chapter 3) and Cuba. In fact the impact of the embargo on the civilian population of Cuba is now well documented and is today provoking widespread outrage among independent observers. For example, in March 1997 the American Association for World Health (AAWH), which serves as the US Committee for the World Health Organisation (WHO) and the Pan

Year	Against	For	Abstain
1992	59	3	71
1993	88	4	57
1994	101	2	48
1995	117	3	38
1996	137	3	25
1997	143	3	17
1998	157	2	12

Figure 2.2   GA votes on US embargo of Cuba

American Health Organisation (PAHO), published a 30-page report detailing the impact of the US embargo on the health and nutrition of the Cuban people.[62]

It was found that the embargo was causing *serious nutritional deficits, particularly among pregnant women, leading to an increase in low-birth-weight babies*; and that the US-contrived food shortages had helped to cause a devastating outbreak of neuropathy affecting tens of thousands of people. The embargo on water-treatment chemicals and spare parts for the water-supply system had seriously reduced the supplies of safe drinking water, which had caused increased morbidity and mortality from water-borne diseases. As particular examples, because of the embargo on nausea-preventing drugs, 35 children in a cancer ward were vomiting an average of 28 to 30 times a day. A man with heart disease needed an implantable defibrillator to control ventricular arrhythmia; the US firm CPI was willing to supply the device but the US government denied a licence and the man died two months later.

American policy on Cuba is causing disease and deaths among the civilian population, particularly among babies, the sick and the old. As such, as with the years-long US-led genocide of the Iraqi civilian population, the American policy on Cuba falls clearly within the defining terms of the UN Convention on the Prevention and Punishment of the Crime of Genocide. Article II(c) notes as one of the examples of genocide 'Deliberately inflicting on the group conditions of life calculated to bring about its physical destruction in whole or in part'. It is important to note that the attempt does not have to succeed in order to qualify as 'genocide'; thus Article III declares that the attempt itself shall be punishable.

The examples given in this section, far from exhaustive, demonstrate that the United States typically exhibits a cynical disregard for the requirements of law and human rights. Brutal states, even if characterised by institutionalised torture and aggression against sovereign neighbours, are aided if Washington calculates there is a prospect of commercial or strategic advantage; and civilian populations – especially the very young, the weak, the sick and the old – are deliberately targeted for 'food denial' (that is, starvation) and disease when a state refuses to acquiesce in US hegemony. Such matters should be borne in mind whenever American politicians or pundits seek to assign 'pariah' status to this or that state for its moral lapses. It is useful in this context to consider the terrorist credentials of the United States.

TERRORISM – US

State terrorism has many forms and many instances, not only those defined by the United States. On 15 April 1986, without any pretence of justification in international law, American aircraft flew from bases in Britain and carriers in the Mediterranean to bomb Tripoli and Benghazi in Libya. This military aggression, a manifest act of war, was a clear violation of the UN Charter (Article 2(4) states: '*All Members shall refrain in their international relations from the threat or use of force … '*. The results, described by foreign journalists, were plain enough. Many private houses were destroyed, the front had been blasted out of an apartment building, and the French embassy had been badly damaged. There were still bodies in the ruins; a child's foot was seen sticking out of the rubble,[63] and bodies were beginning to accumulate in Tripoli's central mortuary. Journalists estimated that more than 100 civilians had been killed and twice as many wounded, far in excess of US claims.[64] Safia, the wife of President Gaddafi, and three of the couple's children suffered pressure shock from a 2000lb bomb which hit their home. Gaddafi's two sons, Saef al-Islam and Khamees, were kept in intensive care for several days; his 16-month-old adopted daughter, Hanna, died from severe brain damage.[65]

The United States does not recognise the bombing of Libya as an act of terror – for the simple reason that *by definition* nothing perpetrated by the US government could be so described. For most purposes Washington relies on the definition of terrorism contained in Title 22 of the United States Code, Section 2656f(d). Here the following definitions are given:

> The term 'terrorism' means premeditated, politically motivated violence perpetrated against noncombatant targets by subnational groups or clandestine agents, usually intended to influence an audience.

> The term 'international terrorism' means terrorism involving citizens or the territory of more than one country.

> The term 'terrorist group' means any group practicing, or that has significant subgroups that practice, international terrorism.

In fact it is easy to see that, even if we exclude US bombings that are clearly premeditated, politically motivated and expected to cause noncombatant fatalities, there are many examples of noncombatant casualties caused by 'subnational groups or clandestine agents' that are directly funded and/or organised by the US government. Today we have even reached the point where the next projected acts of terrorism against Iraq, to be perpetrated by the CIA and other groups, can be openly discussed in the Western media (see below). While Washington constantly rails against 'terrorists' who target American assets, no independent observer doubts that the US government funds and organises terrorists on an international basis as a deliberate political choice. The US State Department claimed that during 1996 there were 296 acts of international terrorism.[66] When we survey the published details we are not surprised to find that US-sponsored acts of international terrorism are omitted from the list.

A principal consequence of the rout and humiliation of the United States in Vietnam was that Washington was forced to re-evaluate its general policies on the use of military force. The much-cited Vietnam Syndrome meant that there would be no more open-ended military interventions with no clear objectives, no new Vietnam-type 'quagmire'. Military force would still be used, but local (or imported) foreign forces – suitably cajoled, bribed or intimidated – would be exploited to the maximum. This new doctrine of Low-Intensity Warfare (LIW), a 'centrepiece' of the Bush Administration's military posture following its development under Reagan, meant that the United States could fight wars 'without declaring them'.[67] In this new strategy, state-sponsored terrorism became a central component. From the US perspective, international terrorism is a 'heinous crime' only when it works against America's hegemonic ambitions. At all other times Washington regards it as a legitimate practical option.

At one level the United States admits its own acts of terrorism. For example, in 1998 it became possible to purchase the CIA's own account of its assassination attempts against Fidel Castro; and various Senate investigations, with findings made public, resulted in a legal ban on attempts to assassinate foreign leaders – a development that has not stopped CIA and other efforts to kill Gaddafi, Saddam Hussein and others. On 27 June 1986 the International Court of Justice ruled that the United States was in violation of international law in running a terrorism campaign against Nicaragua, that it should desist from its illegal acts, and that it should pay compensation. Despite the UN Charter requirement (Article 94(1)) that each Member of the United Nations should 'comply with the decision' of the Court, Washington refused to accept the ruling, thus compounding its dereliction. Other cases of US involvement in terrorism include: the blowing up of an Air India flight in 1985, killing 329 people, by men trained in Alabama; a 1985 car-bombing in Beirut, killing 80 people and wounding 200, arranged by CIA and Saudi agents; the launching of cruise missiles against Afghanistan and Sudan in August 1998; and numerous other terrorist outrages in Nicaragua, Afghanistan, Angola, Mozambique, Guatemala, Cuba and other countries.

The United States' posture on Iraq, a principal theme of the present book, includes support for terrorist activity against Baghdad and other Iraqi cities. At a time when President Bill Clinton was denouncing the Hamas suicide bombers, at an anti-terrorist conference in Egypt in early March 1996, he was continuing to support terrorist bomb attacks inside Iraq. The Iraqi National Accord, one of the main terrorist groups operating against the Iraqi regime, has been described by one of the Iraqi opposition leaders as 'heavily sponsored by the US and under the influence of the CIA'.[68] Abu Amneh al-Khadami, a bomb-maker for the National Accord, has described how he made bombs and sent them to Baghdad; and how he conspired with his American backers. One Iraqi opposition figure commented, after seeing a video in which al-Khadami described the US involvement: 'The people in the [US] State Department will crawl under their desks when they see what Abu Amneh has revealed about the groups they are supporting and co-ordinating.' In 1995 the CIA asked the US Congress for a further $15 million to support terrorist and other covert activities inside Iraq. President Clinton, speaking at Sharm al-Sheikh in Egypt on 13 March 1996, declared: 'We must be clear in our condemnation of those who resort to terror.'[70]

On 14 July 1997 Nizar Hamdoon, the Iraqi ambassador to the United Nations, transmitted a letter from the Iraqi foreign minister Mohammed Said Al-Sahaf to the UN Secretary-General, drawing attention to the actions being taken by the US government 'to undermine the security and sovereignty of Iraq ...'.[71] The letter (Annex) relies heavily on material published in the *Washington Post* (26 June 1997) and on information broadcast on the same day on the American ABC television network. The *Post* article refers to the 'CIA's Secret War on Saddam' and quotes the CIA agent Warren Marik who describes the dropping of leaflets on Iraq and the training of subversive personnel. Millions of dollars were spent on radio and video propaganda, on training, and on arms 'to separate the north from the rest of Iraqi territory', despite the many UN resolutions reaffirming the territorial integrity of Iraq. In particular, Marik relates how he recruited members of the Iraqi National Congress to work for the CIA with the aim of launching sabotage and other terrorist acts against Iraq.

He charged also that in excess of $100 million had been spent in such efforts and that the US Senate Intelligence Committee had been involved in promoting subversive activities against Iraq. A principal aim was to reduce the Iraqi regime's control to no more than the Baghdad area, just as the CIA had worked to reduce the areas of control exercised by the Afghan and Soviet regimes during the Cold War. The *Post* article claimed that the Senate Intelligence Committee had authorised the CIA to establish a secret semi-permanent American group in the north of Iraq to train rebels and mercenaries, and to equip them with *matériel* to conduct sabotage and other tasks, including assassinations, inside Iraq. The CIA was also encouraging Iran to attack Iraq in conjunction with the planned CIA-mounted offensive against the Iraqi regime: 'Washington would look with favour on Iran moving troops along its border to distract Saddam as the offensive began.'[72] In northern Iraq a meeting took place between CIA staff and Iranian intelligence operatives to plan a combined onslaught on the Iraqi regime.

In February 1998 further information on *coup* plots against Saddam Hussein and other terrorist schemes reached the public domain. It emerged that the British MI6 had been involved in a 1996 attempt to overthrow the Iraqi dictator. The consequences of this failure included the execution of at least 100 people in Iraq and an FBI (Federal Bureau of Investigation) probe of the agents involved. One source observed: 'This case was like a paradigm for everything that was wrong with US intelligence policy.' The operation, crushed in June 1996, was reportedly based in Jordan and used the Iraqi National Accord. According to a report in the *Los Angeles Times* the operation was thoroughly penetrated by Iraqi double agents, an Iraqi intelligence triumph that reduced the MI6–CIA plot to fiasco. One opponent of the Iraqi regime commented that the Accord, led by Dr Iyad Mohammed Alawi, a former member of Iraq's ruling Baath Party who has lived in London since 1971, never stood any chance of success: 'A *coup* like this cannot be stage-managed from the outside, as in the 1960s. Saddam has 30 years' experience in keeping power.' Alawi had even publicised his intention to start a mutiny in the Iraqi army; and in any case the Iraqi National Accord had a well-earned reputation for being full of Iraqi double agents.

It is now known that President Bush signed an order in 1991 telling the CIA to overthrow Saddam Hussein, but experienced Agency officers were doubtful that this could be done. Thus Frank Anderson, head of the CIA Near East Division, commented to ABC television: 'We didn't have a single mechanism or combination of mechanisms with which I could create a plan to get rid of Saddam at that time.' General Wafiq al-Samarrai, a former head of Iraqi military intelligence, had a plan to assassinate Saddam as he passed over a bridge in his home town of Samarra; and at the same time the CIA was planning various bombing schemes as a co-founder of the Iraqi National Accord.[73] American, British, Jordanian and Saudi intelligence officers met in Saudi Arabia in January 1996 to plan the *coup* attempt. It was not the first to end in ignominy or the last to be staged. Another *coup* plot failed in November 1997, with the Israeli intelligence agency Mossad reportedly reviving a five-year-old plan to kill the Iraqi president (a 1992 operation was aborted after six Israeli soldiers were accidentally killed during a live-fire training exercise for the mission).[74] In February 1998 yet another CIA plan to topple Saddam Hussein was being discussed in the public domain. This scheme, said to have been 'months in the making' and costing tens of millions of dollars, aimed at enlisting Kurdish and Shi'ite agents to attack economic and political targets inside Iraq. In this plan the sabotage and subversion was to be supported by propaganda, including broadcasts from a 'Radio Free Iraq' (modelled on Cold War transmission), directed at the Iraqi people. George Tenet, the CIA director, had reportedly told President Clinton that the plot was 'risky', with the White House national security advisor Sandy Berger equally sceptical that the plan would be successful. Officials commented at the time that this '*major campaign of sabotage*' would be one of the largest and most ambitious pieces of CIA covert action since the end of the Cold War.[75]

The 1996 Kurdish crisis had revealed the extent of CIA activity in northern Iraq. On 3 September 1996, following alleged Iraqi intervention between the Patriotic Union of Kurdistan (PUK) and the Kurdistan Democratic Party (KDP) in northern Iraq, the United States launched 27 cruise missiles – costing $1.2 million each – against targets south of Baghdad. This manifest aggression, condemned throughout the world, was compounded the next day by the launching of a further 17 cruise missiles from warships and a submarine in the Gulf. The southern 'no-fly' zone, imposed by the US with no United Nations authorisation, was further extended as a vindictive act that did nothing to weaken the strategic position of Saddam Hussein. In fact the Iraqi president had achieved a minor triumph. A KDP–Iraqi pact had resulted in the rout of CIA assets in northern Iraq. As early as 1993 the CIA, following years of involvement in the region, had begun installing surveillance equipment near the Kurdish town of Sallahadine as part of one of the early schemes to depose Saddam. The lack of success was followed by the 1996 coup attempt, when seven CIA operatives had to be plucked by helicopter from a Kurdistan hillside to prevent their capture. The subsequent Iraqi incursions into the area resulted in the eviction of yet more CIA personnel and dozens of their Kurdish collaborators.

The frequent American efforts to promote state terrorism (that is, bombings, sabotage, assassinations) against Iraq are illegal in international law and also (nominally) illegal in US domestic law. This seemingly minor detail does nothing to inhibit the hatching of fresh terrorist plots, including schemes to assassinate the Iraqi president. Today (mid-1998) there are frequent calls for direct terrorist action to be taken against the Iraqi leadership, particularly against Saddam Hussein. The Western media in the United States and Britain have long been tolerant of such a policy.[76] It still remains to be seen whether Washington will be successful in using a particular form of terrorism that it is quick to condemn when it is employed by other states that are not resolutely pro-American.

The bellicose statements issued by American politicians amount to advocating a form of terrorism to solve a political problem. Thus Bob Kerrey, vice-chairman of the Senate Foreign Relations Committee, commented that as a prelude to deposing Saddam (that is, before launching a terrorist initiative): *'I would first of all speak to the 22 million Iraqis who have been terrorised by this dictator and say: "We are going to liberate you".'* In the same spirit Senator John McCain, a Republican on the Senate Armed Services Committee, declared: *'I would say it's our goal to remove him from power because, as long as he's there, we're facing this enormous challenge.'*[77]

The American willingness to resort to terrorism in the pursuit of political objectives should be borne in mind when we hear US politicians and pundits denouncing other states accused of exploiting the same practical option. In this context it should hardly be necessary to emphasise the relevance of law and ethical judgement.

LAW AND DISORDER

The concept of law is problematic at many levels. We may ask, of any society, how did law originate? Is it grounded in metaphysical or purely secular categories? Whose interests does it serve? What is the relationship of law to ethics? Questions of this sort are important but secondary to the purposes of the present book. Here it is necessary to ask only one basic question: how can the demands of acknowledged law be used to constrain the behaviour of a hegemonic power? Law carries ethical weight, and to this extent it can influence behaviour, but in the last resort the law is only effective if it can be enforced. In short, how is (international) law to be enforced to regulate the behaviour of the United States? The problem can be represented as a general one (how is the behaviour of *any* state to be regulated by international law?), but it becomes particularly acute when a nation enjoys unassailable military and economic power.

Companies and/or national governments can combine to resist domestic US legislation intended to have extraterritorial reach; and such a posture may or may not help to reinforce existing international law. Thus in 1992 some of Britain's leading companies were planning a campaign to head off a threat to their US investments from the tax plans of the then President-elect, Bill Clinton.[78] Here the proposed legislation was intended to apply essentially to the American domestic environment, though there were obvious ramifications for foreign companies. In 1996, via the provisions of the Helms-Burton Act (threatening penalties for foreign companies trading with Cuba) and the D'Amato-Kennedy Act (threatening penalties for foreign companies investing in Iran and Libya), Washington was seeking to promote domestic legislation with unambiguous extraterritorial reach. In this case the European Union, as one important trading group, saw the American legislation as an intolerable attempt to impose its foreign policy goals on its trading partners, 'on pain of economic sanctions'.[79] The prospect of a serious trade war between the United States and Europe seemed an inevitable consequence of US arrogance. In the same fashion the Pentagon succeeded in excluding itself from the constraints of the global warming treaty negotiated in Japan in December 1997. In the final hours of the Kyoto conference, despite objections from Iraq and Russia, a provision was gavelled through 'in a bit of diplomatic sleight-of-hand' to ensure that certain types of military operations would remain unfettered by curbs on fossil-fuel emissions. Said one US official: 'It was the one issue the Pentagon cared most about, and we did well on it.'[80]

Such examples illustrate the arrogance of power. The United States assumes – as the self-proclaimed one 'indispensable' nation – that it is entitled to enact domestic legislation with intended consequences for foreign states; and that it can exclude itself from the implications of international law that Washington finds inconvenient. Legal constraints can be massaged away; or, if this proves difficult, they can simply be ignored. Such attitudes are graphically demonstrated in the US posture on 'weapons of mass destruction'. Washington abrogates to itself the right to decide which states will be allowed which weapons (despite the 'sovereign equality' of UN Members, protected by Article 2(1) of the Charter), while at the same time claiming the absolute right to develop and manufacture whatever weapons of mass destruction it chooses.

It is useful to remember that the United States has experimented on unknowing human 'guinea pigs' to research biological and chemical weapons, the very items that today condemn Iraq as a 'pariah state'. We now know that American scientists conducted 'at least several hundred tests with human subjects who were not informed of the nature of the experiments, or of the danger to their health'.[81] In 1993 and 1994 the US government began to reveal the extent of such experiments on human beings during and after the Second World War: *'We now know that American scientists tested humans with mustard gas, other chemical agents, exposed others to radiation tests, and still others to a variety of pathogens without the subjects' knowledge or consent.'*[82] Sheldon H. Harris, Emeritus Professor of History, California State University, commented in 1994 that human experimentation and the production of biological warfare agents appeared to be flourishing in the United States, Russia and Japan despite the international agreements prohibiting such activities.[83] In fact American research has been extensive:

> Scientists were assigned to study botulism, brucellosis, glanders and melildosis, tularemia, psittacosis, coccidioidal granuloma, neurotropic encephalitis, shellfish poisoning ... plague, rinderpest, Newcastle disease and fowl plague, rice brown spot, rice blast, late blight of potato, southern blight, chemical plant growth regulators, and chemical defoliants. It is probable that other possible BW [biological warfare] agents may have been examined ... [84]

In August 1942 George W. Merck of the Merck pharmaceutical company of New Jersey became the head of the newly created War Reserve Service (WRS), set up to co-ordinate all BW work. He commented later: 'All possible living agents, or their toxic products, which were pathogenic for man, animals, and plants were considered.'[85]

The American tests of chemical and biological weapons continued through the decades of the Cold War. In the early 1960s an 'ambitious' test programme covered 'not only trials at sea, but Arctic and tropical environmental tests as well'.[86] Biological tests involving human beings, animals and plants were carried out by American scientists working in the continental United States and also in Cairo, Liberia, South Korea and Okinawa.[87] The United States and China collaborated on BW tests in Hubei province in 1986 or 1987, involving work by Hubei Province Medical University and the US

Department of Defense on 200 'hospitalised volunteers' suffering from haemorrhagic fever.[88]

It is still an open question whether the United States used biological warfare during the Korean War. The International Scientific Commission for the Facts Concerning Bacterial Warfare in Korea and China (ISC), a source generally considered of high quality, found that numerous Chinese and Korean sites suffered unexplained outbreaks of bubonic plague and other diseases accompanied by the appearance of nonindigenous or out-of-season insects. There now seems to be evidence that the Americans used fleas to spread disease among civilian Asian populations, and that some 700 voles that mysteriously appeared in a Chinese village in 1952 after an overflight by an American F-82 fighter might have been used for the same purpose (many of the voles had broken legs).[89] It is known that US researchers experimented with toxic bacteria by spraying serratia organisms over San Francisco: seven people were hospitalised and one died. A lawsuit against the US government by a victim's family revealed three hundred 'open air' germ tests between 1950 and 1969. The US tests included releasing toxic organisms into the Pentagon air-conditioning system and into the New York subways. It is useful to bear such events in mind whenever Washington accuses Iraq of developing a biological warfare capability.

In January 1996 the US Army revealed that it had stockpiled 30,000 tons of chemical weapons (mainly nerve and blister agents) over eight states and that they were being destroyed at a cost of $12 billion. Toxic emissions had already been recorded at various sites, and anxieties were being expressed about the fresh hazards that disposal of the chemical weapons might bring.[90] In April 1997 the US Senate ratified (74 votes to 26) the Chemical Weapons Convention outlawing the manufacture, storage and use of a long list of chemical weapons; but in February 1998 it emerged that the United States, eager for war with Iraq over the weapons-inspection issue, had produced legislation on the inspection of its own chemical arsenal in such a way that the American president would be able to refuse admission to international inspectors. The new legislation allowed the president to pick and choose inspectors and to deny access to individuals from certain countries – precisely the activities which, when urged by Iraq, were enough for Washington to threaten a massive bombing retaliation against Iraqi targets. Senator Joseph Biden commented: 'With few exceptions, denial of a duly authorised inspection would violate the Chemical Weapons Convention.' In the same spirit, Amy Smithson, who had campaigned for US ratification of the Convention, noted: '*We are in violation of the treaty, and it is so ironic that we are about to engage in hostilities against Iraq over the matter of weapons inspections, because Saddam Hussein has registered the same exceptions as we have done.*'[91] Two inspectors, a Cuban and an Iranian, had already been struck off the approved list by the US authorities.

Washington was inviting applause for its ratification of the Chemical Weapons Convention, but in fact the ratification was bogus. US leadership was crucial to the success of the new treaty but Clause 307 of the relevant US bill was headed National Security Exception: '*The president may deny a request to inspect any facility in the United States in cases where the president determines that the inspection may pose a threat to the national security interests of the United States.*' Put another way, inspectors would be allowed to inspect the weapons sites except where they were not allowed to do so. Saddam Hussein could not have said it better. Moreover, as with the Iraqi attitude before the intervention of UN Secretary-General Kofi Annan (see Chapter 6), the president's decision – for example, in objecting to any individual serving as an inspector – 'shall not be reviewable in any court'. Washington would ignore the Convention when it felt like it, and there would be no opportunity for a legal challenge. Smithson dubbed this posture 'sheer folly' and pointed out that if the US 'tears up the treaty, so will all the other countries'.[92]

Hence the US posture on 'weapons of mass destruction' is deeply hypocritical. It remains the case that, despite international agreements, Washington has an unknown and unverifiable capacity in the areas of biological and chemical warfare. The United States is retaining massive nuclear stockpiles and at the same time developing a new generation of nuclear weapons. We have seen that Washington has ignored UN General Assembly Resolution 32/84 (12 December 1977), which prohibits States 'from developing new weapons of mass destruction based on new scientific principles' – such as 'radioactive material weapons' and weapons with 'characteristics comparable in destructive effect to those of the atomic bomb'. Depleted-uranium (du) munitions and fuel–air explosives (FAEs) clearly fall within the definition of prohibited weapons. At the same time the United States was keen to test a wide range of new weapons against Iraqi targets. For example, the GBU-28 'bunker-busting' bomb had not been tested in war conditions before, and military planners were eager to assess its performance. Similarly the improved B-2 Stealth bombers, carrying up to eight GBU-28 bombs, had not been tested in a hostile environment. New guidance systems for cruise missiles had been tested to a limited extent over Bosnia, but the full use of Global Positioning System satellites for this purpose had yet to be evaluated. Washington, whatever the current state of international law and international agreements, was keen to test a massive range of new military hardware. Already a new aircraft, the F-22 fighter, on which $70 billion was being spent, was emerging from development. This weapon too would presumably require a fresh war for real-world testing.

It is significant that many UN-linked bodies recognise items in American arsenals as weapons of mass destruction. There is no ambiguity with *nuclear* weapons but now attention is being given to many devices that the United

States has used for mass slaughter in Iraq and elsewhere. Thus a Sub-Committee on Prevention of Discrimination and Protection of Minorities, working under the auspices of the UN Economic and Social Council, refers not only to nuclear, chemical and biological weapons but also to weapons known to have been used by the United States against Iraq: ' ... fuel–air bombs, napalm, cluster bombs ... and weaponry containing depleted uranium'; expresses concern at the use of such 'weapons of mass or indiscriminate destruction or of a nature to cause superfluous or unnecessary suffering'; expresses concern at the 'repeated reports of the long-term consequences of the use of such weapons upon human life and health'; and urges all States to be guided in their national policies by the need 'to curb the testing, the production and the spread' of such weapons.[93]

In 1996 the International Court of Justice (the World Court), having considered the case on Legality of the Threat or Use of Nuclear Weapons, unanimously ruled that *the use of nuclear weapons was subject to all the rules of humanitarian law*. Such law includes a prohibition on targeting or killing civilians, and damaging non-belligerent States and their people; it prohibits weapons that cause undue suffering, and prohibits damage to the environment. In this context the use of nuclear weapons in war constitutes a violation of humanitarian law and a violation of a crucial World Court decision. The Court ruling also stipulated that states should stop further development of nuclear weapons and eliminate existing stockpiles. The United States, in ignoring the various elements in the Court decision (that is, by continuing to develop a new range of nuclear weapons and by at least implicitly threatening resort to the nuclear option in war), is thus in violation of humanitarian law, the World Court and the UN Charter (Article 94(1), which states: 'Each Member of the United Nations undertakes to comply with the decision of the International Court of Justice...').

Such examples show the US indifference to international law in circumstances where legal constraints might inhibit American foreign policy. At the same time Washington is keen to invoke international law against US-nominated 'rogue states' unwilling to acquiesce in American hegemony. Such cynical hypocrisy is one of the perquisites of unassailable military and economic power: the same phenomenon, or its historical equivalent, has always characterised nations with sufficient power to disregard the legal and moral appeals of weaker states.

In the last resort the integrity of any law rests upon an ethical sanction: the term 'immoral law' is not necessarily oxymoronic and it may be ethically right to ignore such a law. But it is obvious that US derelictions, designed to maximise strategic and economic advantage, occur for other reasons. There is widespread debate about whether capitalist priorities can be consistent with the observance of human rights.[94] The manufacture of American lies about the Cuban regime of Fidel Castro – to the point that *US military advisors recommended shooting down an American civil airliner and blaming it on Castro*[95] – have been exposed. A London-based newspaper, *The Sunday Telegraph* (1 February 1998), can support American 'hawks' by urging the bombing of Iraq in violation of international law: 'Women and children will be killed, and others will be horribly injured... . Bombing Iraq will not look like an exercise in moral purity, because it isn't ... it is the strategically rational option ... *the best course of action is not always the "ethical" one*' (my italics). This is a candid admission. When a powerful State needs to accomplish a strategic goal it does not need to consider what is morally right. The ethical strictures of the dissident Noam Chomsky, which in any decent society would be heard and heeded,[96] can be conveniently ignored. The United States, as the current hegemonic country, has no practical need to reflect on moral categories. There are altogether more important priorities.

THE ECONOMIC INTEREST

It is not simplistic to suggest that the Iraq Question is principally about oil. Following the Iraqi invasion of Kuwait in 1990, Lawrence Korb, a former US Assistant Defense Secretary, declared: 'If Kuwait grew carrots, we wouldn't give a damn'; on 12 January 1991 Congressman Stokes from Ohio commented: 'I venture to say that if Kuwait grew bananas, instead of oil, we would not have 400,000 American troops there today.'

In 1990, prior to the Iraqi invasion, Kuwait was flooding the international oil market in violation of OPEC agreements. One consequence was a massive reduction in Iraqi oil revenues, following the drop in oil prices. Market analysts acknowledged that Iraq was facing economic suffocation. In response Saddam Hussein commented that for every dollar drop in the price of a barrel of oil, 'the Iraqi loss amounted to $1 billion annually ... this is in fact a kind of war against Iraq'. At the same time Kuwait had been illegally extracting oil from the Iraqi Rumeila oilfield, which extends into Kuwait, a violation of agreements and a cost to Iraq of around $2.4 billion. Now it was being suggested that, at the prompting of the United States, certain Arab oil producers had been deliberately exceeding the agreed OPEC quotas, a practice that was costing Iraq $14 billion a year. The main American aim was being achieved: an abundant supply of cheap oil. Iraq, impoverished by the 1980–9 war with Iran – a war funded by Kuwait and Saudi Arabia, and supported by the United States as an active belligerent – was now being subjected to fresh, politically-motivated pressures from Kuwait and the United States. In these circumstances the invasion of Kuwait, unquestionably illegal in international law, can be seen as a desperate act by an increasingly impoverished state facing economic ruin orchestrated by its erstwhile allies in the anti-Iran coalition.

Through the 1990s the world oil markets saw advantage in the absence of Iraqi oil. Any suggestion that sanctions should be lifted generated immediate alarm on the markets. Thus the expert analyst Peter Bogin, at Cambridge Energy Research Associates in Paris, estimated that if Iraq were allowed back into the markets, the price of oil 'would fall by $2 a barrel'; similarly, Michael Sheridan, writing as diplomatic editor of *The Independent* (30 September 1995), noted the commercial pressures to keep the sanctions in place. The priority was simple: the Iraqi people would have to be kept in their diseased and starving condition because the profits of world capitalism demanded it. Iraqi failures to comply with UN resolutions could always be cited (or invented) to justify the years-long genocide of the civilian population.

The morality of this *realpolitik* calculation was plain. While American oil barons consorted with the disgusting Taliban regime in Afghanistan (a regime that is today denying women education, work and hospital treatment),[97] market analysts continued to worry about the commercial consequences of allowing more Iraqi oil to be sold. In the first place the possibility, high in early 1998 (see Chapter 5), of a new Gulf war was alarming enough, though commercial analysts were divided.[98] Then, with the UN-brokered agreement that Iraq be allowed to sell more oil, the international traders reacted swiftly and the oil price slid to a new level.[99] The OPEC cartel was already facing various problems and the warm (1997/8) winter had driven the oil price down by $5 a barrel. The prospect of more Iraqi oil on the market was an added worry. Any humanitarian concern for the desperate plight of the Iraqi people did not rate against the commercial preoccupations of the international corporate world and the mercenary politicians and pundits who serve it.

3 Iraq – The Background

The 1997/8 US/Iraq crisis (see Parts II and III) cannot be understood without an appreciation of recent Iraqi history. The copious snapshots offered by pundits and politicians, seemingly unaware of many detailed and relevant historical circumstances, are often facile and simplistic. It is easy to see the reason: most contemporary commentary in the public domain is intended not to *elucidate* but to *convince*. The main media task through the period of the crisis was to prepare Western publics, primarily those of the United States and Britain (the main intending belligerents), for a further military onslaught on Iraq. Public support for military action would have encouraged the Western political Establishments, but mere acquiescence in further destruction of Arab property and people would have sufficed. The mixed public response to the familiar propaganda, allied to a growing international hostility to American belligerence, is a reason for optimism. Before offering a detailed profile of the crisis chronology it is useful to glance at some of the principal shaping factors in the Iraq Question.

SADDAM: FROM DARLING TO DEMON

It is characteristic of many US-sponsored dictators – Batista, Noriega, Gaddafi, Saddam Hussein and others – that, from the American perspective, they get ideas above their station and seek to escape the hand of the puppet master. It is likely that Saddam Hussein, as a principal player on the modern stage, would never have gained power without persistent American interference in Iraqi affairs; nor would he have emerged as a military threat to his neighbours if he had not been supplied and protected by a Washington more interested in the strategic calculation of the day than in any principled commitment to human rights.

The United States well knew the character of Saddam Hussein as early as 1963, at a time when he was urging the creation of the *Jihaz Haneen* (the so called 'instrument of learning'), a special security body modelled on the Nazi SS and designed to protect the Iraqi Baathist Party by targeting 'enemies of the people', by harassing and intimidating unfriendly factions, and by generally securing power by terror. At this time the Iraqi army staged a successful *coup d'état* against the first Iraqi Baathist president, General Abdul Karim Kassem, who was briskly tried, tied to a chair and shot dead. It is important

46

to note that the *coup* and the events that followed were shaped largely by the American CIA. Thus Ali Saleh Saadi, Minister of the Interior in the new regime, declared: 'We came to power on a CIA train.'[1] This was a characteristic American intervention in Iraq that set Saddam Hussein firmly on the road to power.

The United States, in the throes of the Cold War, had been worried about the possible rise of Communism in the Middle East. In 1961 Syria seceded from the Nasser-dominated United Arab Republic (UAR), so removing the chance of a UAR encroachment on Iraq and the strengthening of the pan-Arabist sentiment. Kassem, also seen as a threat to Western interests, was nationalising elements of the Iraqi Petroleum Company (IPC) while resurrecting the Iraqi claim to Kuwait (Saddam's 1990 claim reflected a persistent theme in Iraqi nationalism). The British responded as the West did in 1991, by sponsoring a Kurdish insurrection against the Iraq government; while at the same time the American CIA was developing its plans for the overthrow of the Iraqi leadership. The CIA scheme included an extensive onslaught on the Iraq Communist Party, not merely through propaganda and the sponsorship of rival groups but through the physical extermination of its active members.[2]

The CIA moved quickly after the *coup* and the execution of Kassem. It had orchestrated a successful civil insurrection involving disaffected Baathists and now it was essential to prevent unacceptable political factions from moving to fill the power vacuum. Thus the CIA prepared comprehensive lists of people to be murdered by death squads after the *coup*. Aburish comments: 'The number of people eliminated remains confused and estimates range from seven hundred to thirty thousand. Putting various statements by Iraqi exiles together, in all likelihood the figure was nearer five thousand and, with some effort, I have managed to gather over six hundred names.[3] The murdered Iraqis included many ordinary men and women who continued to resist after the *coup* had been accomplished, and also what Aburish calls the *crème de la crème* of educated Iraqis (senior army officers, lawyers, professors, teachers, doctors and others – anyone whom the CIA and the *coup* leaders judged to be a possible threat to the new regime and Western interests). The death squads moved from house to house to carry out on-the-spot executions, often after hideous torture. The many victims included pregnant women and old men, tortured in view of their families, and seven out of the thirteen members of the Central Committee of the Iraqi Communist Party. The British Committee for Human Rights in Iraq likened the death squads to 'Hitlerian shock troops'.

The CIA lists of people to be murdered were drawn up in Cairo, Beirut and Damascus, with the help of Iraqi exiles and others. One CIA operative, William McHale, working under the cover of a *Time* news correspondent, was credited with producing the most number of names, many of which were supplied by a Baghdad police officer.[4] It is of interest that McHale was acting under the instructions of his own brother, Don, himself a senior CIA official; that Christian members of the Baath Party in Syria provided names; and that further individuals to be targeted were named by a senior Egyptian intelligence officer. *Saddam Hussein was one of several Iraqis who added names to the CIA death lists.* According to the respected Egyptian writer Mohamed Heikal, King Hussein of Jordan later confirmed that the CIA had set up a radio station in Kuwait to issue instructions to the rebels and to supply lists of people to be murdered.[5] (There is evidence that the CIA again used Kuwait in the economic and propaganda war against Saddam in the prelude to the 1990 Iraqi invasion.) The Kassem threat to Kuwait had been successful: an Iraq/Kuwait federation had been agreed, involving the creation of a single army and the ceding of Kuwaiti foreign policy and some Kuwaiti financial control to Iraq. The *coup* had removed this threat to Western influence, and the subsequent mass extermination served to consolidate the Western grip on the Gulf region.

Saddam Hussein, following the *coup*, returned to Iraq from exile in Cairo and became personally involved in the torture of leftists in the separate prisons for the *fellaheed* (peasants) and the *muthaqafeen* (educated class). This characteristic behaviour of Saddam did not concern Washington. Kassem had angered the Americans by withdrawing Iraq from the anti-Soviet Baghdad Pact, by nationalising part of the Iraqi Petroleum Company (IPC), and by pressing Kuwait into a federal union with Iraq. In such circumstances the torturer Saddam was a darling of the CIA planners: resolutely anti-Communist and ambitious for political power, he was an attractive Washington ally in the *coup* against Kassem and the subsequent murder of leftist Iraqi politicians and academics. With American enthusiasm set to persist through the 1970s and 1980s, the US–Saddam love affair lasted for almost three decades. It had seemed a durable relationship. Through his well-known propensities for torture and arbitrary execution of leftist elements, Saddam had well advertised his anti-Communist credentials and endeared himself to the Washington strategists. When he subsequently displayed reliable anti-Iranian attitudes after the collapse of the Shah (despite being buttressed by CIA-aided terror) and the emergence of the ayatollahs, the United States and its allies were happy to sponsor a Coalition in the war (1980–8) against Iran. The Saudis and Kuwaitis contributed around $50 billion to Saddam Hussein – with the undisguised approval of the United States, which itself became an active ally of Saddam in the first substantial Gulf war of the last half-century.

This war left Iraq impoverished, unable to pay its debts, and facing mounting economic pressures. Brief reference has already been made to Iraq's grievances during the prelude to the invasion of Kuwait.[6] Some observers (allowed little exposure in the Western media) came to believe that the illegal Iraqi aggression, far from being the work of a 'new Hitler', was the result of deliberate and calculated provocation. For example, there is evidence that in 1990 King Fahd of Saudi Arabia judged that *'the Kuwaitis had brought the invasion upon themselves by being too inflexible ... '*.[7] And no-one doubted that the United States was the principal influence behind any attitude that the feudal Kuwaiti rulers chose to adopt. In the event Washington decided to orchestrate another Gulf war, this time building a Coalition against Iraq rather than against Iran. By August 1990 Saddam Hussein had moved full circle: from being a fêted and funded darling of the West he had become a hated demon.

The response for this dramatic but not unprecedented transformation can be debated. It now seems undeniable that in the months leading up to August in that fateful year Iraq was being subjected to massive and growing political provocation.[8] This, in conjunction with the celebrated American 'green light',[9] seemed designed to maximise the likelihood of war. There were good reasons why the United States, like any militarised system, should have welcomed a suitable war: there was the ever-present need to demonstrate military hegemony, the need to justify a massive military budget, the need to test new weapons in a 'real-world' environment, the need to stimulate factory production by depleting existing munitions stockpiles, etc. The Oil Issue was important but perhaps not decisive. Saddam would have been obliged to sell his newly-acquired Kuwaiti oil at a price to safeguard stable revenues: with the pressures within OPEC, and the diminishing role of OPEC itself in world markets, he would have been pressured to impose realistic pricing levels. What seems clear is that the 1991 Gulf War had little to do with human rights or naked aggression. Such things are vitally important but not to Washington planners unless there are attendant issues that affect perceived US 'national interest'.

The character of Saddam Hussein was well known in the West before his reckless invasion of Kuwait: if the political leaders in Washington, London and elsewhere had been genuinely interested in democracy and human rights they would have had little truck with one of the most ruthless political operators in the Middle East. The pattern had been laid down long ago. Abdul Salaam Arif had emerged as Iraqi leader following the 1963 *coup*, only to be killed in a helicopter crash three years later whereupon his brother Abdul al-Rahman assumed the reins of power. A fresh *coup* in July 1968 was staged by General Ahmad Hasan al-Bakr with the support of Saddam Hussein, which led to purges, show trials and public executions: some 200,000 citizens attended the hanging of fourteen 'counter-revolutionaries', with Bakr and other Baathist leaders making violent anti Zionist speeches against the backdrop of corpses hanging from the gallows. Saddam was now working ruthlessly to impose the Baathist will on the other factions of the Revolutionary Command Council (RCC) and on the country as a whole.[10] To the muted international response Baghdad Radio retorted: 'We hanged spies, but the

Jews crucified Christ'; and Saddam later commented that the men were hanged 'to teach the people a lesson'. The message was plain: now Saddam Hussein was in charge of the internal security and the Baathists were here to stay.

Throughout the 1970s Saddam worked to secure his power base; and on 17 June 1979 felt strong enough to declare himself president of Iraq. Bakr, having resigned 'owing to poor health', was under house arrest; and five days later Saddam launched a fresh terror purge. At a closed session attended by one thousand cadres the Party was purged in a dreadful exercise of terror. Saddam slowly read out the names of the doomed men, pausing over his list for maximum dramatic effect (these televised proceedings were later shown in Britain and elsewhere). Finally a body of 'convicted men' was completed and forced to face the firing squad. Saddam's methods were brutal and unambiguous: possible rivals were targeted as 'traitors', marginalised and executed, often after torture. Public confessions were used to 'legitimise' the ruthless process; now no-one could doubt that the era of Saddam Hussein had been consolidated through terror and was set to endure. The West was well pleased. Now it was plain that a reliable anti-Communist had assumed total control in a vital region of the Middle East. The harshness of his methods was seen as entirely justified in the fraught circumstances of the Cold War.

The pattern persisted through the 1980s/90s. Saddam knew how to use the internal security apparatus to consolidate his position.[11] In March 1993 the special UN rapporteur Max van der Stoel declared that Iraq was guilty of massive human-rights violations and that the blame could be laid squarely on Saddam Hussein's system of government. In a report to the UN Human Rights Commission he noted that the abuses included economic deprivation, torture and mass executions of ethnic minorities: 'Such violations are effected through a variety of means, but for one overriding reason: the present order of government in Iraq tolerates no real opposition.' It is significant that Mr van der Stoel, a former Dutch foreign minister, was not allowed to visit Iraq for his investigation and was forced to rely on outside evidence and on documents seized after the 1991 Gulf War. Sceptics may conclude that for this reason the results of the enquiry were unreliable, but further evidence has accumulated in the years that followed.[12] For example, in 1998 the Abu Ghraib prison remained notorious. One victim has related how guards were bribed to say which prisoners would be on the execution list for the next day. If 10 or 20 people were to be executed the guards would talk of tomorrow's 'meal', typically arranged to occur on Saturdays and Tuesdays.[13]

The methods persist, a feature of the Saddam regime. But they were known about through the decades when Saddam was a darling of the West. And now that it is the period of his comprehensive demonisation it is rarely remarked that Iraq had one of the best national health systems in the region, before it was destroyed by war and economic sanctions; and that Iraq, home to one of the world's oldest Christian communities, shows considerably more religious tolerance to non-Muslim commitments than do Kuwait or Saudi Arabia.[14] In this respect at least, Saddam Hussein is 'closer to our values' than were our Coalition allies during the 1991 Gulf War.[15]

The point is made. When Saddam Hussein was a *darling* of the West his gross abuses of human rights were of no concern in Washington and London: even the currently much-advertised slaughter at Halabja did nothing at the time to damage the scale of Western support for the totalitarian Baathist regime in Iraq. And when Saddam was comprehensively transformed into *demon* his social reforms in education and health provision, and his tolerance for non-Muslim religion, were discounted; and no attention was given to any Iraqi grievance, however legitimate. There is nothing in this shifting Western posture of a principled concern about human rights; there is only the *realpolitik* machination for commercial and strategic advantage, the covert pursuit of commercial benefit for this or that identifiable social élite.

THE WEAPONS PRETEXT

The 1997/8 US/Iraq crisis was essentially about whether the Iraqi authorities would allow UN weapons inspectors to enter various 'sensitive' sites, including the so-called 'presidential' compounds. Whether the United States was really keen to gain such access for the publicly-declared reasons is open to debate: there are certainly grounds for thinking that some of the UN personnel were more interested in espionage than in conventional inspection activities (see Parts II and III). During the entire period of the crisis the West maintained a bombardment of propaganda designed to show that Saddam possessed vast stockpiles of prohibited weapons, that he retained the capacity to manufacture more, and that therefore he represented a threat not only to the countries of the region but to the entire world. Part of the American propaganda was to publicise plans of the US military to inject every member of the armed forces against anthrax bacteria. Thus a Pentagon official declared: 'We know the threat is out there. We need protection before we go to war and not afterwards.'[16]

At the same time little publicity was given to the minor matter that there seemed to be no evidence that Iraq actually possessed biological and chemical weapons. It was plain that Iraq had run biological and chemical development programmes, in the past had stockpiled a vast number of weapons, and had lied about its activities; but it was equally clear that the UN inspectors had located substantial quantities of weapons, subsequently destroyed, and that many UN personnel were suggesting that what was left was of little consequence. In February 1998 British diplomats were admitting that they did not know the location of Iraq's supposed stockpiles of weapons,[17] which to independent analysts was tantamount to saying that they did not know for certain whether they actually possessed any.

A British Foreign Office document (released on 4 February 1998) said that Iraq was known to have 'ingredients' to make 200,000 litres of the VX nerve gas (sufficient, noted various commentators, to kill the entire population of the world); and to have the 'capacity' to produce more than 20,000 kg of anthrax (experts were happy to note that an aerosol spraying 100 kg of anthrax in a densely populated area could kill three million people). The document declared: 'Iraq has four plants which have been used to produce chemical weapons and 30 which could be converted to produce chemical weapons materials. These factories cannot be destroyed because they have legitimate alternative civilian use.' This statement, typical of the genre, while superficially daunting, is in fact totally vacuous: part of it refers to the past (no longer threatening) while the rest deliberately evokes a dire situation that is purely imaginary. This is the stuff of propaganda and does nothing to support a responsible policy on weapons inspections. It is further noted that of the 819 Scud missiles acquired by Iraq in the 1970s and 1980s, all but two had been either destroyed or fired; and that six launchers and 30 warheads adapted for carrying chemical or biological weapons had been destroyed. This all suggested that Iraq might have *two* out-of-date missiles for the possible delivery of chemical and biological weapons that *might* exist – a purely hypothetical scenario that in 1997/8 the Washington planners were using to justify a further resort to war.

There are suggestions that Iraq deployed anthrax during the Gulf War, but did not use it: 'UN officials launched the investigation after more than 100 sheep died in unusual circumstances after being allowed to graze in an area that formed one of the Iraqi's main defensive positions during the war.[18] Bedouin shepherds and their flocks in the region were later found to be contaminated with anthrax. An official 'close to the UN investigation' concluded that this incidence – suggesting the stockpiling of anthrax weapons in Kuwait and southern Iraq – proved that Saddam was prepared to use such devices, and that he had been deterred only by the threat of a US nuclear response. At the same time it was being pointed out that Britain had supplied large quantities of growth medium to Iraq which could have been used to assist in the production of anthrax,[19] and that this supply continued until as late as 1996.[20] At one level this was unremarkable. The West had long supplied Iraq with many of its war-making facilities – which is why some Western companies were able to suggest the scale and scope of Iraq's weapons potential.[21] At another level it seemed surprising that the United States was suddenly becoming agitated about a range of possible Iraqi weapons that – if they existed at all – had been known about for years.

It was hard to ignore the possibility that the weapons scare was no more than a pretext: to test newly developed American weapons (guided bombs, 'bunker-busting' bombs, new satellite-guidance systems for Tomahawk cruise missiles, an 'earthquake' bomb capable of devastating an area a mile across – the 12,000 lb Storm bomb, a new generation of incendiary devices, new laser-guidance systems, etc.). The weapons crisis also served to provide justification for the ongoing genocidal sanctions policy, to be sustained in perpetuity just as long as a single military planner in Washington imagined that Saddam Hussein might have an evil thought in his head (even if there were *no* weapons of mass destruction in Iraq, *Saddam would want to possess some* – so sanctions must remain). The character of the sanctions regime must be appreciated in any attempt to understand the nature of the 1997/8 weapons crisis.

SANCTIONS: TARGETING THE PEOPLE

The economic sanctions on Iraq did not begin with UN Resolution 687 (see Appendix II) at the end of the 1991 Gulf War, as many commentators have suggested. They began almost immediately after the Iraqi invasion of Kuwait on 2 August 1990. Before any sanctions had been agreed by the Security Council the United States took its own immediate unilateral action: President George Bush signed two executive orders to freeze all Iraqi and Kuwaiti government assets (the latter now under nominal Iraqi control following the invasion). The US banks and other financial institutions at once moved to take the necessary actions. On 6 August the UN Security Council passed Resolution 661 (no votes against, Cuba and Yemen abstaining), the first of the sanctions resolutions; now many states enacted domestic legislation to give effect to the mandatory sanctions specified in the new resolution. Iraq now faced a pre-war sanctions phase (that was soon having a crippling effect on the Iraqi economy), the 1991 war itself, and then long years of draconian sanctions enforced by the merciless and unassailable might of the United States.

The (mainly) US war against Iraq began on 16 January 1991, the prelude to the dropping of some 88,000 tons of bombs, an explosive tonnage equivalent to seven Hiroshima-size atomic bombs. Thus for the period of the war (16 January to 27 February) Iraq was subjected to the equivalent of one atomic bomb a week, *a scale of destruction that has no parallels in the history of warfare*; and this scale of destruction was not concentrated on a few sites but ranged over the whole of Iraq – a totally disproportionate policy of devastation in view of the declared American aim of expelling Iraqi forces from Kuwait.[22]

Following the rout of the Iraqi forces the Security Council passed Resolution 687, the so-called 'ceasefire resolution', reinforcing the sanctions regime and specifying the destruction of Iraq's 'weapons of mass destruction' (essentially chemical, biological and nuclear) and the means of producing them.[23] There now began a massive onslaught on the Iraqi civilian population – denied the means to rebuild a totally shattered social and industrial infrastructure, denied uncontaminated drinking water, denied medical facilities, and denied food in adequate quantities. The US policy represented one of the most comprehensive campaigns of *biological warfare* – denying relief to a diseased and starving people – in modern times.[24] The situation was exacerbated by the scale of the environmental damage that the war had caused. Massive publicity was given in the West to the oil pollution in the Gulf (much of it caused by the Coalition forces) and to the firing of the Kuwaiti oil wells by the retreating Iraqi forces. Little has been said about the prodigious pollution caused by allied attacks on Iraq: the burning of millions of litres of crude oil, the burning of millions of litres of gas oil, the spillage of millions of litres of crude oil into rivers, the spillage of thousands of litres of other substances (kerosene, transformer oil, HCL, NaOH, engine oil, heavy oil, acids, fluorocylicic, etc.), the burning of liquid sulphur, the burning of solid sulphur, the burning of car and bicycle tyres, the ruining of agricultural and other land.[25] To all this has been added the widespread radioactive contamination caused by the Coalition's use of depleted-uranium (du) munitions over much of Iraq. In some estimates around 1.2 million uranium-coated bullets and shells were fired in the Gulf War, leaving a lethal residue of some 750 tons of radioactive dust – now judged to be a principal cause of the soaring cancer rate in the Iraqi civilian population.

The sanctions regime operating under nominal UN auspices, has been supervised by the UN Iraq Sanctions Committee with the main aim of denying the Iraqi people any substantial relief from their polluted environment, the soaring rates of disease, and the totally inadequate nutrition available to the bulk of the civilian population.[26] In these circumstances – according to a massive and growing body of crucial evidence (supplied by aid workers, UN bodies, visiting academics, journalists and others) – a US-orchestrated genocide is being accomplished: Iraqi-supplied statistics, supported by UNICEF, showed that by 1998 about one million children had been killed by the years-long economic siege of Iraq.

The American policy has been plain enough. With unquestioning support from Britain alone, Washington has worked to block food and medical shipments nominally allowed under the terms of the so-called 'oil for food' resolution (Resolution 986), has blocked the supply of free medicines that US corporations have been prepared to supply to Iraqi hospitals, and has worked to intimidate American aid workers active in trying to supply medicines and toys to dying Iraqi children. Thus a letter from the US Department of the Treasury (signed by an Acting Supervisor, Office of Foreign Assets Control, 22 January 1996) threatens US aid workers with imprisonment and fines. Acting Supervisor David H. Harmon writes (to Kathy Kelly of the aid charity Voices in the Wilderness):

> This Office has learned that you and other members of Voices in the Wilderness recently announced your intention to collect medical relief supplies for the people of Iraq at various locations in the United States and to personally transport the supplies to Iraq ... you and members of Voices in the Wilderness are hereby warned to refrain from engaging in any unauthorised exportation of medical supplies and travel to Iraq. Criminal penalties for violating the Regulations range from up to 12 years in prison and $1 million in fines.

The likely consequences of the years-long sanctions regime have been accurately predicted by many informed observers. The published report of a mission (10–17 March 1991) to Iraq led by Martti Ahtisaari, UN Under-Secretary-General for Administration and Management, included the comments: '... nothing that we had seen or read had quite prepared us for the particular form of devastation which has now befallen the country. The recent conflict has wrought near apocalyptic results ... the flow of food through the private sector has been reduced to a trickle. ... Many food prices are already beyond the purchasing reach of most Iraqi families ... widespread starvation conditions are a real possibility.' Two years later a UN Food and Agriculture Organisation (FAO) report (July 1993) declared that '*the continued sanctions, have virtually paralyzed the whole economy and generated persistent deprivation, chronic hunger, endemic undernutrition, massive unemployment and widespread human suffering ... a grave humanitarian tragedy is unfolding ... large numbers of Iraqis now have food intakes lower than those of the populations in the disaster stricken African countries.*'

Many other studies, reports and testimonies have provided evidence and commentary in the same vein through the 1990s. Thus in September 1995 the UN World Food Programme (WFP) noted that '*70 per cent of the population has little or no access to food. ... Nearly everyone seems to be emaciated*'; in December 1995, from which time conditions have continued to deteriorate, Sarah Zaidi and Mary Fawzi, writing in the prestigious medical journal *The Lancet* (London), commented that since August 1990 some 567,000 children in Iraq had been killed as a result of the determination '*of an international community intent on maintaining sanctions*'; and in 1996 the UN World Health Organisation (WHO) reported that the health conditions in Iraq were continuing to deteriorate 'at an alarming rate under the sanctions regime ... the vast majority of Iraqis continue to survive on a semi-starvation diet'. In May 1997 some 5600 children under five were dying every month because of sanctions, with the number still rising.[27] Monthly adult deaths had risen by more than 6000 as a direct result of sanctions-induced disease and starvation.[28]

In June 1996 a note verbale sent by Iraq to the Centre for Human Rights at the UN Office in Geneva recorded the effects of sanctions on education (the closing of many Iraqi schools, the collapse of school sewerage systems, the difficulty of providing paper and children's toys, the inability to provide heating and cooling services, an increase in the disease incidence among students, a soaring student drop-out rate, etc.).[29] A letter (22 March 1997) from Mohammed Said Al-Sahaf, the Iraqi foreign minister, addressed to the UN Secretary-General, recorded the continuing deterioration of health and other services in Iraq as a result of the economic embargo. The evidence continued to accumulate. In April 1997 a UN-linked Committee on the Elimination of Racial Discrimination acknowledged that by as early as August 1995 the US-orchestrated sanctions had killed some 600,000 Iraqi children (*'A slow genocide, the more dramatic than a swift genocide, was clearly under way'*).[30] At the same time the Iraqis continued to record how the United States was working to block the implementation of humanitarian contracts ('On ... 15 May 1997, it placed contracts Nos. 368, 372, 399 and 435 on hold without giving any reason for doing so. On 16 May 1997 the United States delegation placed contracts Nos. 473, 487, 489 and 492 on hold without giving any clear reason. ... On 19 May ... contracts Nos. 365, 505 and 561 ... without providing any reason ... it also blocked contract No. 312 without giving any reason').[31] In a letter (25 May 1997) addressed to the UN Secretary-General, Mohammad Said Al-Sahaf highlighted the American policy of blocking Iraq's access to free medical supplies:

> The representative of the United States of America ... has placed on hold the contracts for supply of pharmaceuticals numbered 252, 253, 391, 428, 429 and 553 and has done so on the pretext that they would include free merchandise or free medical samples. ... There is no doctor's office in the world, not even in the United States, that is without medical samples of this kind. ... Mr Yasushi Akashi, Under-Secretary-General for Humanitarian Affairs, referred to the disgraceful state of the hospitals he visited ... from 3 to 9 May 1997. Mr Nakajima, Director General of WHO ... also said that the country's health system was on the verge of collapse. These facts have not been enough to persuade the representative of the United States of America to desist from using irresponsible methods to prevent thousands of sick children, older persons and women from obtaining the medicines they need to alleviate the suffering brought on by the disease they have contracted as a result of ... the unjust embargo ...[32]

In a subsequent letter (30 May 1997) Antonio Monteiro, the chairman of the Security Council Committee established by Resolution 660 (1990) concerning the situation between Iraq and Kuwait, expressed concern at the slow pace of approval for humanitarian contracts under the terms of Resolution 986.[33]

It was plain that Washington was working to block the access of the Iraqi civilian population to food, medicine and other humanitarian supplies. A few days later a report from the UN Secretary-General acknowledged *'the slow and partial arrival of medicines and medical supplies'* and commented that *'the continuous degradation of the health sector has been exacerbated by this situation'*.[34] And even if the agreed contracts were speedily implemented, they would still be *'urgent needs'* that were not covered by the scheme.[35]

The Iraqi authorities, often in conjunction with UN agencies, continued to report the plight of the civilian population. In April 1997 the Iraqi Ministry of Health, working with UNICEF, recorded a total of 750,000 children under five suffering from malnutrition, with available nutrition funds for less than a third of these. At a UNICEF/Iraqi meeting on 20 July 1997 it was agreed that donor support had diminished because of the false expectations regarding the impact of Resolution 986. In August the Iraqi Ministry of Health published figures, showing that the US-run embargo had so far killed some 878,856 Iraqi children (see Table 3.1).

The various UN bodies (UNICEF, WFP, FAO, WHO, etc.) were now acknowledging the consequences for the Iraqi civilian population of the economic embargo. And this was the supreme paradox, as it had been for nearly eight years: while the many humanitarian agencies were trying to relieve the growing suffering of Iraq's helpless people the UN Security Council (that is, the United States), was striving to maintain the sanctions-induced genocide in perpetuity. In August 1997 the UN Commission on Human Rights (Economic and Social Council), via the mechanism of the

Table 3.1   Total number of child deaths due to embargo

	Age Groups		Total
	Under 5	Over 5	
1990	8,903	23,561	32,464
1991	27,473	58,469	85,942
1992	46,933	76,530	123,463
1993	49,762	78,261	128,023
1994	52,905	80,776	133,681
1995	55,823	82,961	138,784
1996	56,997	83,284	140,281
1997 Jan.–Aug.	39,353	56,865	96,218
Grand total	338,149	540,707	878,856

Source: Iraqi Ministry of Health with UNICEF support.

Sub-Commission on Prevention of Discrimination and Protection of Minorities, adopted a resolution noting the *Adverse Consequences of Economic Sanctions on the Enjoyment of Human Rights* (see Appendix I). Sanctions, the resolution declared, 'most seriously affect the innocent population, in particular the weak and the poor, especially women and children'.

In September the Iraqi authorities were still complaining about how the United States and Britain were acting to block the implementation of humanitarian contracts: ' ... *the Secretary-General describes this situation very clearly. He states that uncertainties in the arrival of food and other items have caused great difficulties. ... Although more than 100 days have elapsed since the end of the first phase of the procurement and distribution plan, the secretariat of the Security Council Committee ... still has around 60 contracts that it has yet to process. ... More than 70 contracts are still on hold at the request of the representatives of the United States and the United Kingdom, and these countries have blocked a further 21 contracts.*'[36] At the same time the various aid charities were striving to relieve the suffering of the Iraqi civilian population. Thus the Chicago-based Voices in the Wilderness ('A Campaign to End the UN/US Economic Sanctions Against the People of Iraq'), already cited, noted how it was acceptable in the United States to care about the human rights of Chinese dissidents or to protest on behalf of individual victims of child abuse in America, 'yet unacceptable to care about over one half million Iraqi children, under age 5, who have died at the hands of US policy makers'. It was noted (September 1997) that pockets of resistance to the sanctions were growing in various parts of the United States: activists included the Gulf War veteran Erik Gustafson and the 8-year-old Grace Schaeffer-Duffy (Worcester, MA), organising bear fairs for the collection of toys for Iraqi children; some 96 teach-ins had been organised by the Iraq Action Coalition and the International Action Center. More than one activist and aid worker has noted the irony that Hiroshima Day (to commemorate the dropping of the first atomic bomb on civilians) falls on 6 August, the day (in 1990) that economic sanctions were imposed on the civilian population of Iraq.[37]

Further UN-linked reports continued to highlight the increasingly desperate plight of the Iraqi people, with focus on the failure of Resolution 986 to address the scale of the tragedy. An FAO/WFP report (3 October 1997) declared that the situation for most of the people had become 'deplorable', with beggars, street children and undernourished children commonplace. Children in hospital wards were seen to be suffering from 'severe wasting' ('especially visible in the ribs, limbs and head'), and the mothers accompanying such children were themselves undernourished.[38] A comprehensive Iraqi/UNICEF report (November 1997) concluded:

> ... *it would appear that there has been no consistent evidence for improvement in nutritional status in infants since the start of SCR986/1111 imple-*

mentation. The same situation is also likely for children aged under five years.[39]

Here was further proof that the so-called 'oil for food' resolution (986) and the subsequent Security Council resolution (1111), designed to extend its scope, were doing nothing to improve the overall nutritional condition of the Iraqi child population. On 26 November UNICEF issued a statement declaring that almost one million children in southern and central Iraq were chronically malnourished. Thus Philippe Heffinck, the UNICEF Representative in Baghdad, commented that *'there is no sign of improvement since Security Council Resolution 986/111 came into force'.* He added that it was the Iraqi children that were bearing the brunt of the current economic hardship: 'They must be protected from the impact of sanctions. Otherwise, they will continue to suffer, and that we cannot accept.'[40]

The evidence of the suffering of the Iraqi people had swelled massively through 1997. The aid agencies, the UN organisations, systematic studies, journalistic accounts and the rest all combined to depict a consensual picture. The US-sustained sanctions were wreaking a catastrophe of genocidal proportions. A report in the prestigious London-based *British Medical Journal* (29 November 1997) noted the virtual collapse of the Iraqi health system. All the public hospitals were closing beds and experiencing 'serious problems with lighting, cleaning, water supply and sewage'; at Baghdad's Ibn El Baladi Hospital the absence of air conditioning systems meant that 'any child who comes to the hospital without a fever ends up with one'; the plumbing in most hospitals had been 'without repairs or maintenance for years', and every visited hospital had leaking sewage pipes; some entire wards lacked a working toilet; there was reluctance to begin surgical operations that might need much suture material; and one surgeon had developed an appendectomy that used one suture thread instead of the usual three.[41] In such an environment, with 'disinfectants and antiseptics almost non-existent', it was inevitable that mortality rates among sick and malnourished children would continue to rise. Mustafa Harith, a director of the Samarra General Hospital, was quoted: 'With sanctions, people are dying every day, and we haven't the means to cure them.[42]

It was widely known by 1998 that the Iraqi people were being denied not only the desperately needed medical attention but also food in adequate quantities. The deliberate starvation of a national population was now being questioned throughout the Western media:

Iraq: Who do sanctions hurt?
('Whilst Britain and the US bleat about the rights of the UN inspectors, they might also reflect on the UN Convention on the Rights of the Child'.)[43]

Why do we support starvation?
('... the UN's own observer teams inside Iraq have been so shocked by the results of the [sanctions] policy in terms of undernourishment and collapsing medical services that they are now urging a relaxation on their bosses in New York'.)[44]

Sanctions are not the way to beat Saddam
('... we keep on with a policy which leads nowhere, except to the destitution of a country whose people deserve better'.)[45]

Food crisis worsening, UN warns
('... the seven-year embargo had created malnutrition which was getting worse one year after the start of "oil-for-food" sales intended to meet urgent food and medical needs'.)[46]

Suffer the children
('What to do with this economic weapon [sanctions] needs as much attention as the military weapons question. it is not getting it – while the children continue to die.')[47]

Sick and dying in their hospital beds, the pitiful victims ...
('Dr Juad Rashid, the hospital's consultant paediatrician ... "Why are you making war on our children?"')[48]

Such commentary through the period 1997/8 helped to raise public awareness of the sanctions issue. For the first time, despite Washington's eagerness for war, the matter of sanctions was firmly on the agenda of UN and other international discussion of the Iraq Question. Perhaps, some observers were now suggesting, an end to sanctions might follow real Iraqi co-operation with UN inspectors working to abolish Iraq's capacity to develop and stockpile weapons of mass destruction. In any event the 1997/8 US/Iraq crisis was shaped in large part by the growing Iraqi desperation over a merciless sanctions policy that would continue to ravage the civilian population seemingly in perpetuity. We need to remember that a nation being deliberately starved to death will have a legitimate sense of grievance.

DEFINING THE LAW

We have seen that the United States is powerful enough to observe or ignore international law, as it thinks fit. In short, Washington is happy to find that law can be a suitably negotiable commodity to accord with current American foreign policy. At one level this state of affairs is unremarkable: the only reason that political factions seek power is to win the licence to define the law. In the last resort it is *power* that defines the law. Iraq's invasion of

Kuwait was a violation of international law, as was the American method of prosecuting the subsequent war. Since Saddam Hussein was defeated by Washington he is almost universally known as a liar, an aggressor, a demon; had he emerged victorious, Kuwait would have been licitly subsumed in a Greater Iraq justified by the *vilayet* pattern of the ancient Ottoman Empire. Where power has its way, there is a will ...

If, ignoring fashionable demonisations and the propaganda of mercenary journalists, we glance at the record we find that the US derelictions in the legal sphere are copious, continuous and unashamed. Some have already been mentioned and will not be rehearsed here. It is enough to recall that in conducting the 1991 Gulf War and the subsequent sanctions-blighted peace the United States was in comprehensive violation of the Geneva Convention, the UN Genocide Convention, the UN Charter, the Hague Convention, the Nuremberg Charter, and many UN General Assembly Resolutions, Conventions, Declarations and Statements.[49] Here it is enough to highlight a theme that is discussed later in the present book: *the failure of Washington to establish an adequate legal basis for its belligerent posture during the period of the 1997/8 crisis.*

It is arguable that Iraq committed many violations of Security Council Resolution 687 (3 April 1991), the so-called 'ceasefire' resolution designed to accomplish many objectives, including the abolition of all Iraq's 'weapons of mass destruction'. It is equally arguable that these violations *in toto*, while betraying both the spirit and the letter of 687, were relatively minor when compared with the extent of the Iraqi positive co-operation and the minimal post-war threat that Baghdad posed to its neighbours in the region. No party to the 1990/1 crisis, and certainly not the United States, was acting in conformity with all the relevant international law – though this obvious and demonstrable circumstance does not provide excuse or mitigation for any Iraqi failure to observe the law.

It is clear that Resolution 687 provides no explicit authorisation for the use of force, as threatened by Washington through the 1997/8 crisis. Even the British, normally incapable of questioning American Divine Right in foreign affairs, hinted at times that a new US bombing war against Iraq may not have enjoyed unambiguous legal authorisation. Foreign Secretary Robin Cook declared in the House of Commons that he would seek a new Security Council resolution before agreeing to a US/UK bombing campaign, and then forgot that he had ever said any such thing. And even the United States, keen enough to proclaim the legal UN authorisation – by virtue of existing Security Council resolutions – for the slaughter of more Iraqis, began to have doubts: in the face of opposition from other Permanent Members of the Security Council, Washington eventually wilted and placed ever-diminishing emphasis on UN authorisation, relying instead on the doctrine of *national interest* (see Parts II and III).

In these circumstances no pundits or politicians chose to revisit Resolution 678 (29 November 1990), the Security Council resolution that supposedly provided UN authorisation for the 1991 Coalition war against Iraq. Resolution 678 (Paragraph 2) authorises Member States co-operating with the Government of Kuwait, '*to use all necessary means to uphold resolution 660 (1990) and all subsequent relevant resolutions ...*'. This seemingly clear provision remains in fact deeply ambiguous. No hint was given as to who should judge what was 'necessary'. Could *any* Member of the United Nations decide on unilateral action? If China had decided to drop an atomic bomb on Baghdad would that have enjoyed 678 authorisation? Who was to decide? Again the situation seemed to invite the question:

Quis iudicabit ipsos iudices? ('Who will judge the judges?')

In reality if more care been taken to observe the specific wording of the UN Charter the problem could largely have been avoided. When, under the mandatory Chapter VII of the Charter, the Security Council has decided to use force (Article 44) it is required to establish a Military Staff Committee (Article 47) to advise and assist the Security Council; and which 'shall consist of the Chiefs of Staff of the permanent members of the Security Council ...' and 'be responsible ... for the strategic direction of any armed forces placed at the disposal of the Security Council ...'.

Hence the Charter defines a mechanism to ensure that any military action taken by the Security Council remains under the joint control of *all* the Permanent Members. This vital provision was clearly ignored by the United States; no attempt was made to construct the Charter-defined Military Staff Committee; and, from the moment that 678 was passed, the United States illicitly assumed a full and unilateral right to control all the subsequent military and political decisions concerning the treatment of the Iraqi regime and the Iraqi people. When the 678-defined expiry date (15 January 1991) for Iraq's withdrawal from Kuwait had been reached, the Security Council should have convened to decide what action was then judged to be 'necessary'; and any subsequent military action should have been conducted under the control of the Military Staff Committee. This would have maintained the response to Iraq's aggression as a proper United Nations initiative, with full observance of the rights of all the Permanent Members, and without any single nation assuming powers to which it had no legal entitlement under the UN Charter or any other international provision. Instead Washington seized control of the rapidly unfolding events; and thereupon bribed and intimidated Coalition members into acquiescing in what was in reality a unilaterally orchestrated war beyond all United Nations control.

The importance of such considerations is that since Resolution 687 (the ceasefire resolution stipulating the destruction of all Iraqi weapons of mass destruction) inevitably derives its authority from Resolution 678 (the resolution that in all the conventional wisdom authorised the 1991 war), if the implementation of 678 is seriously flawed then the authority of 687 is seriously compromised. In fact the preamble to 687 explicitly cites 678 as relevant to its subsequent judgements and statements; so the soundness of 687 must rest on a careful assessment as to the soundness of 678. In particular, for the purpose of the present book, if there was no UN authorisation for the 1991 war *in the manner it was decided upon and conducted* (there is no reference to 'force' or 'military action' in 678) then the terms of any (purportedly UN) ceasefire resolution are necessarily weakened. It follows that any Iraqi derelictions from the terms of a deeply flawed UN imposition must be evaluated with care. And it follows also that if the 1991 war *as initiated and prosecuted* lacked proper UN authorisation, then there could certainly never have been any UN authoriation for resuming military action at any time during the 1997/8 crisis.

If it is required that international actions should be conducted within the proper confines of a legal framework, then the above arguments should be considered against the crisis chronology outlined in Parts II and III. If, alternatively, the conduct of international affairs is solely a matter of *power* exploiting an unassailable sway, then we should admit that the United States is indifferent to law and concerned only with protecting and extending the privileges of a small plutocratic élite.

Part II
Crisis Chronology

4 From UN Coalition …
(June to November 1997)

PREAMBLE

The relationship between the Iraqi authorities and the UN weapons inspectors had been difficult from the outset. Despite a broad measure of Iraqi co-operation with the United Nations in the post-war period there were many occasions when the Iraqi authorities were reluctant to allow foreign inspections of sensitive sites. This was hardly surprising. A proud Arab people were being humiliated and starved by powerful nations overtly and covertly committed to the overthrow of the Iraqi regime. There were also periodic bombing raids, causing further fatalities and despair, and the years-long sanctions regime designed to deny an entire civilian population the very means of survival. In such dire circumstances it is perhaps the degree of Iraqi compliance that is surprising rather than the frequent incidents of recalcitrance and obstructionism born of a mounting desperation.

The international political attitudes to the Iraq Question shifted gradually through the 1990s. The suffering of the Iraqi people became more widely known and the devastated wilderness that Iraq had become was no longer universally regarded as a diabolical threat to its neighbours, the region and (as hyped in much US/UK propaganda) the entire world. Gradually most of the Arab states, the Non-aligned Nations, most of the UN General Assembly and even some Permanent Members of the Security Council were coming to believe that the deeply malevolent pariah politics practised by Washington was no longer appropriate. It cannot be assumed that the 1997/8 US/Iraq crisis represented an end to the brutal US policy of military intimidation regarding Iraq, but the crisis clearly demonstrated the political isolation of the United States and the diplomatic scope of a resurgent United Nations led by a new and unexpectedly effective Secretary-General (see chapter 6).

CHRONOLOGY

The growing sensitivity to the plight of Iraqi people was reflected in the wording of Security Council Resolution 1111 (4 June 1997), designed to extend the scope of the so-called 'oil for food' Resolution 986. Where 986 referred to the need to address the humanitarian requirements of the Iraq people, 1111 expressed the determination of the Security Council 'to avoid *any further deterioration of the current humanitarian situation'*. Here was the Security Council, formerly denying that humanitarian supplies were obstructed by UN resolutions, now admitting the deterioration in the humanitarian situation. It was still only words, and the Iraqi authorities had good reason to think that there would be little or no improvement in the humanitarian situation. It was already obvious, to those who cared to notice, that Resolution 986 was supported by Washington only to the extent that it was useful for public-relations purposes ('look how caring we are') and for exposing Iraqi capital assets to US-friendly claimants. There was little evidence to suggest that Resolutions 986 and 1111 were introduced to improve the situation of the Iraqi people to any large extent.

The tensions had been mounting. Iraqi frustration at the seemingly endless embargo and the American eagerness to adopt spoiling tactics wherever possible were combining to shape a new crisis. The Security Council (that is, Washington) was frequently complaining, often with cause, that the Iraqi authorities were denying the UN inspectors access to designated sites. Resolution 1060 (June 1996), while noting the progress made by the Special Committee (UNSCOM) 'towards the elimination of Iraq's programmes of weapons of mass destruction', noted 'with concern' occasions (11 and 12 June) when the Iraqi authorities had denied access to the inspectors (the Security Council 'Deplores the refusal of the Iraqi authorities to allow access ...' and 'Demands that Iraq cooperate fully ...'). For its part, Iraq was becoming increasingly irritated by what it rightly perceived as US-led tactics to frustrate any favourable report by UNSCOM to the Security Council which may have prepared the ground for a lifting of sanctions (as explicitly specified in Paragraph 22 of Resolution 687).

A letter (18 June 1997) from Mohammed Said Al-Sahaf, the Iraqi Foreign Affairs Minister, addressed to the President of the Security Council, drew attention to particular inspections made by UN teams. On 17 June the inspectors entered the Za'faraniyah telephone exchange, a dormitory for students, a theatre, a cinema, and a cinematographic store and laboratory belonging to the Ministry of Information. Then the UNSCOM team entered Saint Joseph's Monastery in Za'faraniyah and began a radiometric survey of the gardens and grounds. While the inspectors were demanding the attention of the priest and the sister, pupils were being taught aspects of Christian religious doctrine (this in Muslim Iraq). On the same day, UN inspectors entered the Sayyidat al-Sanabil Convent and demanded access to all the buildings, despite protests that this was an affront to a place of worship. The Iraqis were later horrified to learn that Rolf Ekeus, the then Executive Chairman of UNSCOM, had subsequently denied responsibility for the sacrilege, even though he had personally signed the authorising order. Mohammed Said Al-Sahaf then called upon the Security Council to put an end to 'the deliberate pattern of unprofessional conduct' on the part of the

UNSCOM inspectors.[1] The charge was later supported by UN Secretary-General Kofi Annan in seeking to resolve the 1997/8 crisis (see Chapter 6).

On 28 August 1997 the annual report on the work of UNSCOM claimed that 'high priority' had been given to the supply of essential humanitarian necessities for the Iraqi civilian population. The perceived need to make reference to this aspect was significant but the claim was clearly absurd. Even in the 52-paragraph report itself there is evidence that humanitarian initiatives had been blocked. Thus the Sanctions Committee had not been prepared to accede to two requests made by the United Nations Development Programme (UNDP): one concerning a project entitled 'Provision of consultancies and training to essential humanitarian sectors'; the other a project entitled 'Rehabilitation of seed multiplication system through the strengthening of seed quality control in Iraq'. Nor was the Committee prepared to grant the World Food Programme (WFP) permission to import equipment necessary for its work in Iraq (individual items would be considered on a case-to-case basis, with all the delays and US obstructionism that this implied).[2]

In the same negative spirit the Committee had found it impossible to permit a Jordanian request for one or more weekly flights between Amman and Baghdad to carry UN personnel '*and for humanitarian reasons, that is, to transport the sick and elderly to and from Baghdad, to provide means of transportation for pilgrims in their pilgrimage to Moslem shrines in Iraq, to transport medical, pharmaceutical and food supplies from Jordan*'.[3] The request was rejected when it was first submitted on 24 September 1996; and rejected when it was again submitted in March 1997. A request made by the World Health Organisation (WHO) for medical evacuation flights for seriously-ill Iraqi nationals was considered by the Committee on 21 February 1997 and was 'still under the Committee's consideration' in August.

By September 1997 the Iraqi authorities, increasingly frustrated by the tactics of the US-dominated UNSCOM inspectors and Security Council, had decided not to export oil under the terms of Resolution 1111, increasingly perceived as yet another device for delaying the lifting of sanctions. The Security Council response was Resolution 1129 (12 September 1997), noting the Iraqi decision and expressing deep concern 'about the resulting consequences for the Iraqi people, since the shortfall in the revenue from the sale of petroleum and petroleum products will delay the provision of humanitarian relief and create hardship ...'. This new bout of Security Council crocodile tears convinced no-one; and the Russian Federation even went so far as to abstain in the vote on 1129 on the reasonable ground that the text of the resolution failed to reflect the reasons for the humanitarian crisis and the need to change the situation in the Sanctions Committee, currently blocking the delivery of urgently needed humanitarian supplies for no valid reason. This hinted at the shape of things to come. Moscow, whatever its motives, now seemed ready to chart an independent course in the Security Council. This development was highly uncongenial to Washington: the last thing that the United States wanted was another Permanent Member prepared to veto the American manipulation of the Council in the interest of US foreign policy.

In Iraq most of the UNSCOM-run inspections of designated sites continued without hindrance, a detail that received little publicity in the Western press. It seemed of more interest to the outside world that the 60-year-old Saddam Hussein had swum across the Tigris three times on 15 September 1997 to demonstrate his fitness; that three Iraqis had been arrested in Baghdad for using carrier pigeons in an extortion attempt; and that five men and woman had been sentenced to death for running a prostitution and alcohol-smuggling racket for Saudi Arabians. Iraq was protesting that its aircraft, parked in Iran during the 1991 Gulf War, had been repainted in Iranian colours and were being used by Tehran. Mohammed Said Al-Sahaf, the Iraqi Foreign Minister, declared that Iran's failure to return the 115 military and 27 civil transport planes was a 'grave breach of the most elementary principles of international law'. A week later, Iran was confirming that it had attacked opposition groups based in Iraq in a series of dawn raids; while at the same time more than a hundred Turkish tanks and other military vehicles had invaded northern Iraq to attack separatist Kurdish forces. Over a four-day period several Turkish military convoys had entered northern Iraq and were continuing their military operations.[4] Such matters – Iranian bombing of Iraqi targets, Turkish tank invasions of Iraqi territory – were of no interest to the Security Council, continuing in late-1997 to punish Iraq for its 1990 aggression.

On 2 October 1997 the United Nations noted that Iraqi officials had barred UNSCOM weapons inspectors from three designated sites in the past week. Now there were signs that a fresh US/Iraq crisis was brewing. US officials hinted at the likelihood of further UN sanctions, with Richard Butler, the chief inspector, warning Tariq Aziz, the Iraqi Deputy Prime Minister, that the incidents were serious and could not be ignored. A comprehensive report submitted by Butler to the Security Council noted that Iraq's recent submission of a 640-page account of its work on biological weapons fell short of being a 'full, final and complete disclosure', as required. The Butler report acknowledged that the majority of the inspections '*were conducted in Iraq without let or hindrance*'; but claimed that the situation still remained very unsatisfactory. The Iraqi submission 'was incomplete and contained significant inaccuracies ... The outstanding problems are numerous and grave ... It is the view of the panel that Iraq has not compiled with Security Council resolution 687 (1991) as regards BW [biological warfare].'[5] The barring of inspectors from the designated sites, added to the hostile Butler report, had given Washington what it wanted: now Washington was preparing the ground for additional sanctions against Iraq – and for a comprehensive bombing campaign against the 'pariah state'. The Americans, as was usually the case, had something to prove; hopefully the technical niceties of international law would not be allowed to stand in their way.

On 5 October four gunmen launched a grenade attack on the UN office responsible for the administration of the 'oil for food' programme in Baghdad. There were no casualties and one of the men was taken into custody by the Iraqi army, who claimed that he was an Iranian agent. Denis Halliday, the UN's humanitarian co-ordinator in Baghdad, condemned the attack on the WHO building, commenting that it was the responsibility of the Iraqi government to protect UN personnel and property. No-one claimed responsibility for the attack but the building is located in the al-Wahda district, where an Iranian opposition group in exile is known to operate. The incident had no serious repercussions but did little to help an already worsening political climate. A New York-based diplomat, responding to the negative Butler report, declared: 'It's a complete mess. There may well be pressure from the US and Britain for tougher action.'⁶ Now there was the suggestion of a travel ban on Iraqi officials, though Russia and France were known to be hostile to fresh sanctions measures. At the same time, while Turkish pilots were bombing targets inside Iraq with impunity, Washington was warning Iraq that it would 'bear the consequences' if its aircraft continued to violate the US-declared 'no-fly zones' in southern Iraq.

By mid-October the United States, with the sole support of Britain in the Security Council, was calling for new sanctions to punish Iraq for failing to comply with the demands of the UNSCOM weapons inspectors. Foreign Office officials were now confirming that Britain was fully behind American demands for the imposition of travel restrictions on all members of Iraq's armed forces, police and intelligence services, as well as employees of the Iraqi Ministry of Defence and its Military-Industrial Commission. It was inevitable in these circumstances that Washington and London would continue to do everything possible to maintain the sanctions regime, despite the growing international awareness of its genocidal impact on the Iraqi civilian population. Iraq's ambassador to the United Nations declared on 16 October that Iraq would 'cease all further co-operation' with the UNSCOM teams if a new batch of sanctions were imposed on Iraq. A British official, echoing the increasingly belligerent American posture, commented: 'We think there is a strong need for a robust response to show that the UN means business.' No attempts were being made by either the United States or Britain to negotiate with Baghdad or to address the questionable legality of any fresh bombing strike against Iraq.

It was now plain that, following American and British agitation in the Security Council, a new resolution would emerge to enshrine further condemnation of Iraq. On 23 October 1997 Resolution 1134 (see Appendix III) was passed with a vote of 10 in favour and none against, but with five abstentions (Russian Federation, France, China, Egypt and Kenya). Now it was clear that the 1990/1 Coalition was in ruins. Three of the five Permanent Members of the Security Council (Russia, France and China) were not prepared to support a relatively moderate resolution. Here the Council expressed 'grave concern', stressed the 'unacceptability of any attempts by Iraq to deny access' to designated sites, took note of UNSCOM progress, reaffirmed the Council's determination 'to ensure full compliance by Iraq', and threatened to adopt measures to prohibit the international travel of Iraqi officials and members of the armed forces deemed responsible for Iraqi non-compliance. Sir John Weston (for the United Kingdom) cited Richard Butler and emphasised that the Security Council would not be deflected 'by unacceptable Iraqi attempts at blackmail'. It was soon clear that the US/UK posture had not come close to achieving a consensus in the Council.

Nabil A. Elaraby (for Egypt) pointed out that he would have liked to have seen a number of other issues included in the resolution. Why was there no mention of the positive results already achieved by the UNSCOM inspectors? Why was the Council failing to define the 'end goal' of both UNSCOM and the International Atomic Energy Agency (IAEA)? There should be agreement on the degree to which Iraq was fulfilling its obligations, with an attempt to resolve existing difficulties between UNSCOM and the Iraqi government. Egypt was opposed to the imposition of any additional sanctions. Antonio Monteiro (Portugal) urged Iraq to co-operate fully 'so that sanctions would finally be lifted'; Hans Dahlgren (Sweden) supported the resolution, suggesting that innocent Iraqi citizens would not be affected; Zbigniew Matuszewski (Poland) gave the usual reason of Iraqi compliance to justify Poland's co-sponsorship of the draft resolution; Liu Jieyi (China) opposed fresh sanctions and Sergey V. Lavrov (Russia) emphasised 'an obvious lack of balance' in the resolution. After the vote, Alain Dejammet (France) pointed out that the Butler report itself had not asked for further sanctions and had included details of progress made by UNSCOM. The Commission should be encouraged to work with the Iraqi government to improve the situation.

The United States was obviously irritated that Washington's usual blandishments and threats had not produced a consensus in the Security Council. Bill Richardson (for the US) expressed his amazement that after six and a half years the Security Council was still forced to consider new approaches to convince Iraq to comply with its international obligations. It was Baghdad, and Baghdad alone, that was responsible for the current situation: Iraq, according to Richardson, had resorted to 'bullying, burning and blackmailing'. If Iraq did not understand that the Security Council would brook no challenges, new mechanisms must be considered to make it understand: 'compliance with international obligations was not a voluntary act'.

Richardson, declaring that *'our goal remains to help the people of Iraq, but
...'*, expressed regret that some Council Members had chosen not to give
support for the new resolution (1134, 23 October 1997). Again it seemed
clear that American influence in the Security Council was ebbing fast. Now
Washington could no longer rely on bribery and threat to dragoon the
Council into sullen acquiescence behind a persistently vindictive anti-Iraq
posture.

The Iraqi government was quick to advertise the low level of support in
the Security Council for Resolution 1134. In a letter (29 October 1997) to
Juan Somaria, President of the Council, the Iraqi Deputy Prime Minister
Tariq Aziz emphasised how the abstention of three Permanent Members
(Russia, China and France) and two other members (Egypt and Kenya)
'clearly demonstrates the arbitrary position imposed by the United States
against Iraq by all means of pressure and blackmail'.[7] Here it is pointed out
that the Special Commission, over a period of more than six and a half years,
had destroyed tens of factories, thousands of instruments and items of equipment ('claimed to be related to proscribed weapons'): *'Moreover, many factories, equipment and instruments of civilian use have also been destroyed through
arbitrary decisions, thus depriving Iraq of them while it has been under comprehensive embargo for seven years.'*[8] Thousands of intrusive inspections had
been conducted and a comprehensive and strict monitoring system put in
place. Yet despite the scale of this massive operation spread over many
years, the Commission had not been prepared to submit a fair report to the
Security Council to allow the implementation of Paragraph 22 of Resolution
687 (that is, to allow the lifting of sanctions). The reason for all of this is the
position of the United States and personnel in UNSCOM who implement
American policy:

> The United States insolently declares that it is determined to change the
> national government of Iraq and to maintain the embargo against Iraq
> regardless of the implementation of the resolutions of the Security
> Council. The ... personnel of the Special Commission, who occupy senior
> and influential posts and whose number is very large, are executing this
> policy. This renders the Special Commission an institution influenced to a
> large extent by the American hostile policy aimed at fulfilling the
> American illegal and illegitimate objectives ... the Special Commission ...
> is no longer a neutral institution operating impartially and objectively to
> implement the provisions of Security Council resolutions ...[9]

There is abundant evidence to support the Iraqi charges, not least the declarations by Secretary of State Madeleine Albright and other American leaders
that the years-long embargo will continue until Saddam Hussein disappears
from the political scene. The Iraqi claim that UNSCOM staff have behaved

provocatively and to an illicit US agenda has been supported by journalistic and other observations, by UN Secretary-General Perez de Cuellar in reprimanding UNSCOM staff as early as 1991, and by UN Secretary-General Kofi Annan in 1998 (see Chapter 6).

As a response to this situation Tariq Aziz made specific proposals (set to be influential in the 1998 UN/Iraq agreement negotiated in Baghdad by Kofi Annan):

1. Iraq is ready to receive a specialised committee or committees from the Permanent Members of the Security Council (with the exception of America), as well as any other member states of the Security Council individually or collectively within the framework of the Special Commission or outside it, to verify the claims of concealment in a decisive and final manner and to ascertain that Iraq is fully clean of proscribed weapons.

2. Iraq is ready to ensure the visit by the committee or committees ... to all sites they wish to visit in order to verify this matter. We are ready as well to answer all their questions and enquiries in a manner that ensures credible means of verification within the framework of respecting Iraq's sovereignty, security and the dignity of its people.

These specific proposals did not form part of the subsequent negotiated agreement but an essential theme – that UNSCOM staff should not be allowed sole discretion over sensitive sites – was enshrined in the Annan settlement.

At this time (late-October 1997) Turkey was still launching air raids against Kurdish targets in northern Iraq. The Patriotic Union of Kurdistan (PUK), long in dispute with the rival Kurdistan Democratic Party (KDP), was claiming that bombing raids by the Turkish air force were covering a wide area, while fresh fighting had broken out between the two Kurdistan groups. The Turkish authorities were asserting that the attacks were essentially against the forces of the Kurdistan Workers' Party (PKK), which had been waging an independence struggle in south-east Turkey since 1984. It has long been plain that the Turkish attempts to contain minority disaffection – analogous to Saddam Hussein's struggle to contain the southern Shias and the northern Kurds – was deeply embarrassing to Washington and London. How were the United States and Britain to respond to a Turkish invasion of Iraq, a manifest aggression that relied upon a copious supply of NATO-provided arms, and to Turkish attempts to establish an illegal security zone on Iraqi territory? Such circumstances were making it increasingly difficult for Washington and London to maintain the necessary pressure on Baghdad. Declared one Western source: '*Turkey is playing fast and loose with international law in many respects*.' But since Turkey, far from being a US-defined 'pariah state', was a crucial strategic member of NATO, there was no reason for the United States to agitate the Security Council over the issue. Turkey might be a political embarrassment but its current illegalities posed no substantial threat to US national interests.

The Iraqi authorities were continuing to complain about the American political agenda in the manipulation of UNSCOM and other UN groups. Tariq Aziz had declared on 29 October that no Americans would be allowed to work with the Special Commission inside Iraq: they would not be permitted to take part in inspections, interviews or aerial and ground surveillance.[10] Again reference was made to what the Iraqis perceived as the espionage agenda of the United States. Aziz cited the case of the U-2 plane, 'an American spying plane which has been spying on Iraq and its leadership in order to execute America's hostile policy against Iraq under cover of the Special Commission's operations'.[11] On 12 October Tariq Aziz had suggested that the American U-2, universally acknowledged as a spy plane under sole US control, be replaced by an Iraqi plane supervised by the Special Commission or by a plane from a neutral State 'that has no special objectives against Iraq'.

The crisis was now beginning its remorseless escalation. In prohibiting UNSCOM access to particular sensitive sites and in proposing that certain UNSCOM teams should not include American personnel the Iraqi authorities had enraged the United States. Saddam Hussein then chaired a crisis meeting of his top officials to decide whether to end all co-operation with UN inspectors, while Washington threatened 'grave consequences' if Iraq carried out any such measures; Britain predictably echoed the US line and France and Russia conceded that the situation was becoming more hazardous. The Iraqi newspaper *Babel* commented: 'Any measures [against Iraq] considered by the wicked dictatorship of America would be of limited effect.'

On 29 October the Iraqi authorities ordered the removal of 10 Americans from an UNSCOM inspection team and declared that Iraq was also asking the United Nations to stop using American reconnaissance planes to monitor Iraq's alleged weapons sites. The UN immediately suspended its operations in Iraq, with Richard Butler commenting: 'Who's next? Today the United States? Tomorrow the United Kingdom? This is wrong.' In London the Foreign Office generated its familiar echo: 'This is completely unacceptable. It is not for Iraq to dictate who should be in UN teams.' In fact it was not for Washington or Britain either, acting in isolation, to determine the composition of the UNSCOM teams. Paragraph 9(b) of Resolution 687 calls on the Secretary-General to submit to the Security Council for approval a plan for the forming of the Special Commission. In short, it was the UN Secretary-General, not the US or the UK, who had the authority to propose the make-up of the inspection teams. The Security Council could then approve or not, but the initial discretion clearly lay with the Secretary-General – a 687 provision that gave substantial authority to Kofi Annan's subsequent peace moves (see Chapter 6). Such legal niceties were of only minimal concern to Washington and London. Perhaps, reasoned the US/UK strategists, it was time for another war. A totally dishonest 'preference for a diplomatic solution' would be advertised while at the same time all the efforts of the American and British politicians would be focused on preparing the ground for military action.

For a brief period it seemed that the United Nations was developing a consensual response to Saddam's latest initiative. In London a Foreign Office minister, Derek Fatchett, threatened a 'serious response'. The Iraqi decision to deny access to two US officials expecting to join the UNSCOM teams could not go unanswered: 'The rest of the world cannot sit by idly while Iraq develops its weapons of mass destruction. The response will be serious. It will be commensurate with the action.' No actions, including military strikes, would be ruled out. Typically, no effort was made to consider the possible illegality of such a course or whether the implied threat of such bombing strikes constituted a violation of Article 2(4) of the UN Charter ('All Members shall refrain in their international relations from the threat or use of force ...').

In Paris a foreign ministry spokesman declared that France was willing to examine 'any appropriate measures', a relatively unhelpful tautology (appropriate measures might well be judged appropriate); Russia, in the same non-committal spirit, branded Iraq's action as 'unacceptable', urged Baghdad to abide by Council resolutions, but proposed no practical measures to end the crisis. Nonetheless it was helpful to Washington and London to be able to represent the critical consensus, though luke-warm, as a victory for the US/UK posture. One US official declared, with evident optimism: 'Every time Saddam has been presented with a unified strong position he has backed down. He has once again totally misunderstood his situation. If he thought he could divide the Council he has miscalculated horribly.' It remained to be seen: the test would come when proposals for unambiguous military action were presented by the United States and Britain to the Security Council. By November 1997 few observers believed that anything like the 1990/1 Coalition of anti-Iraq countries had survived or that states like Russia and France had any residual appetite for a fresh military adventure in the Middle East.

The current crisis was rooted in seemingly trivial detail. Most of the UNSCOM inspections were being allowed to continue; and of the approximately one hundred weapons inspectors in Iraq only ten were Americans. A mere two US officials had been turned back at Habanniya airport, west of Baghdad, and American pride was deeply affronted: if two US officials were denied access to Iraq today then perhaps Saddam would blow up the world tomorrow. There was a point of principle involved. It was certainly arguable that the Iraqi authorities were in violation of Paragraph 96(b)(i) of Resolution 687, but any reasonable observer would have acknowledged that such manifest dereliction should be assessed against the known UNSCOM provocations and the covert and overt agendas of the Washington strategists. The contrived moral outrage in Washington – after years of political manoeuvring and genocidal sanctions – was risible. But the United States knew what it was about. While James Rubin, the US State Department spokesman, would not elaborate on American plans, he called the Iraqi move 'an attack on the very fundamentals of the UN system'. No-one doubted that Washington was already planning a military response.

There was now growing speculation about the causes of the crisis. It had begun in June with the banning of UNSCOM personnel from sensitive sites, in particular the 'presidential' precincts; then the Iraqi authorities began objecting to the role of the Americans in the inspection teams. It was known, and scarcely disguised by Washington, that the United States had funded various *coup* attempts – involving assassination if necessary – against the Iraqi leader. Could *any* regime tolerate *coup* plotters crawling over its most sensitive security sites? At one level the whole situation was a matter of high farce. The CIA wanted to kill Saddam but its various attempts had been foiled by poor intelligence. Now here was Washington indignantly insisting that American personnel with obvious access to the American espionage services be allowed to scrutinise the installations at the heart of Iraq's state security. How keen would Washington be to let Iraqis or Libyans or North Koreans prowl round the Pentagon.

The Iraqi reluctance to expose the regime to the likelihood of US orchestrated sabotage and *coup* plots was one powerful reason for the current political moves. Another was born out of sheer desperation. The sanctions had been in place since early August 1990; and had so far produced – quite literally – millions of civilian casualties. Was there no light at the end of the tunnel? Was the embargo set to last in perpetuity? What could be done to draw the attention of the so-called 'international community' to the worsening plight of the Iraqi people? Co-operation , to a substantial extent, with the UNSCOM teams had brought the lifting of sanctions no nearer. Perhaps a serious bout of non-compliance would concentrate the minds of Western leaders who claimed to have concern for human rights and the suffering of innocent civilians. On 30 October 1997 Barzan Tikriti, Saddam's half-brother and a Geneva-based ambassador, commented that Iraq was 'an ice tray under the sun, melting away day by day'; it was 'the government's right and duty to take a stand against attempts to perpetuate' that situation.[12] The pathetic 'oil and food' deal had done virtually nothing to relieve the suffering of the Iraqi people. Did the West expect them to die quietly, without disturbing Washington's strategic and commercial ambitions? What was to be done?

It seemed that Saddam was resigned to the likelihood of a further wave of US-led bombing strikes. An Iraqi exile commented: 'What does he care about 40 cruise missiles in the desert, especially if, like last time [September 1996], it is accompanied by what amounts to a clear redefinition of US policy – in his favour.' Now it seemed probable that the United States, well aware of the ineffectiveness of earlier bombing strikes, was planning a much more comprehensive onslaught. It was time surmised some pundits, for Gulf War II. No American land forces would be involved (corpses of American 'boys' arriving back home tended to cause local distress) but the planned bombing would range over the whole of Iraq and last for days or weeks. It was an increasingly cheerful scenario.

Washington continued to stress that the barring of the two American arms inspectors had been a 'mistake' by worsening an already serious situation, but the Iraqi authorities were standing firm. The ruling Baath Party newspaper in Baghdad said that the leadership had taken the action after losing all hope that the genocidal sanctions would be lifted. Said the daily *al-Thawra*: *'There is no other alternative before Iraq to get out of the dark tunnel of the embargo in which America put the country.'* Now it was emerging that the US-hyped 'consensus' in the Security Council was unreal. Russia, while condemning the Iraqi move, was opposed to fresh bombing strikes. Yevgeny Primakov, the Russian Foreign Minister, declared in Cairo: 'We are against any use of force against Iraq. I speak about this because some voices appear, particularly in the United Kingdom, to be speaking about the use of force against Iraq. We strongly object to this.' Nor were any other states, beyond America and Britain, enthusiastic about further military strikes against Iraq. Richard Butler, the current head of UNSCOM, was suggesting that if Iraq were to co-operate with the UN inspectors the whole process could be over 'in six, nine or 12 months'. He presumably intended this as an encouraging message: it meant in reality that the genocide would be allowed to claim perhaps another one hundred thousand children through starvation and preventable disease. The Iraqis were not impressed.[13] A grim resignation was now settling over Baghdad. A legislator, Said Kasim Hamoodi, represented the general mood: 'We are on the defensive, but if they push the issue towards a military confrontation ... we will not back down.'[14]

The United States and Britain continued to wage a propaganda war. They claimed that a 'diplomatic solution' was the preferred option, but at the same time they refused to negotiate meaningfully with the Iraqi regime and did all they could to assemble a new Coalition for Gulf War II. The propaganda was well rehearsed. If Iraqi children were dying it was Saddam's fault. Everyone knew that the Iraqi regime was brutal and intolerant and no-one would mourn its passing, least of all the hapless Iraqi people. Saddam – or his son or both – were making a killing by selling drugs on the black market, while their people suffered. One piece of investigative journalism revealed that large quantities of the UN-approved medical supplies were being smuggled onto the black market 'to finance Saddam's dictatorship'. It was claimed that the Jordanian capital Amman was the main outlet for drugs produced by the State Enterprises for Drug Industries, Iraq's main pharmaceutical production complex at Samarra. Profits from the enterprise were allegedly being collected by the *Mukhabarat*, Iraq's main intelligence service.[15] If this were not enough to demonstrate the perfidy of the Iraqi regime, the Western media was working hard to stimulate a general anxiety – if not hysteria – about Saddam's military potential. Journalists were eager to report that the Iraqis now had sufficient stockpiles of biological weapons to kill *millions of people*. This was seemingly well known to the journalists but impossible for the UNSCOM officials to verify, though unnamed 'international weapons inspectors' were cited as believing that Saddam now had a 'doomsday arsenal' (the word *'doomsday'* had the right sort of emotive ring to it and was deployed as a journalistic device in several articles[16]). Some of the claims about Saddam's 'doomsday' potential were little more than farcical (see below).

Now we were being told that Iraq had secret stocks of nerve agents, chemical weapons and, in some accounts that even the UNSCOM officials would have branded as risible, nuclear weapons.[17] A UN team in Iraq reportedly informed *The Observer* (London) that it had been on the verge of uncovering the VX liquid nerve agent when Saddam Hussein had ordered the American members of UNSCOM to leave the country. Richard Butler commented: 'I think we were getting hot, and maybe that's part of the reason why they took this decision in the last couple of days. I think we are getting closer and closer.' Documents found by the UN inspectors had established that Iraq had imported tons of VX precursors, essential to the manufacture of the nerve agent. Iraq claimed that most of the chemicals had been destroyed by the Gulf War bombing, with the rest of the chemicals unilaterally destroyed at a later date. The inspectors also discovered that the Iraqis had imported 40 tons of growth media to produce enough anthrax and botulism cultures 'for a cocktail of weapons to kill everybody in the world'.[18] (In April 1998 Tony Lloyd, a Foreign Office minister in the British government, declared that an investigation would be held into claims that anthrax cultures manufactured in Britain had been exported to Iraq. Said Menzies Campbell, the Liberal Democrat defence spokesman: *'There is now clear and credible evidence that Britain laid the foundations, not just for the nuclear and the chemical programme, but for the biological weapons programmes being pursued in Iraq.'*[19])

There was now little doubt that the United States was planning a military response to the Iraqi moves. The Americans working for the UN inspection teams had been told to leave the country, with Taha Yassin Ramadan, the vice-president of Iraq, saying that within days 'there will be no American inside Iraq in inspections'. Now it was plain that Saddam was deliberately escalating the crisis, preferring conflict with Washington to an unchallenged continuation of the open-ended sanctions that were devastating the country. In Baghdad several thousand Iraqis demonstrated outside the offices of the United Nations Development Programme (UNDP), shouting anti-US and anti-Israel slogans and burning flags. But despite the developing crisis there still seemed uncertainty about how the Security Council would react. When Richard Butler commented that he considered Saddam's action a violation of Resolution 687 he was rebuked by the French, who declared that it was up to the Council to assess the situation. Ramadan predictably accused Butler of taking sides in the dispute: 'Butler cannot order Iraq around, nor does he control it.' Saddam had manifestly exposed the divisions in the Security Council: the situation in late-1997 was very different from that of 1990/1. The prospect of agreement among the Permanent Members of the Council on what action to take seemed to be fading by the day. The principal American aim was to contain the situation, to resist any challenge to the sanctions regime, and to enlist sufficient international support for military action. Now it seemed increasingly likely that Washington would be pushed onto the defensive, able to take unassailable military initiatives but likely in so doing to attract the condemnation of a growing part of the international community. Most States were urging Saddam to observe the terms of Resolution 687; none, apart from a supine and jingoistic Britain, was eager to join with the United States in launching Gulf War II.

The so-called international community remained uncertain how to respond to the developing crisis. Washington continued to exert pressure on other States to adopt a belligerent line on Iraq, but American sabre-rattling was a largely isolated phenomenon. In an attempt to enlist powerful allies, Bill Richardson, the United States ambassador to the United Nations, called for 'incremental pressure' on Baghdad and declared: 'This is not an attack against the United States. This is an Iraqi attack against the UN and the Security Council.' If other Council Members agreed with this analysis they were not rushing to say so in public. Many observers continued to suspect that all the American talk was intended as a moderate and reasonable public-relations exercise, with military preparations continuing apace in the real world of strategic planning. Tariq Aziz commented that US policy was directed at toppling Saddam and that an American military strike would make no difference to Baghdad: 'The US has its special objectives on Iraq, whether we co-operate with the UN Security Council or not, whether we co-operate with UNSCOM or not.'[20] The total refusal of Washington to talk directly to Baghdad suggested that a peaceful solution to the crisis was the last thing in the minds of the US strategic planners.

On 2 November the Iraqi authorities ejected three American UNSCOM inspectors from the country, reinforcing the growing perception that Saddam was willing to risk a military confrontation in order to extend his control in the country. Again the United States, frustrated at the lack of support in the Security Council for firm military action, resorted to the familiar propaganda line. Richardson emphasised that Washington wanted to resolve the situation 'diplomatically' but condemned the actions of Iraq as 'serious, unacceptable and outrageous'. But now the American mask was slipping: while emphasising the primary role of *diplomacy* and at the same time refusing to talk seriously to the Iraqi leadership, Richardson was hinting that the United States might be prepared to take unilateral military action.[21] The Iraqi vicepresident Ramadan, reflecting the general Iraqi assumption that a US military strike was imminent, declared: 'Our noble people, under the leadership of President Saddam Hussein, will remain steadfast and are capable of foiling all evil chapters of American aggression.' The situation was becoming increasingly fraught. American vanity, always a delicate accoutrement, was increasingly under threat in circumstances where it seemed impossible to generate a consensual response to the accumulating perfidies of the Iraqi dictator; and the Iraqis, a proud people, were growing increasingly impatient with a group of strategic planners in Washington who seemed determined to starve the Iraqi people and to reduce the national economy to permanent ruin. It was clear that the crisis, escalating through 1997 and beyond, represented a watershed in Iraqi relations with the rest of the world. The central underlying question remained: whether another US military onslaught on Iraq was now inevitable.

The Iraqi authorities were now being forced to reduce yet further the rations of food and basic commodities, already below the nutritional minimum, being distributed to the civilian population. Official blame was laid on the United States for 'delaying or freezing' many contracts under the terms of the so-called 'oil for food' deal. At the same time there was a growing fear that Washington might restrict yet further the pathetic trickle of food and other humanitarian supplies reaching the increasingly desperate Iraqi families. Few Iraqis who had endured the years-long embargo doubted that the United States typically acted with a vindictive malice. The US-dominated Sanctions Committee had blocked Iraqi access to children's pencils, hospital disinfectants, and shroud material for the dead. It seemed likely that now Washington would sabotage the humanitarian programme in its entirety 'as part of its policy of "starving" the Iraqi people'.[22] And against this situation of worsening misery and destitution was the growing likelihood of bombing raids that would inevitably involve civilian casualties. The Iraqis remained defiant, with the army newspaper *al-Qadisiyah* declaring: 'The Iraqis don't care about America's absurd and odious threats.' Long years of substantial co-operation with UNSCOM had accomplished nothing, said the official publication *al-Jumhouriyah:* '*So any confrontation will certainly be easier than the extermination of a million and a half Iraqis during the years of the embargo.*' And Tariq Aziz was again stressing that while the United States dominated the Sanctions Committee there would be no lifting of sanctions: there had been co-operation with UNSCOM but 'why should we continue?'[23]

On 4 November 1997 the UN Secretary-General Kofi Annan spoke by telephone with Tariq Aziz, urging him to postpone the deadline set by Iraq for the expulsion of the American UNSCOM members. It was announced that three UN envoys were being sent to Iraq to emphasise the importance of compliance with Security Council resolutions that related to the current situation. Kofi Annan's appeal was successful (just as his February 1998 mediation was triumphant): 'The Secretary-General is pleased to announce that Mr Aziz has informed him that the Government of Iraq will comply with his request. He has been assured that no members of the [UNSCOM] team will be expelled from Iraq while his envoys are in the country. The Secretary-General welcomes this action as a positive beginning of the talks that will take place starting tomorrow [5 November], when the envoys will meet the Deputy Prime Minister [Tariq Aziz] in the afternoon. Their task will be both delicate and difficult. Let's all wish them success.' Kofi Annan requested also that a scheduled U-2 flight be postponed. Richard Butler (statement, 5 November) acceded to the request (noting that the flight 'would have occurred during the period', while Annan's 'Personal Envoy's were emphasising to the Iraqi authorities that UNSCOM operations 'must be fully and unconditionally reinstated'), but stressed the importance of the U-2 flights and that they would be resumed the following week. Again, few independent observers doubted that the U-2 aircraft, manned solely by American pilots and with data links to US intelligence units, were performing a characteristic espionage function for Washington.

The pundits, where not mired in propaganda, continued their efforts to analyse the situation. Some stressed the need for a diplomatic solution, though acknowledging that the United States might be prepared to 'go it alone' (Britain's poodling support scarcely affecting the international position). Anti-Saddam commentators took comfort from the general agreement that Iraq was in violation of 687 and other relevant Security Council resolutions, but since many countries conventionally take a 'pick and mix' approach to Council decisions this circumstance did not amount to much. And the pundits were forced to admit that the 'no-fly' zones did not enjoy UN authorisation, that the innocent civilians in Iraq were being harshly punished by the US-sustained sanctions regime, and that military action under UN auspices properly required a majority vote in the Security Council without a veto from any of the Permanent Members. These details, difficult to gainsay, combined to undermine US efforts to drum up support for military strikes. The Iraqi authorities had lied for years about their weapons programme and related matters (did not the various mostly indifferent publics know that *all* politicians lied?). So did this mean that a few hundred more innocent Iraqi men, women and children should be bombed to death? Saddam had already been characterised in Western propaganda as oblivious to the suffering of his hapless people. Would he really be punished if they were to be made to suffer more? The rationale for a further episode of US-induced carnage seemed increasingly unclear.

On 3 November Saddam had threatened to shoot down the American spy planes but had offered a dialogue over the question of the UN weapons inspectors. Dialogue was the last thing on the minds of the American strategists. Bill Richardson expressed the general US attitude: 'This is an irresponsible escalation which we view with grave concern'; and Britain, still eager not to loosen its grip on American coat-tails, declared that it was prepared to use force against Iraq but only after all the 'diplomatic avenues' had been explored (which did not of course include the reckless gambit of actually sending a minister to Baghdad for talks). US spokesmen were keen to assert that no action, including unilateral military strikes (presumably in the absence of UN authorisation), was ruled out. The international community looked on, seemingly adjusted to the inevitability of a new war, further destruction of Iraqi property, and yet more civilian deaths. For example, in Abu Dhabi, Nabil Nijem, the Iraqi ambassador to the Arab League, voiced the opinion of much of the Arab world and beyond: 'When we took this decision we were expecting, as in the past, that America would take hostile positions, including the use of military means against Iraq.' In early November it was estimated that the United States had approximately 18,500 troops, 200 aircraft and 15 ships, headed by the aircraft carrier USS *Nimitz*, in the Gulf.

It was clear that Saddam's proposed dialogue ('that will put things in their proper perspective, where rights and obligations will be clarified') would be bitterly opposed by the Americans. In tolerating the mission of the UN envoys sent to Baghdad by Kofi Annan, Washington emphasised that they were not expected 'to negotiate'. The envoys were to convey a single message: that Saddam Hussein was under obligation to observe all relevant UN resolutions (said a Foreign Office spokesman in London: 'The team is there to insist on compliance ...'). Again it was being stressed that the use of force was a 'possibility', though the US/UK preparations for war – still with no real diplomatic initiative visible in Washington or London – were increasingly hampered by objections from Russia, France, Turkey and most of the Arab world. President Clinton, as befitted the US threat posture, declared that Saddam would make 'a big mistake' if he took action against the American U-2 spy planes; while UN Secretary-General Kofi Annan, set to have a significant shaping influence on the course of events, called on 'all sides' (including Washington) to hold down their rhetoric.

The Americans were in no doubt that they had every right to inspect every inch of Iraq – including, presumably, the intimate living quarters of the man against whom they had already launched abortive *coups d'état*. Clinton was insisting that the UNSCOM teams must have every latitude ('We have to be very firm about it'), with James Rubin, a US State Department spokesman, determined to underline the sentiment: the Security Council 'should be prepared to take firm action to bring about Iraqi compliance in the event they don't change their mind in the next day or so' ('*firm*' is of course one of the approved terms in the rhetorical lexicon).

The UN envoys (an Algerian, an Argentinian and a Swede) were charged with the task of bringing the Iraqis back into compliance. Kofi Annan had not hinted at any other objective, though the Iraqis plainly intended to exploit the mission. The government newspaper *al-Jumhouriya* declared that Iraq would use the visit to extract a timetable for the lifting of UN sanctions, at the same time emphasising that following Iraq's success in the laboratory preparation of the (Western-advertised) VX material it had not been developed into an active product or used in armaments. Now it was the turn of the US Defense Secretary William Cohen: to the talk of 'firm action', 'big mistake' and suchlike, Cohen noted the 'serious consequences' that would flow from any aggressive Iraqi initiate (over Iraqi territory). And Washington remained committed to sanctions as a foreign policy tool, as applied not only to Iraq but to other countries that refused to acquiesce in American hegemony. Thus during the escalation of the US/Iraq crisis the United States took steps to tighten its sanctions on Sudan, a desperately poor country racked by civil war. Madeleine Albright declared that sanctions would be tightened because of Sudan's alleged involvement in international terror and its 'abysmal record' on human rights (Sudan had not learned one of the cardinal principles of politics in the global environment: that only US allies are allowed abysmal records on human rights). Mustafa Osman Ismail, the Sudanese foreign affairs minister, commented on state radio: 'This is one of the injustices that the United States is imposing on other countries which do not submit to it'; while Seifuddin Fadlullah, a producer of gum arabic, Sudan's main export to the United States, declared that if Washington intensified the embargo then other markets, in Europe and Japan, would be found.

On 5 November further Iraqi violations of the terms of Resolution 687 were being reported. Thus according to an UNSCOM inspector the Iraqis had moved arms-related equipment out of sight of surveillance cameras and also tampered with the cameras themselves. The equipment included items that could be used to balance prohibited missile gyroscopes, and now the cameras were unable to perform as UNSCOM intended ('… cameras may have been intentionally tampered with, lenses covered and lighting turned off in the facilities under monitoring'). Doubtless the US-led UNSCOM teams would be forced to take 'firm action'. Richard Butler was quickly involved, saying that his officials would try 'to establish the whereabouts' of the material that had been moved. Now, in addition to the possibility that inspection cameras 'may' have been tampered with, Butler was warning that Iraq 'could have' produced seed stocks for biological weapons with some of the equipment that had been removed – yet more trivial hypotheses to justify the continued starvation of a national people.

The UN envoys, urging Iraqi compliance, had seemingly achieved ambiguous results. While one Baghdad-based diplomat was suggesting a 'positive outcome',[24] other commentary noted that the talks had 'failed to make any progress'.[25] On 6 November the Iraqi authorities turned back UN inspectors for a fourth successive day and admitted moving some equipment from UNSCOM-monitored sites, but only to protect it from the expected American air strikes; the cameras, asserted the Iraqis, had not been tampered with but one had been damaged by an accidental explosion of a missile engine. On the following day the UN envoys gave a press conference in Baghdad. It included the following commentary:

> **Mr Brahimi**: '... We have asked them [the Iraqi authorities] to consider going back to the status quo ante that prevailed before the 29th October and to allow UNSCOM to come to Iraq, to discuss with them how cooperation ... can resume in a better atmosphere, so that UNSCOM can finish its work as soon as possible.
>
> We told them that the Secretary-General realizes and understands that the Iraqis consider that the work of the Commission has been going on for a very long time, six and a half years, and that we understand their impatience and their desire to see to it that this work is finished, so that Article 22 of the resolution [687] can be implemented and perhaps ultimately the sanctions can be lifted ... .
>
> We have conducted our discussions with the Iraqis in a very good atmosphere. ... We are taking these ["concerns and grievances"] back to the Secretary-General, who will inform the Security Council and then we will see where that will lead us ... '

Mr Brahimi (speaking variously in English, French and Arabic) noted the concern of the Iraqis about how UNSCOM was carrying out its duties, confirmed the Iraqi reluctance to tolerate American inspectors, and emphasised that the Iraqis wanted the Security Council to consider specific grievances. Throughout the press conference (7 November) the envoys were circumspect, as befitted diplomats. The various Iraqi grievances were seen as a matter for the Security Council, the issue of the provocative U-2 flights was 'beyond our mandate', the question of 'a fixed timetable to lift the embargo in order to alleviate the suffering of the Iraqi people which has lasted so long' did 'not fall within our responsibilities'. Nonetheless the atmosphere of the dialogue had been seemingly cordial, the Iraqis had managed to voice their concern about the UNSCOM posture, and further publicity had been given to the worsening plight of the Iraqi civilian population. Mr Eliasson, one of the envoys, stressed the importance of gaining a deeper understanding of the Iraqi grievances, 'which in some instances was legitimate'.

The political climate continued to deteriorate. As far as Washington was concerned Iraq *by definition* had no legitimate grievances: such a theoretical fantasy was prohibited by pariah politics. And so the main American focus was on comprehensive preparations for war. The UN envoys had left Baghdad 'with little to show from two days of talks',[26] while a senior Iraqi official repeated the threat that U-2 spy planes would be shot down if they ventured over Iraqi territory (that the Iraqis would probably be technically unable to accomplish this did nothing to diminish the political weight of the threat). Both sides were reportedly 'making contingency plans for combat'; the USS *Nimitz* had cancelled a scheduled port call and remained in the Gulf, while Iraqi forces were dispersing around the country to minimise the effects of a concentrated bombing attack.[27] The suspended U-2 flights were soon to resume, primarily with the aim of selecting targeting data for planned American air raids (Aziz: 'I know the U-2 is entering Iraqi air space to take photographs to enable the Americans to attack the Iraqi targets'). The Iraqi position appeared to be resolute (Aziz: *'We have been in a situation since 1991 until now where the adversary is the judge. The American government says openly, clearly, that it's not going to endorse lifting the sanctions on Iraq until the leadership of Iraq is changed'*). Washington remained intransigent, with many observers now speculating on the likely countdown to war. Premier Tony Blair, speaking for Britain, was reaffirming that 'all means' were legitimate to achieve Iraqi compliance with anything and everything that Washington demanded, while other states were circumspect. Thus at the end of the Anglo-French summit in London, President Jacques Chirac, while emphasising the importance of Iraqi compliance with UN resolutions, stressed that France was opposed to 'brutal methods', such as sanctions and military force.

President Clinton was now content to discount any reason for optimism. Asked if he saw any reason for hope that Iraq would move to comply with American demands he replied: 'No, I don't.' Many American strategists, keen for a fresh war, would have been deeply disappointed with any other answer. The mission of the UN envoys was now being depicted as 'abortive', and at least Clinton could be relied upon not to disturb the war planners by generating any hint of constructive or original thought: 'I think it is important that we be resolute and I think it would be a mistake to rule in or rule out any particular course of action at this time' (it was heartening to know that when the US President was not being 'firm' he was being 'resolute').

William Cohen had developed a detailed analysis: on ABC's *Good Morning Today* he declared that 'some action has to be taken'. When, on 7 November, President Clinton declared that the international community had to be 'resolute *and* firm' it was obvious that matters were moving to a head. It was equally plain that unless 'some action' was taken Saddam Hussein would continue to threaten his neighbours, the region and the entire globe – not least because of his development of the 'doomsday option', a fearsome device apt to strike terror into the hearts of strong men everywhere. I refer of course to the propellor-driven crop-duster aircraft, a modified Polish M18, probably capable of all of 150 mph and now equipped to spray enemy forces (and enemy cities) with the most deadly germs.[28] This is the pitch that anti-Iraq propaganda has reached – to propose that a small, slow, short-range aircraft could represent a *doomsday* scenario by outflanking, outflying and outwitting the prodigious armed forces of the most powerful nation the world has known. Are we really expected to treat such a risible absurdity as a matter for serious concern? And if it is not an ancient propellor-driven crop-sprayer, it is a suitcase: 'The fear that Iraq has developed a "suitcase bomb" with chemical or biological components to attack Western cities is now a priority for Western security experts.'[29]

The United States and Britain, terrorised by the thought of crop-sprayers and suitcases, were now hastening the military preparations. Hundreds of US aircraft, equipped with a vast array of hi-tech ordnance, were assembled in the Gulf region and supplied with copious data collected from AWACS, satellites and ground assets; cruise missiles, earthquake bombs, napalm incendiaries, fuel–air bombs, cluster bombs, depleted uranium ordnance, nuclear weapons (?) – all were being assembled and programmed for possible use against an already-ravaged country with virtually no air defences. It was the sort of military scenario relished by aggressive war planners everywhere. The British government, having declared its new 'ethnical' foreign policy and keen not to be left out of a piece of imperial nonsense, judged it might be ethical to kill a few more innocent Arabs – and so gave orders for its small number of Tornado jets to be made ready. Washington was now making it plain that military action was imminent, and London, keen to prolong the Blair/Clinton honeymoon, was keen to join in. It was now the turn of a British official to rehearse the mantra: 'We are going to be resolute and firm. We are not looking for a violent conflict and see the next step as being at the Security Council. We are certainly hoping for a diplomatic solution. But there should be no doubt that nothing is ruled out.'[30] *Resolute and firm ... diplomatic solution ... nothing is ruled out ...* This sort of 'speak-your-weight-machine' contribution was being supplemented by a range of proposals designed to alarm and outrage. Saddam was allegedly secreting equipment and experts (in chemical and biological warfare) in Sudan, Algeria and Libya (or was it Libya, Algeria and Sudan?); he was responsible for an anthrax scare in New York (or was it Paris?); he was about to lob a ton of VX nerve gas into Tel Aviv (or was it Cairo or London?). The sooner we bomb Iraq back to a pre-Stone Age the better.

On 8 November thousands of Iraqis demonstrated in Baghdad as UNSCOM were prevented from entering suspected weapons sites for the sixth day. The chants were enthusiastic, if unoriginal: 'Yes, yes for Saddam, the sword of the Arab nation. No, no for American spies.' One of the UN envoys, Jan Eliasson, observed that the escalation could end in an armed conflict that would cause terrible suffering. Now the Iraqis were introducing suggestions that would be influential in shaping the final peace agreement (see Chapter 6): the UNSCOM teams could be better balanced by including more members from other countries and fewer Americans; perhaps also the surveillance planes, as already suggested, could be manned by non-Americans (to reduce the likelihood that espionage information would be fed directly to Washington instead of to the United Nations agencies in Baghdad and New York). President Clinton, faced with this escalating crisis, knew what to say: 'It would be a mistake to rule in or out any particular course of action.' Blair, the world was impressed to learn, was determined to stand 'absolutely firm'.

The Western media were now eager to portray the escalating crisis as a 'Who blinks first?' drama. Already newspapers and television networks were gearing up to offer entertaining coverage: *you saw Gulf War I, now for the sequel!* The crisis was a 'trial of strength' where two nations (or, more likely for theatrical purposes, two men) were 'reaching the point of no return'. Clinton was declaring that to shoot down a U-2 pilot would be 'murder'; and Saddam was telling Iraqis that they had to choose between 'sacrifice' and 'slavery'. Again the Iraqis were making a central and important point: they had co-operated with the United Nations for years, and where had it got them? They were still a pariah state, sanctions were still killing many thousands of civilians every month, and there was no end in sight. Divisions in the Security Council were serving as some sort of brake on US military action, but Kofi Annan was well aware of the gravity of the crisis: 'It is serious; no one should underestimate it.'

President Clinton continued to assert that *nothing* could be ruled 'in or out'. Was this really what he meant? Thermonuclear weapons? He proclaimed also that the United States was not going to be 'bullied' by Saddam – an unremarkable comment in circumstances when the world's only superpower was planning the systematic pulverisation of an already devastated land. Secretary of State Madeleine Albright was happy to convey the perception that Saddam Hussein was a 'pariah' caught in 'a box that is tightening'. (Another useful metaphor: in October 1995 a Western diplomat noted: 'Our policy is to keep Iraq in its box.') She added, with evident relish: 'He [Saddam] is in much worse shape than he was six-and-a-half years ago. He has lost hundreds of billions of dollars in oil revenues. His country is a mess. People who have been there recently say it has been completely devastated. Of course he is still building his own palaces at great expense. But the people are suffering.' It was heartening to find that the woman who had said it was justified to kill half a million Iraqi children (CBS, *60 Minutes*, 12 May 1996) had noticed that the Iraqi people were suffering. She added for good measure, speaking to reporters: 'Saddam is a congenital liar who cheats and steals.'[31] Some observers persisted that in these circumstances it might have been more ethnical to protect the hapless Iraqi population from the demon rather than to torment them.

Again it was made plain that the United Nations would seek the 'strongest possible action' against Iraq when the Security Council convened; but that Washington was prepared to take unilateral military action if a Council consensus could not be built (Albright: 'I think we are going to work on having an international accord, but we cannot afford to have anybody doubt our resolve'). Now Iraq was hinting that the ban on American members of UNSCOM might be flexible – if a more balanced make-up of the inspection teams could be constructed for investigation of the most sensitive arms sites. But there had to be some movement from the United Nations (Aziz: *'We are in a long dark tunnel. There is no end in sight ... there will be no retreat by Iraq'*). The Iraq position was plain and gaining increasing publicity. UNSCOM members were often deliberately provocative, with Richard Butler, the head of the teams, a blunt and uncompromising operator, insensitive to Arab feelings and to any (UN-specified) concept of Iraqi dignity and sovereignty. For the Americans, Butler was ideal. As an Australian he was nominally independent of the American UNSCOM caucus (Sandy Berger, US National Security Advisor: Butler is 'a total professional' running the operation in an 'apolitical way').

On 10 November the United Nations called Saddam's bluff by sending a US-piloted U-2 reconnaissance plane over Iraq to collect surveillance data. Other American planes escorted the U-2 to provide a fighter escort, a precaution that in the event proved unnecessary. After a three-hour flight without incident the spy plane returned to its Saudi base, with William Cohen subsequently admitting that there had been 'no indication' of any Iraqi threat. This was hardly surprising since, as predicted, the U-2 had been well out of range of anti-aircraft batteries (an Iraqi military spokesman commented that 'our defences are being prepared to confront the situation'). Again Baghdad was emphasising that such surveillance flights, in the past associated with subsequent bombing raids, were not a proper part of the UNSCOM operations. Now the Iraqis were continuing to prepare for the expected air attacks. Hundreds of Iraqi civilians carrying food, blankets and Saddam portraits assembled at the presidential compound in Baghdad, seemingly offering themselves as 'human shields' against aerial attack.

Western sources depicted the event as a contrived propaganda exercise orchestrated by the Iraqi authorities, with the Iraqi News Agency describing the gathering as spontaneous: 'Hundreds of Iraqi families have expressed their readiness ... in defiance of any American military aggression ... to sacrifice for their country and leader Saddam Hussein.' CNN, already gearing up for the television spectacular of the anticipated war, was invited to film Iraqi boys volunteering for military service in Saddam's Commando units. At the same time women and schoolchildren chanted anti-American slogans as they paraded in organised demonstrations. Iraqi military units had been put on maximum alert, all leave had been cancelled and commanders had been ordered to prepare for a military attack.

The mutual abuse continued. Tariq Aziz objected to Albright calling Saddam Hussein a 'congenital liar' and hoped that Mrs Albright 'wasn't a liar herself' but 'unfortunately she is'. Bill Richardson, US ambassador to the United Nations, commented that Aziz was trying to create confusion by means of 'delay, deception and denial'. It was all somewhat less than constructive diplomacy. Now the Pentagon was announcing that Defense Secretary William Cohen was postponing a trip to China, and that General Henry Shelton, chairman of the Joint Chiefs of Staff, was also postponing a scheduled trip to Asia. Pentagon sources were leaking their plans for a massive bombing onslaught on a largely defenceless Iraq. Some US military planners wanted to rely on dozens of sea-launched Tomahawk cruise missiles (costing $1.2 million each), though their limitations were well known. Other strategists assumed that the imminent onslaught would include wave upon wave of fighter bombers in a days-long campaign that would range over the whole of Iraq.

Throughout this period the Iraqi authorities were emphasising their willingness to tolerate the activities of USCOM teams that did not include American ('espionage') personnel. Thus in a letter (11 November 1997) from Mohammed Said Al-Sahaf, the Iraqi Minister for Foreign Affairs, addressed to the President of the UN Security Council, stress was laid on the assumed right of UNSCOM officials (apart from US staff) to inspect the designated sites. Emphasis was given to the USCOM decisions not to proceed with particular inspections, despite the encouragement given by the Iraq authorities:

> Each time a group was preparing to depart from the Baghdad Monitoring and Verification Centre, it was informed by the Iraqi authorities that the Americans were not permitted to carry out inspection activities. At the same time, the Iraqi authorities informed the group that they were ready to lend their full cooperation and assistance in order to facilitate inspection by the remaining members of the team, and to ensure the success of their mission. In addition, the Iraqi authorities reiterated their position each time a group arrived at the designated inspection site, and on each occa-

sion, the group cancelled its activities immediately, or while travelling to the inspection site, or after its arrival at the site, without true justification.[32]

The matter seemed relatively trivial. Some inspectors were banned but encouragement was being offered by the Iraqi authorities for UNSCOM to continue its work. Because of the exclusion of a few American personnel – which in any reasonable judgement would not have seriously degraded UNSCOM's work – Washington was prepared to plan for the comprehensive bombing of an entire country. The technical violations of Resolution 687 were minor and questionable, and the spirit of the inspections could well have been preserved; but US hegemonic conceit was not to be flouted, even if a vast new war was the consequence.

On 12 November 1997 the Security Council, under massive American pressure but with a fair degree of accord, adopted Resolution 1137 (see Appendix IV). Here, as usual, a reference was made to earlier resolutions and to the commitment of all Member States 'to the sovereignty, territorial integrity and political independence of Kuwait and Iraq'. Then, acting under Chapter VII of the Charter (the mandatory chapter), the Council condemned Iraqi violations of the 'relevant resolutions' and the blocking of certain UNSCOM officials 'on the grounds of their nationality'; and demanded an immediate change in the Iraqi position. As a punitive gesture, Resolution 1137, adopted unanimously, imposed travel restrictions on all the Iraqi officials and members of the Iraqi armed forces 'responsible for Iraq's failure to cooperate with the United Nations Special Commission (UNSCOM) ... '. this further sanction was a relatively puny restriction, even with the Council intending to list the names of the individuals whose 'entry or transit through the territory of Member States would be prevented'.[33] It was however the most that an increasingly frustrated Washington could accomplish. Now it was plain that the rest of the Security Council, Britain apart (as a presumed element in the US State Department), had no appetite for a further military adventure in the Gulf.

Resolution 1137 (Paragraph 8) expressed also the 'firm intention to take further measures' that may be required. Such measures were not defined but at least allowed the United States to continue the pressure on Council Members for a robust response to continued Iraqi derelictions. In response to 1137, Mohammed Said Al-Sahaf in Baghdad declared that Iraq would not lift its ban on US weapons inspectors, would not rescind its threat to U-2 spy planes, and would not be intimidated by further American threats. In Washington President Clinton inserted a new warning to Iraq in his commemoration address for Veterans' Day at the Arlington National Cemetery; while 61 per cent of Americans polled in a Wirthlin Worldwide survey expressed their approval for US military action against Iraq. Now Clinton was asserting that the United States had 'inherent authority' under existing

UN resolutions 'to carry out such strikes, should it be necessary'; and American commanders were boasting of their military capacity. Thus Rear Admiral John Nathman, overall commander of USS *Nimitz*, declared: 'We are at a relatively high state of readiness. We are ready and well-trained and the women and men understand they are doing the right thing. If there is a military option, we are very much part of the answer ... We have a message to Saddam Hussein that we have a tremendous combat capability.' The *Nimitz*, steaming 100 miles off the Iraqi coast, carried 75 aircraft, including 14 F-14 fighters and 36 F/A-18Cs, used to patrol the illegally-declared 'no-fly' zone in southern Iraq. The military option was receiving more attention by the day, even in the commentaries of supposedly liberal newspapers: 'Sooner or later, the [Security] Council will almost certainly have to consider military action, a choice which is far from satisfactory and yet may well be necessary, because not to take it would lead to an even worse situation.'[34]

Other matters were now receiving scant attention in the Western media: two Muslim terrorists had been convicted in Fairfax, Virginia, of killing two CIA workers in retaliation for the US role in bombing Iraq during the 1991 Gulf War; the US/UK 'diplomatic efforts', 'exploring every avenue', 'searching for a peaceful solution' comprised nothing more than pressurising possible allies into support for a further military onslaught on a defenceless nation; and Mary Robinson, UN High Commissioner for Human Rights, was trying to keep the sanctions issue alive by expressing her deep concern at reports of the suffering of the Iraqi civilian population. (*'I want to bring to the public's concern the incredible suffering of the children and the old people. These are the people who don't wield the levers of power, but who suffer from the results'*).[35] The sanctions issue had helped to stimulate Iraqi recalcitrance. Substantial co-operation over many years had brought the Iraqi nation no hint of a light at the end of the tunnel. What would non-compliance with US/UN demands achieve?

The situation now seemed to be moving towards a climax. The United States was moving a second carrier, the USS *Washington*, to the eastern Mediterranean with two cruiser escorts, bringing a further 76 aircraft within striking range of Iraq. The British were sending 800 troops to exercise in Kuwait, of minimal military significance but indicating political solidarity with Washington. In Baghdad, Tariq Aziz 'condemns and rejects' the travel restrictions imposed by Resolution 1137, and gave every indication that Iraq was prepared for a military confrontation. Now it seemed that Washington was increasingly 'tired of words' and that the American people, suitably agitated by the constant propaganda, wanted to see an end to the 'Beast of Baghdad', the 'Butcher of Baghdad', a 'bad man' (said one correspondent in the *New York Times*). Perhaps, reasoned the *Wall Street Journal*, there should be another attempt to stimulate another anti-Saddam revolution in Iraq (Sure there would be bloodshed. 'But one thing is clear. There is no cost-free way to depose Saddam'). Even the expected military action, in the absence of a comprehensive ground-troop occupation, seemed an unlikely way of toppling the Iraqi regime.

By mid-November, with Iraq seen by Washington as 'raising the stakes', the military preparations were well under way. Clinton was commenting that Baghdad's moves were 'clearly unacceptable' and Premier Tony Blair was having emergency meetings. Bill Richardson was warning of 'serious consequences', albeit undefined; and Clinton knew where he stood: 'I intend to pursue this matter in a very determined way.' Britain had ordered the aircraft carrier *Invincible* to sail from the Caribbean to the Mediterranean as a 'purely precautionary measure'; and Bill Richardson was soon contributing further detailed analysis (the Iraqi action was 'outrageous and irresponsible', pushing the crisis 'to the brink'). An unnamed British official offered his own penetrating assessment ('At this stage we don't rule anything in or out'); and Foreign Secretary Robin Cook noted the 'seriousness' of the crisis and conveyed his own illuminating insight: 'Poisoning whole cities is not ethical.'[36] (This left aside the moral status of *starving* whole cities to death, which for some reason the ethical Foreign Secretary chose not to address.) The banal commentaries multiplied – on the lips of US/UK politicians and pundits, and throughout the pliant Western media. If platitude and cliché, issued *ad nauseum* in tones of mindless gravitas, were all that were required to defeat the demon then the Iraqi case would have crumbled long ago. On 13 November the United Nations ordered all but a skeleton crew out of Iraq. It seemed plain that the countdown to war had begun.

The United States and Britain continued to threaten the use of force (in constant violation of Article 2(4) of the UN Charter) and to insist that Saddam was a hazard to the entire globe (Blair declared that if Iraq was not prevented from gaining access to weapons of mass destruction '*the whole of the world*' would face disaster). Iraq's foreign minister Mohammed Said Al-Sahaf commented that Baghdad was now expecting an attack from the United States and its 'British stooges', and called on the UN Security Council to stop 'reiterating American rhetoric' and to enter into 'real, serious dialogue with Iraq' (this too was rhetoric: Washington was as likely to allow serious dialogue as Saddam was to abdicate). The United States continued to cultivate the fantasy that Saddam Hussein was ranged not just against Washington and London but '*against the world*' (Albright). It was a congenial doctrine. The virtuous US/UK axis was selflessly defending the entire planet, safeguarding 'the security of the 21st century' (Clinton). It must have seemed odd to Washington strategists that the nations of the Arab League, the Non-aligned organisation, the Security Council and the General Assembly were not more grateful. Nonetheless it was vital that virtue prevail.

It was now clear that, far from being supportive of US/UK warmongering, the former Gulf War allies were 'falling away'.[37] The Russians were reportedly furious at Butler's decision to pull out the UN monitoring teams after the Iraqi expulsion of the Americans, and France and Egypt were equally critical as Security Council Members. In one assessment: 'Mr Butler has been too keen to stamp his authority on UNSCOM in an effort to emerge from the shadow of Mr Ekeus [the former head of the inspectors].'[38] The United States was even losing the support of its most loyal allies in the Gulf, most of whom had expected the Israel/Palestine question to be seriously addressed by Washington. A final straw had been American efforts to force its Arab allies to attend an economic convention in Qatar designed to improve the relations between Israel and Arab world. Thus Fahed Fanek, Jordanian economist, summarised the general Arab feeling: 'America is going down the drain in the Middle East. It is losing its credibility rapidly.' By contrast, Iran, frequently dubbed a 'pariah' by Washington, was enjoying a wave of diplomatic successes. Now it increasingly seemed that the US policy of 'dual containment' (of Iran and Iraq) was melting under the Middle East sun: European ambassadors, but not the Americans, had returned to Tehran; and Washington was finding it impossible to build anything like a plausible coalition against Baghdad.[39]

The doubts were now beginning to accumulate. Would the planned American military action even accomplish its goals, forgetting about whether bombing was legal or ethical?[40] In November 1997 publicity was given to a highly critical report from the American General Accounting Office (GAO), a monitoring arm of the US Congress. This report, *Operation Desert Storm: Evaluation of the Air Campaign*, systematically criticised the company and government claims made for the effectiveness of the weapons systems used against Iraq in 1991. For example, the GAO pointed out that the ability of the F16 fighter bomber's Maverick air-to-ground missile (costing around $100,000 each) to hit anything was seriously impaired by cloud, haze, humidity, smoke and dust. More severe criticisms were levelled at the much-hyped Stealth bomber, with suggestions that its performance features were much less impressive than the hyperbole had proclaimed. The implication was that it would be much easier to hit the civilian infrastructure than small mobile military targets – a poor commentary on the massive investment (around $58bn) made by the US armed services in guided munitions.[41]

Other doubts related to the proportionality of the planned US response to Iraqi provocations: 'Can six slighted Americans be worth a war?'[42] And should the United States really be prepared to take unilateral military action without a consensus, or at least substantial support, in the Security Council?[43] The Americans and Richard Butler remained perplexed that the US/UK propaganda had not succeeded in generating a broader base of support for the planned US military strikes: 'I refuse to believe that the international community is going to simply walk away from the large problem of Iraq's weapons of mass destruction.' In fact the so-called international community did not share America's apocalyptic claims, real or invented. To a growing number of states it was Washington that represented a threat to international peace, blundering around with more military muscle than was good for it or the world, and totally disinclined to resolve the crisis through responsible diplomacy. US vanity was at stake, a hazardous situation in circumstances where unassailable military power seemed to be totally unconstrained by any countervailing force: *'Better, the hawks argue, to act unilaterally and mend fences later ...'*[44] The Iraqis had no doubt that a new war was imminent: Saddam Hussein had put the country on a war footing and his son Uday was urging fellow Arabs to attack American and British targets across the Middle East. There were no signs that the Iraqis were seriously deterred by US threats of a comprehensive bombing campaign.

The Iraqi Foreign Minister Al-Sahaf expressed a common view: the United States wanted to replace Saddam with a 'US-sponsored regime. ... They want this, and nothing else'; Richard Butler was in Baghdad 'to provide the appropriate cover for an evil act by the American administration'; and Iraq remained ready to shoot down the U-2 spy planes that were expected to fly over Iraqi territory for espionage purposes. Still Washington seemed uncertain how to proceed. The countdown to war was under way, but precisely what was the objective? A senior Pentagon official reportedly said that 'no one – from the President down – has said what we are going to do'. Part of the problem stemmed from the many conflicting claims. Did Saddam have an arsenal of prohibited weapons, or simply the capacity to produce them? In any event where was the evidence? Documents proving the existence of past weapons programmes – often aided by the United States, Britain, France, Russia and others – could not be used to prove a current capacity. And if anthrax or VX nerve weapons could be easily hidden in small containers, exactly what was a comprehensive bombing raid supposed to accomplish? No-one doubted that whatever Saddam was up to was happening inside Iraq and – despite the UN-authorised encroachments – Iraq was still declared a sovereign state. What was a new war supposed to achieve? Punishment? Of whom? The desperate civilian population? The US case was crumbling fast.

The Western propagandists did their best. It was easy to demonstrate that Saddam could not be trusted: from the Arab perspective he had little enough reason to co-operate with Western and other powers that had built him up into a powerful Middle East force and then betrayed him. Now it was again being suggested that he was dispersing his 'secret arsenal',[45] manufacturing poison gas in Sudan,[46] and that in consequence Clinton and Blair would have no option but to 'stand tough together'.[47] They had little choice. Desultory support was offered to Washington and London by various other states, and the US/UK propagandists eagerly listed their names as co-opted members of a new anti-Saddam coalition. But this public-relations ploy carried little conviction: there was nothing in this of the comprehensive 1990/91 Coalition, no

Security Council fig-leaf equivalent to Resolution 678, and growing doubt that a new bombing campaign could be carried out either legally (without an explicit Security Council authorisation) or effectively (without ground-troop involvement or well-defined objectives).

The crisis was continuing to escalate. Iraq was yielding nothing in its attitude to the American members of UNSCOM or its insistence on the inviolability of the so-called 'presidential' sites. The country was on a war footing while senior Iraqi officials taunted Washington to do its worse. The United States, having assembled a vast armada in the Gulf, seemed unclear how to proceed. There was no international support for a sustained bombing campaign, but Washington was not ready to scurry off like a chastened child. The hawks were urging unilateral military action, and their influence was being felt in Washington. If the United States could not rely on realistic international support or the imprimatur of the Security Council, perhaps it would suffice to justify a fresh bombing campaign on no more than 'national interest'. Simple slogans had worked in the past – Divine Right, Manifest Destiny, *inter alia*. Perhaps National Interest would do the trick. But Washington was now grossly misjudging the times and misjudging also the inconvenient skills of the most senior United Nations official, Secretary-General Kofi Annan ...

5 ... To US Military Countdown (November 1997 to February 1998)

PREAMBLE

The 1997/8 crisis had many of the features that characterised the preamble to the 1991 Gulf War. The United States, with Britain in tow, seemed bent on conflict. Efforts at diplomacy by Washington and London were desultory, intended not to achieve any worthwhile results but to create the false impression that a peaceful solution was deemed preferable to war. Various states – Russia (the Soviet Union in its final gasp), France and members of the Arab League – made important attempts to halt the inexorable slide into a devastating military conflict. And Washington had been quick to ignore any signs that the 1990/1 crisis could be resolved through negotiation. In General Norman Schwarzkopf's own account of events, an Iraqi representative, Ahmad, at the 1991 ceasefire talks asked him *why Iraq had been invaded 'after we had withdrawn from Kuwait and announced it on the television and radio'.* Schwarzkopf made no attempt to dispute this version of events, saying only 'I think we will leave it to history.' And Ahmad replied: '*I have just mentioned it for history.*'[1] The historians, for the most part, have decided: the 1991 Gulf War was necessary to drive out the Iraqi invaders. Little attention has been given to the many signs that a diplomatic solution was possible. Had it not been for the efforts of UN Secretary-General Kofi Annan, contending all the time with US/UK spoiling tactics, the 1997/8 crisis would have terminated in another 'unavoidable' war. This is what Washington wanted; and, in the event, this is what Washington was denied.

CHRONOLOGY

Through November 1997 the United States struggled to drum up Arab support, in the increasing likelihood of a military attack on Iraq – this being the well-rehearsed American route to constructive diplomacy. But now Washington was finding that the 1991 Coalition had almost completely collapsed under the pressures of the moribund Israeli–Palestinian peace process, the growing international awareness of the dire effects of the US-sustained sanctions on the Iraqi civilian population, and an increasingly widespread resentment at American arrogance. It was now more and more obvious that a unilateral US bombing campaign against Iraq would generate massive resentment throughout the Arab world and beyond. The Egyptian president Hosni Mubarak represented the general regional view when he declared that the use of force to resolve the crisis was 'not appropriate'; the Syrian foreign minister Farouq al-Shara was calling for a solution that avoided military escalation; Saudi Arabia was expressing its reluctance to allow air strikes to be launched from its territory, as was Turkey; and the Iranian foreign minister Mohammed Kharrazi said: 'We believe that threats to use force do not solve anything. ... Iran is against any military strike on Iraq.' The US ambassador to the United Nations, Bill Richardson, characteristically oblivious to such international commentary, was again repeating the mantra: 'The message has been clear: Iraq must comply or face consequences ... We are not precluding any operation, including the military option.' In fact it was *only* the military option that was being given serious attention by the Washington strategists. The point was not lost on Arab commentators. Thus the Jordanian economist Fahed Fanek observed that US policy was 'to control and confiscate Arab oil and protect Israel from any change of a power balance in the Middle East'; and others were questioning why Israel, with its own nuclear and chemical weapons programmes, was not being subjected to the same UN inspection policy.

The Arab response to the US-sponsored Qatar conference (mid-November) highlighted the extent of the obvious American humiliation. Designed to improve Arab–Israeli relations, the whole enterprise was rapidly descending into farce. President Clinton was pleading by telephone with the Saudis; and the American Martin Indyk, a former ambassador to Israel and a pro-Israeli activist, was touring the Middle East in an increasingly vain attempt to garner Arab support for the conference. But now the Middle East states were lining up in opposition to the US plan: Saudi Arabia, Syria, Morocco, Tunisia, United Arab Emirates, Bahrain, Sudan, Libya, Algeria, Lebanon and Egypt – all were now resisting the American appeals and blandishments. Perhaps Oman, Yemen and Jordan might turn up, but any unilateral US military strike would reduce even this Arab rump to a humiliating ruin. Perhaps Kuwait could be relied upon, but even here, the erstwhile victim of Saddam, many reservations were being voiced. And Qatar itself was being condemned by the Saudis, the Egyptians and many others for even agreeing to hold the conference at a time when the Israelis were continuing to expand onto Arab land.[2]

The increasing isolation of Washington was doing little to erode the characteristic American enthusiasm for war. Now it seemed plain that a military countdown was in progress, with journalists and others vying to list the items of hardware available to the US war planners: Tomahawk cruise missiles on surface ships and submarines, missiles designed to home-in on air-defence missile radars, F-117 Stealth fighters; carrier-borne aircraft equipped with an expanded range of so-called 'smart' weapons; RAF Tornados (under *de facto* US orders) carrying their own laser-guided bombs; and so on. But the constraints on US/UK power were apparent: many military assets in the region were effectively neutralised by the reluctance of Saudi Arabia, Turkey and others to become involved in offensive military actions; while there were suspicions that the Iraqi ploy of hiding sensitive equipment in residential areas might mean substantial civilian casualties from US air strikes – an embarrassing scenario that would not play well in public-relations terms. The military planning, the defining of strategic objectives, the attempt to build a new Coalition, the usual propaganda campaign – none of this was going well for the Washington strategists. That Saddam, though comprehensively demonised and operating with sanctions-depleted assets, was seemingly 'winning the crisis' added to American frustration and increased the likelihood of war. The banning of US weapons inspectors and the blocking of UNSCOM access to 'sensitive' sites were relatively minor matters (few observers imagined that Saddam Hussein would have stacked anthrax warheads under his bed); but American vanity, bruised by the frustrations of a seeming impasse, was well capable of transforming itself into an agent of mass destruction.

France and Russia continued to insist that, while Iraq should observe all the relevant UN resolutions, force was not the answer to the crisis. President Chirac urged an end to the 'Iraqis' obstinacy' but Anne Gazeau-Secret, a foreign ministry official, emphasised that French forces in the Gulf region were not on the alert: 'There is no explicit mention of resort to force [in the latest Security Council resolution]. The Security Council will decide the future measures, taking into account Iraq's attitude.' Now, through the posture, Saddam was emerging throughout the region and in wider circles as a *victim* of American obduracy – a most unlikely role for the most comprehensively demonised character in recent times. It was plain that Washington had no interest in real negotiations and that the economic embargo was being maintained in order to topple the Iraqi regime. In a letter (16 November 1997) the Iraqi foreign minister Mohammed Said Al-Sahaf again emphasised to the Security Council that US policy was to uphold sanctions as a means of destabilising Saddam:

... I should also like to refer to the report from Agence France-Presse in Washington on the same day [14 November 1997] that President Clinton had once again stated that the sanctions imposed on Iraq would remain in place as long as President Saddam Hussein was in power ... the United States of America is endeavouring to act against the will of the international community in the context of its pursuit of a policy of exercising hegemony over the Security Council, the United Nations and the world as a whole.[3]

This confirmed, at least to Iraqi satisfaction, that Baghdad's complaints were 'true and well-founded': even if Iraq were to comply with UN resolutions there would be no lifting of the economic embargo. The US attitude was itself a violation of Council resolutions that affirmed Iraq's 'sovereignty, territorial integrity and political independence'. The President of the Security Council should intervene to halt the 'frantic military campaign' of the United States.[4]

On 16 November Tariq Aziz, the Iraqi Deputy Prime Minister, declared that Iraq would allow the return of the US weapons inspectors providing they were on an equal footing with UN experts from other countries: the five Permanent Members of the Security Council 'would all have the same weight' in the new team. And while Aziz was demanding no more than a 'fair' hearing by the Council, Secretary of State Madeleine Albright was doing little for the American case by denouncing Iraq against the backdrop of the Star of David in London. Now Muslim fundamentalist groups in Jordan were urging suicide attacks against American targets. Said Hamzeh Mansour, speaking for the Islamic Action Front, '*The Arab nation must stand up and fight against the coming aggression. ... Another independence war is needed.*' The direction of US policy was clear: the Washington strategists were succeeding in converting the demonised Saddam into the sword of pan-Arabism, a new Gamal Abdul Nasser. Where the United States wanted to isolate the Iraqi dictator in the Middle East they were achieving exactly the opposite result: Saddam was succeeding in uniting substantial sectors of Arab opinion against the presumptions and arrogance of US hegemony. This was demonstrated in many ways, not least by the fiasco of the Qatar conference: not a single Arab foreign minister – apart from the Qatari host – was in Doha to greet Madeleine Albright. Washington had guaranteed the attendance of the Saudis and other Western allies, and had been humiliated. The discomfiture of the Qatari authorities was equally plain.

Such events were combining to sow confusion in Washington. Now it seemed that even Kuwait, perhaps the harshest critic of the Iraqi regime, could not be relied upon to support a military attack on Baghdad. Nonetheless, the American propagandists now had no option but to continue their rhetoric as a prelude to war. Samuel Berger, a White House National Security Advisor, commented that all the military installations were on 'a higher state of alert', and of Saddam: 'I don't think he's been exactly a George Washington or Thomas Jefferson for his own people. Let's remember this is a man who was a weapons-of-mass-destruction repeat offender.' Washington continued to emphasise the American preference for a diplomatic solution, while refusing to talk constructively with any senior Iraqi officials. Perhaps the French or the Russians might be able to coax Baghdad into agreeing some formula that would force the US strategists to abandon the countdown to war.

On 16 November Saddam Hussein declared that Iraq was not seeking a confrontation with the United States and that he wanted to achieve a solution through dialogue. In Doha, Madeleine Albright continued to go through the motions, urging international solidarity against the Iraqi dictator: 'This is not a dispute between Iraq and the US, but between Iraq and the law, Iraq and the world.' The suffering of the Iraqi people was no fault of the United States but a direct consequence of Iraqi policies. Most of the rest of the world persisted in seeing matters in a different light: the humiliation of the United States in Qatar – where even Israel had down-graded its representation – was complete. This served as a dramatic symbol of America's waning influence in the region.

Other political developments were also combining to weaken the US posture. The tensions between the various Kurdish factions in northern Iraq were again erupting into violence, so undermining yet further any Western attempt to build a Kurdish bulwark against Saddam. The troops, planes and artillery of the Turkish armed forces continued their advances into Iraqi sovereign territory, a matter of little interest to a Washington allegedly opposed to foreign incursions into other lands. On 16 November Turkish troops were moving further into Iraq: ' ... *the Turkish government is breaking international law, but its strategic importance in the region means that Washington and London seem prepared to look the other way ...* '.[5] Turkish forces were violating the US-declared 'no-fly' zone in northern Iraq, and some 7000 Turkish lorries were reportedly waiting in the region for fresh oil supplies. Such events received scant attention in Washington or London, where the principal focus remained on the preparations for Gulf War II, the surest way to convince the Iraqis that they could not flout the American will with impunity.

On 17 November an apparent shift of emphasis emerged in the US/UK posture. Perhaps chastened by the absence of international support for military action, diplomats in Washington were reportedly softening their hard-line stance in order to avoid the expected resort to force. Perhaps, it was hinted, there might be some lifting of the punitive sanctions if Saddam were to comply fully with all the relevant UN resolutions. A British diplomat conveyed the shift of mood: 'People got terribly wrapped up in the military option last week. We have had discussions with the Americans and agreed that more can be done to alleviate the suffering of the Iraqi people. We want to make clear that, once Iraq complies with Security Council resolutions, we can begin to look at a process of lifting sanctions.' (It was difficult to avoid the thought that this was no more than a further public-relations ploy. The suggestion that compliance might result in a lifting of sanctions was in any case completely superfluous – since this proposition was already explicitly stated in Paragraph 22 of Resolution 687, agreed by all parties in 1991. Why parade a seeming concession as though it were not already enshrined in the principal UN resolution?)

The seeming shift in the US/UK attitude did little to change the course of events. Few observers doubted that the countdown to war was continuing – as most of the endless propaganda and the banal interviews with US service personnel so graphically indicated. The United States and Britain were reinforcing their military capacity in the region, though the uncertainties about how to use it were obvious: 'A limited attack is not going to get weapons inspectors back into Baghdad. Saddam would love to have military strikes, in which he loses only a bit of hardware in the desert. He would gain sympathy in the Arab world, and create antipathy among some Security Council members towards American unilateral action.' The London-based daily *al-Hayat* noted that America's Gulf allies were 'in a state of acute alarm' over the crisis: '*What they fear are limited US military strikes which don't seriously hurt the regime but enable it to exploit the situation to make trouble for them. They don't want a military strike aimed at teaching the regime a symbolic lesson. They want the regime to be dealt a fatal blow, or no blow at all.*'[6] A Jordanian columnist, Tarek Massarwa, emphasised – as others had done – the relevance of proportionality by suggesting that the United States could not wage a war against Iraq 'for the sake of six American inspectors'. It remained to be seen. The unexpected shift of emphasis had already hit the oil markets, though no observers imagined that the crisis was over. Perhaps, suggested US officials, there could be 'modest adjustments' in the oil-for-food programme – by most accounts a largely useless scheme. But in reality the shift was inconsequential. British officials continued to emphasise that 'an iron fist was still contained within the softer new glove. The emphasis was still on "readiness to consider use of force if all other measures fail".'[7] War, despite any countervailing public-relations rhetoric, was still Washington's preferred option.

The Western media worked to indicate that perhaps diplomacy might succeed in preventing a new US/Iraq war:

Diplomacy paving the way in Iraq crisis[8]

West offers sweeteners to head off Iraqi clash[9]

Clinton builds up air power as US edges towards deal on Iraq[10]

The possible deal was ambiguous but was linked at least in part to an extension of Resolution 986, the 'oil for food' agreement. Perhaps the revenue from increased oil sales could be used to increase the flow of humanitarian supplies to aid the desperate Iraqi civilian population. British officials were calling the new ideas 'a major initiative' to alleviate the suffering of the Iraqi people, 'with whom we have no quarrel'. But again the deal was soon exposed as little more than Western propaganda, devised to give Washington and London some breathing space in the countdown to war. We have seen that Paragraph 22 of Resolution 687 made provision for the lifting of sanctions, but now Washington was insisting on more than simple observance of 687. In addition there would have to be action on human rights (in accord with the non-mandatory Resolution 688), which have never interested the United States outside the cynical calculation of commercial/strategic advantage; and there would have to be increased compensation to Kuwaiti claimants (which often meant no more than supplying them with Iraqi revenue in order to fund the activities of US contractors). The deal – insofar as one was emerging – was bogus, as was Resolution 986, to which it would be linked; the Iraqis, having witnessed the total inadequacies of 986 (and how in any case it had been emasculated by Washington), were in no mood to underwrite another US propaganda stunt.

It was plain also that the United States was continuing to reinforce its military power in the region. On 18 November President Clinton approved the development of 40 to 45 more combat aircraft in the Gulf, including F-117 Stealth fighters and B-52 bombers, weapons that were used in the 1991 Gulf War. The Iraqis, perhaps increasingly sensitive to the scale of the American forces being marshalled close to their borders, seemed interested in pulling back from a further confrontation with US forces. A letter (20 November) from the Iraqi ambassador to the United Nations, addressed to the President of the Security Council, suggested that the excluded UNSCOM members would be allowed back into the country. Thus Nizar Hamdoon referred to a meeting of the Iraqi Revolutionary Command Council, chaired by 'Mr Saddam Hussein, President of the Republic of Iraq': '*That meeting produced a statement containing a decision by the Council to issue an invitation to the Special Commission, with its full complement of members, to return to Iraq to pursue its work there.*'[11] Reference was made also to a Russian–Iraqi Joint Declaration (of 20 November 1997) indicating that agreement had been reached by Iraq on the return of the Special Commission, 'with its full complement of members ... '.[12] And included also (as Enclosure I) was the statement issued by the Revolutionary Command Council (RCC).

The RCC statement denounces 'the forces of evil, headed by the United States of America, that modern incarnation of evil', resorting 'to the conduct of cowards devoid of all humanity'. Here it is recorded that 'factories, workshops, assembly lines, equipment and private laboratories' have been destroyed at the whim of the Americans, who have 'mocked the destiny of a whole people in order to delay a review of one of its most elementary and legitimate rights, the lifting of the embargo ...':

The embargo claimed more than a million victims among the Iraqi people, who were also deprived of countless opportunities to progress and to live. The Americans destroyed all that they wished to destroy under the aegis of the Security Council which ... has been sunk until recently in a kind of torpor. In the face of such arrogant, vile and immoral behaviour, Iraq has no other way of making its voice heard and claiming its rights but to expel the Americans from the country. In so doing it is merely exercising its right of sovereignty, which gives all States the right to expel foreigners whom it considers personae non gratae, even if they are members of the diplomatic corps.[13]

This suggested that the Special Commission would not be allowed to continue its work unless UNSCOM was prepared to redefine the composition of the inspection teams. The foreign ministers from the United States, Russia, Britain and France had met in Geneva to discuss specific Russian proposals; while Prime Minister Tony Blair, speaking in London, made his usual constructive contribution: Saddam 'has to back down. ... Because if he doesn't back down ... we will simply face this problem, perhaps in a different and far worse form in a few years time'. At the same time RAF Harrier jump-jets were ordered to augment the British forces in the Gulf.

It was now increasingly clear that a principal US/UK task was to disparage the Russian attempts to secure a diplomatic solution to the crisis. Washington and London were quick to express their doubts that any 'deal' with Saddam brokered by Russia would secure full Iraqi compliance with the relevant Security Council resolutions. Officials at the Geneva talks worked hard to play down any expectations of a diplomatic success: 'no breakthrough Geneva Declaration' should be anticipated. Nonetheless the US/UK analysts now had doubts about their earlier decision to withdraw all the UNSCOM inspectors with the expelled Americans. Without any residual international scrutiny, Saddam, according to a memorandum circulating among Western diplomats, 'could produce within a matter of months a small number of chemical and biological weapons, including missile warheads'. 'Symbolism', said one European official, 'is one thing, but there's a technical job to be done.' The UNSCOM staff were now convinced that an immediate restoration of inspections was a priority; while an American spokesman was emphasising that full Iraqi compliance with Resolution 1137 (see Appendix IV) was essential. It now seemed that Washington was operating on two parallel tracks: renewed efforts were being made to advertise the 'diplomatic option' (with commentators like former US president Jimmy Carter saying that Clinton would be making a 'serious mistake' if he ordered a military strike), while at the same time American forces in the Gulf were being constantly enlarged and prepared for a sustained bombing campaign.

The American propaganda offensive was not helped by fresh revelations about the style of UNSCOM boss Richard Butler in particular and about the behaviour of UNSCOM staff in general. Butler, known to be in trouble with Baghdad on account of his blunt and offensive methods, was also reportedly in trouble with New York.[14] Here it was suggested that it was Butler's handling of the crisis that had put the United States on the brink of war. He had 'failed utterly to lower the temperature ... by refusing to moderate his confrontational style, he had provoked and offended almost everyone involved'.[15] Commented one diplomat: 'The feeling now is unanimous that Butler has lost it. He shoots from the hip and it is just not helpful at a time like this.' Some observers had accused him of racism, of being so pro-US as to yet further damage Washington's reputation in the region, and of being prone to excessive alcohol consumption ('I've given all that up,' he claimed). It was Butler who withdrew all the UNSCOM inspectors in sympathy with the expelled Americans – without first consulting the Security Council. In an interview with the *New York Times* he asserted that 'truth in some cultures is kind of what you can get away with saying' – a seemingly racist observation that invited a host of criticisms from individual Arab observers and governments.[16]

Again the UNSCOM interference with the life of Baghdad convents was receiving publicity.[17] Sister Francis Clare, at 88 years of age a frail Chaldean nun, was quoted. Between 15 and 20 UNSCOM officials arrived at the gates of her Zafaraniya convent, and a man stepped forward: 'He explained that they had flown from Washington to search our convents and church for weapons. I was stunned ... I told them that even the bishop requests permission in advance to visit us ... They walked the corridors, entered every room, even our bedrooms ... Then they went out into our gardens and sank stick-like implements into the ground. When they found our cemetery where we bury our Sisters, they even sank them there.'[18] Perhaps the gravesites, with their large granite blocks, might have been confused with a missile silo when seen by a U-2 spy plane.[19] Such events, more desecrations, were further eroding the reputation of the UNSCOM teams. In such circumstances it was hardly surprising that the Arab world was slowly coming together, combining in opposition to the constant US-inspired infringements of national dignity in Arab lands. Now the crisis was accelerating the reconciliation between Iraq and Syria – a further alarming threat to US policy in the Middle East. Tariq Aziz was discussing a possible visit to Damascus, increasingly sensitive to encirclement by the growing accord between the hated Israelis and the Muslim state of Turkey. Both Syria and Iraq were concerned that Turkey, perhaps under Jewish pressure, would use its control of the headwaters of the Euphrates as a weapon against them.

It now appeared that Saddam was pulling back from the brink of agreeing to allow US UNSCOM members to return to Iraq. Washington remained predictably sceptical. Madeleine Albright all but discounted the new Iraqi proposal ('I will believe it when I see it. Actions speak louder than words'), and the United States continued to enlarge its forces in the Gulf. Tariq Aziz was suggesting that Russia would become Iraq's advocate in the Security Council (Aziz: 'They are a permanent member of the Security Council and they promised they would do their best to get sanctions lifted'). President Clinton promptly affirmed that the United States would remain 'resolute' and that Saddam must be prevented from 'threatening the world' with nuclear, chemical and biological weapons. (Again Clinton's hyperbole had little connection with the real world: an IAEA report, published on 13 April 1998, said that Iraq had complied with all the specified requirements to declare and destroy its nuclear weapons.) Butler declared that UNSCOM inspections would resume as soon as possible, and implied that Saddam would have taken the opportunity to commit illegalities. Premier Blair, as always echoing Washington from the margins, stressed that it was essential to remain 'firm and tough'. The success, if success there were, belonged to the Russian foreign minister Yevgeny Primakov: it was he who had urged Saddam Hussein to allow the US UNSCOM members to return to Iraq. The Americans, now miffed at further difficulties for their military policies, remained resolutely sceptical; and hoped that soon they would have another pretext for war. In London, Foreign Secretary Robin Cook rushed to declare that Saddam Hussein had 'not won any concessions' (far be it for American or British politicians to compromise on anything). But in fact it was clear that the Iraqis had so far turned the crisis to their advantage. Saddam had defied the Americans for some weeks; the inspectors had been expelled, albeit temporarily; and the patent divisions in the UN Security Council had been further prised open for all the world to see. Moreover, it was now apparent that Baghdad had enlisted the Russians as committed advocates in the Council, a development that served not only Moscow's long-term commercial plans but also the resurgent Russian desire to play a leading role on the world stage. Saddam had 'not done badly';[20] and in consequence US frustration and bellicosity were set to grow in the week and months ahead.

On 20 November 1997 the UNSCOM inspectors returned to Baghdad to continue their work. In most commentary it was suggested that Saddam had backed down in return for a Russian promise to work for an end to the punishing economic embargo. There was little ground to assume that the crisis would not resurface before long and in another form: the basic conditions (sanctions, Saddam's duplicity, US vindictiveness, the moribund Arab–Israeli peace process, etc.) were all in place. Madeleine Albright's declaration that the embargo would not be lifted while Saddam was in power had revealed the US indifference to Security Council resolutions: Iraqi compliance was an irrelevance, since all that would satisfy Washington was Saddam's demise. But with the Iraqi dictator seemingly more secure than ever the world was waiting for the next eruption of the running crisis. Bill Clinton was conveying the news that all the world was waiting to hear: the United States was 'resolute'; and Bill Richardson again rehearsed the American policy: 'The United States and the United Nations have made no deal, no concession. No carrots have been offered. We are not ready to lift sanctions until all Security

Council resolutions are complied with. If necessary we will use our veto to achieve that.' The military moves were continuing, perhaps stimulated by a further Saddam provocation: he declared 20 November 'The Day of the People' to establish an annual celebration of 'the glorious and brave stand of President Saddam Hussein and his sincere people to face up to the United States' threats of aggression'. The inspectors were back at work, but their authority was tarnished and the Iraqis had turned the situation to considerable propaganda advantage. Russia, in its joint communiqué with Iraq, pledged to 'energetically promote the speedy lifting of sanctions against Iraq on the basis of its compliance with UN Security Council resolutions'; Primakov noted this 'great success of Russian diplomacy'. An editorial in *The Independent* (London), 21 November 1997, carried the score – '*Bill Clinton 0, Saddam Hussein 1*'; and asked – '*So what is the US strategy?*' Washington, discomforted, was not in despair. There would soon be another opportunity for war.

As the UNSCOM inspectors resumed their work, Washington and London were 'firmly' digging in their heels. They would resolutely resist any Russian attempt to pressure the Security Council into a relaxation of sanctions: it was essential to US/UK policy that the Iraqi civilian population continue to be denied food and medicine in adequate supply. David Kay, an earlier truculent UNSCOM inspector, commented that the oil-for-food deal should not be extended, since 'feeding carrots to a totalitarian dictator is a great way to strengthen him, not weaken him'. It was this sort of pressure, deriving from many American sources, that made it unlikely that the Iraqi people would be granted any significant relief in the near future. Soon, the Washington planners were pleased to note, there were further reasons why only a belligerent attitude to Iraq could be allowed to shape US policy.

Now increasing emphasis was being given to the Iraqi refusal to allow the UNSCOM inspectors to enter Saddam's private palaces – the very places, US officials were arguing, where the Iraqi dictator would be likely to hide evidence of his weapons of mass destruction. (We may speculate on how keen Saddam might have been to live in close proximity to chemical and biological weapons that would attract American air strikes in the event of war.) In fact a letter (22 November 1997) from Richard Butler, UNSCOM 'Executive Chairman', was acknowledging that in important areas it was likely that the work of the inspectors was complete. Thus the letter cites an earlier IAEA report (8 October) declaring that '*there are no indications that any weapon-usable nuclear material remains in Iraq and that the ongoing monitoring and verification activities of IAEA have not revealed indicators of the evidence in Iraq of prohibited materials, equipment or activities*'.[21] If IAEA were to be subsequently satisfied on a few relatively minor matters it 'would have been a basis for an early favourable report to the Security Council'.

There were still matters to clear up but the general tone of the report was plain: there had obviously been substantial Iraqi compliance with UNSCOM over the years-long inspection regime, though this fact was never reflected in US/UK propaganda. Thus UNSCOM was *'satisfied that 817 of the 819 proscribed missiles imported by Iraq have been effectively accounted for'*. (Was Saddam really going to threaten the world with two out-of-date Scud missiles?) And UNSCOM recognized the 'significant progress' that had been made in the area of chemical weapons ('Considerable quantities of chemical weapons, their components and chemical weapons-related equipment have been destroyed by Iraq and UNSCOM, in cooperation'). Only in the area of biological weapons were accusations made that Iraq had 'disregarded its obligations to the United Nations', but even the UNSCOM caveats in this sector seemed a poor ground for the continuation of sanctions on an entire nation. Even considering a worst-case scenario of Iraq's possession of biological weapons, how were such devices to be delivered to vulnerable cities? UNSCOM had admitted that the Iraqi missiles had been accounted for. Or were we back to the 'doomsday suitcase' scenario?

The report emphasised that 'immediate, unconditional and unrestricted' access to any site was essential if UNSCOM was 'to accomplish any of its tasks'[22] – as if the tasks already described in the report had not already been accomplished. Now the scene was being set for a further bout of US/Iraqi confrontation. Where the presidential palaces, manifest symbols of Iraqi sovereignty, had been regarded as inviolate for seven years, they would now be targeted as obvious places for Saddam to stockpile vast quantities of nerve agents and lethal organisms. If the exclusion of US inspectors had not yielded Gulf War II perhaps the banning of UNSCOM staff from Saddam's living quarters might do the trick. At the same time, declared the Butler report, the surveillance of Iraq should be increased – a direct provocation to Baghdad (already highly sensitive to the U-2 espionage missions): ' ... additional aerial surveillance, with additional aircraft, could enhance UNSCOM effectiveness, including night surveillance ... '.[23] A sovereign Iraq was expected to endure increased day and night surveillance by a hostile state committed to the overthrow of the national government. Here again was a recipe for increased US/Iraqi tension and yet another seemingly inevitable slide to war. Iraq would be allowed no early relief: the November report concluded by stipulating the next scheduled meeting for April 1998, 'if this were considered to be helpful'. Again the impression was deliberately created that the surveillance activity, the constant infringements of sovereignty, and the genocidal sanctions regime were to be maintained (strengthened even) in perpetuity. And if Iraq were to resist such unending impositions, war would be the inevitable consequence.

The Iraqis continued to convey their concerns to the UN Secretary-General and the Security Council. In a letter (24 November 1997) from

Nizar Hamdoon, the Iraq ambassador to the United Nations, the usual grievances were expressed: here it was asserted that the Russian Federation had
made intensive efforts

to extinguish the flames which have been and continue to be fanned by
the United States of America; that country, rather than demonstrating the
wisdom of one who has learned a genuine and useful lesson, has behaved
more foolishly than wisely. It has built up its military presence in the Arab
Gulf area and sent the U-2 aircraft to violate Iraqi airspace and carry out
not only espionage activities, but also acts of provocation, in order to
escalate tension and hostility to the point where the situation becomes
explosive.[24]

On the same day Nizar Hamdoon submitted a detailed letter to the
President of the Security Council in response to the report (22 November
1997) from Richard Butler, summarising UNSCOM progress. The 15-page
Iraqi response (which cannot be reproduced in the present book) deserves
careful consideration, totally absent in Western propaganda intent on exacerbating US/Iraqi tensions. Apart from the occasional items of rhetoric ('The
accusation and suspicions the Special Commission directs against Iraq are
endless, and they are constantly and continually being nourished by circles
hostile to Iraq'), the report includes much detail about the character and
scope of Iraqi activities in the weapons field. In particular, in response to the
UNSCOM accusations that inadequate information had been provided on
the extent of the Iraqi biological-weapons sector, the report appends a list of
192 documents presented by the Iraqis 'concerning declarations in the biological sphere'.[25] It is difficult in these circumstances, and without expert
assessment (a capacity absent in many of the UNSCOM staff), to avoid the
conclusion that the Iraqis, despite some areas of concealment, had offered
substantial co-operation with the inspectors – in the biological-weapons area
as elsewhere. This years-long degree of compliance had earned Iraq no
credit. Soon there would be yet another United States countdown to war.

Again Washington was rejecting Russian proposals for a timetable to be
drawn up for the lifting of sanctions (a 40-minute telephone conversation
with President Yeltsin yielded a curt rebuff from Clinton: 'No way'). Later
Clinton and Bill Richardson, America's UN ambassador, emphasised that
they would continue to feed the tensions: 'The crisis is not over' (and they
added that it was now necessary to get tougher on Saddam). Richardson
commented, with no UNSCOM-supplied evidence, that Iraq was continuing
its secret development of chemical and biological weapons of mass destruction; and now there was a growing focus on the presidential palaces (one
said to have 100 square miles of enclosed grounds, presumably not previously noticed over the seven years that the UNSCOM staff had been

combing the country). On 23 November the United States demanded unobstructed access to Saddam's palaces, with Defense Secretary William Cohen declaring that those 'cannot be off-limits'. He noted that as soon as UNSCOM staff sought access to the restricted sites they were 'either delayed or simply obstructed and refused'; that this state of affairs 'cannot continue'; and that the crisis, which had led to the massive US military build-up in the region, was 'not over by any means'. The US strategy was plain: Washington intended to prolong the crisis through propaganda and vast military deployments, with an ultimate bombing campaign the preferred option.

It was now being reported that President Clinton had shown Boris Yeltsin U-2 spy photographs of Iraq in an attempt to deflate Russia's support for Saddam Hussein.[26] This extraordinary revelation confirmed the Iraqi charges that the U-2 missions were primarily designed to serve US espionage purposes, rather than to support the proper UNSCOM role. How was Clinton in a position to exploit what was supposed to be UN-protected data authorised by Resolution 687? The American exploitation of such spy data was reminiscent also of how the Bush Administration had drummed up Saudi support for the hosting of US troops in 1990/1 by using doctored satellite photographs showing alleged Iraqi troop movements on the Saudi border.[27] No details were given of what the U-2 pictures were supposed to reveal, apart from the possible movement of Iraqi lorries, but the CIA was reportedly involved in the espionage activity.[28] It was plain that the U-2 overflights, far from being under explicit UN control, were an important element in the American spying activity. No publicity was given in the Western media to the fact that Iraqi accusations in this regard had been well justified.

The United States, for its part, persisted with the propaganda campaign. The Pentagon was warning that Saddam Hussein might have enough chemical weapons *'to kill every man, woman and child on the face of the Earth'*. This sort of consideration was quite sufficient to convince President Clinton that the Iraqi presidential palaces ('huge compounds') should be accessible to UNSCOM staff. Soon the US alarmist propaganda was reaching risible proportions, with William Cohen indicating that the US national guard had been ordered to draw up emergency response preparations against possible Iraqi-backed chemical or biological attacks in 120 American cities, plans that would involve the co-ordination of police, firefighters and officials: 'The front lines are no longer overseas; they can just as easily be in any American city'. This sort of alarmist nonsense omitted all mention of the fact that it was Iraqi cities, afflicted by US-contrived starvation and disease, that knew most about the practical effects of biological warfare.

The Iraqis continued to protest that the Americans were lying about the presence of chemical and biological weapons in the presidential palaces ('... there is no truth to their false claims and allegations ... The United States officials have always lied and they are not ashamed of lying ...'; the lies were sent up 'like balloons ... to see if they will float ...'). Despite all this the Iraqi authorities had decided 'to invite two diplomats and experts from each State represented on the ... Special Commission and five representatives from each State member of the Security Council to visit these palaces and sites ... so they can discern the truth for themselves ...'.[29] At first Washington did not know how to react to this new Iraqi proposal. A senior official in the State Department described the move as a 'major climbdown', but then James Foley in the Department emphasised that the inspectors must be allowed unconditional access. Britain's UN envoy, Sir John Weston, stressed that he was not interested in 'political tourism'. The US/UK front was holding: the Iraqi dictator would do as he was told or there would be war.

The US/Iraqi tensions were again growing, while the international community gave no serious attention to the appalling plight of the Iraqi civilian population. A report (28 November 1977) issued under the name of the UN Secretary-General provided an assessment of the civilian situation following the passing of Resolution 1111 (intended to extend the scope of 986).[30] After thirteen pages of broadly factual presentation the report indicated the state of affairs prevailing among ordinary Iraqis. Extracts from the final sections of the report conveyed something of the plight of a suffering people:

> ... The erratic arrivals of foodstuffs have led to the reduction in the amounts of some commodities ... The processing 'and distribution of flour was again subject to marked difficulties. Insufficient grain stocks, erratic power supplies, inadequate back-up generators and shortages of spares ... late arrival of wheat grain ... Transport problems continue to hamper the regular flow of medicines and medical supplies ... resolution 986 inputs to assist in water purification are insufficient for the sector's needs ... With the delays in the arrival of water and sanitation supplies ... there is hardly any measurable improvement ... there is concern over the functionality of electricity, cold storage facilities and transport available for the cold-chain distribution of ... vaccines and ... drugs ... out of some 40 items normally provided to health centres only some 4 or 5 had been provided from resolution 986 supplies ...[31]

In such circumstances little was being done to address the high rates of sanctions-induced malnutrition. *Acute* malnutrition in children under five now stood at 11 per cent, with chronic malnutrition causing stunting affecting 31 per cent of children in this category. An Iraqi/UNICEF study supervised by international observers found no improvement in the child malnutrition levels, just as the FAO/WFP assessment (June 1997) had confirmed high and enduring levels of malnutrition in children and adults.

The food ration at the end of 1997 was continuing to fall 'far short of meeting the nutritional needs of the Iraqi population', with UN observers reporting 'an exceptionally serious deterioration in the health infrastructure, a high infant mortality rate and high rates of morbidity and mortality in general ...'.[32] In addition even the available supplies could not be properly stored, electricity supplies were unreliable, air-conditioning systems were faulty or inoperative, water supplies were unreliable, sewage systems were leaking, and hospital waste-disposal systems were inoperative. Even the paltry humanitarian inputs under the terms of Resolution 986 would have little impact 'if other related areas, such as proper treatment of water supply and sewage, electricity, improved quality of food rations and critical environmental problems, are not adequately addressed'.[33]

Vaccines for animals were either totally lacking or impaired through the 'excessive age of the mother seed'. Some power stations and parts of the electricity distribution system were continuing to deteriorate: 'output and distribution in 1998 are expected to be lower than in 1997'. A half of all rural children were now not entering school; many schools were short of desks (in 150 surveyed schools half the children were obliged to sit on the floor), teaching aids and working sanitation facilities. Severe and chronic malnutrition among children was drastically affecting the entire education sector, despite the efforts of WFP and UNICEF to establish a countrywide feeding programme for malnourished children and adults. It was estimated that a third of all children under five and a quarter of all adults under 26 years of age were suffering from malnutrition, with all other age groups affected to a comparable degree.

The report, issued by the UN Secretary-General, noted that the humanitarian programme was unique, 'being implemented within the context of a sanctions regime with all its attendant political and commercial dimensions ... the population of Iraq continues to face a serious nutritional and health situation ... there is an urgent need to contain the risk of a further deterioration ...'.[34] On 26 November 1997 a press release was issued by UNICEF to highlight the deepening crisis among the children of Iraq:

> The most alarming results are those on malnutrition, with 32 per cent of children under the age of five, some 960,000 children, chronically malnourished – a rise of 72 per cent since 1991. Almost one quarter (around 23 per cent) are underweight – twice as high as the levels found in neighbouring Jordan or Turkey.
>
> 'What we are seeing is a dramatic deterioration in the nutritional wellbeing of Iraqi children since 1991', says Philippe Heffinck, the UNICEF representative in Baghdad. 'And what concerns us now is that there is no sign of any improvement since Security Council resolutions 986 (1995) and 1111 (1997) came into force'.

In a letter (28 November 1997) to the President of the Security Council, Iraqi ambassador Nizar Hamdoon emphasised the dreadful facts: almost one million children were suffering from malnutrition; Resolutions 986 and 1111 were doing nothing to improve the situation; a quarter of children (6-to-11 age group) were not able to attend school; that it was the Iraqi children that were bearing the brunt of the current economic hardship (without relief from sanctions 'they will continue to suffer'); and that only 50 per cent of people in rural areas had access to potable water. In all these sectors, and in all the other humanitarian-linked areas, the persistence of the sanctions regime had caused a dramatic deterioration in the lives of the Iraqi people.

The known state of the Iraqi civilian population did nothing to erode the keen US/UK enthusiasm for the years-long economic blockade. The priority in Washington and London was to gain UNSCOM access to Saddam's palaces, if only to provide fresh espionage information for further *coup* attempts (see pp. 35–7). The crisis was again beginning to escalate. The White House was insisting that UN inspectors must have 'unconditional and unfettered access' to all sites in Iraq and at all times. This meant that a group of American spies would have every right to invade Saddam's bedroom in the dead of night. This was not an approach well judged to resolve all outstanding problems by diplomatic means.

The propaganda continued to emphasise that Saddam Hussein might be equipped to kill every human being on earth. There was no evidence for such a gargantuan scope but it was judged politically useful to assert the proposition from time to time. According to UNSCOM the Iraqis had already admitted to producing biological-weapons materials in substantial quantities (just as many other States, including America and Britain, had done the same): 19,000 litres of botulinum, 8500 litres of anthrax, 2200 litres of aflatoxin, 340 litres of clostridium perfringens and 10 litres of ricin – agents that variously paralyse the lungs, cause liver cancer, rot the flesh and induce circulatory collapse. The Iraqis were claiming that all these substances had either been destroyed in the 1991 war or subsequently abolished. It was an easy matter for the US/UK propagandists to disseminate suitable horror stories: did we not all know that Saddam was a 'congenital' liar?; what if such lethal agents had been secreted away somewhere (perhaps in a presidential palace)?; would it not be foolish to relax the sanctions regime while such uncertainties remained?; would it not be prudent to starve another million Iraqi children to death (just in case the Iraqi dictator had a flask of anthrax spores under his bed)? The questions never provoked rational discussion; Washington remained committed to the sanctions regime – for reasons best known to the strategic planners (perhaps they were *experimenting* with the effects of creeping starvation on a national population – much as in earlier times the United States had experimented with biological, chemical and nuclear agents on its own unsuspecting nationals).[35]

On 3 December UN Secretary-General Kofi Annan conveyed to the President of the Security Council a communication received from the Director General of the IAEA. An Appendix to the document included the words: *'The information so far provided by Iraq is incomplete, but the provision of the missing information should be a simple administrative matter. This is not a matter of major significance'*.[36] And so it proved: as already noted, the IAEA declared in April 1998 its willingness to close the Iraqi nuclear file. Iraq's compliance in this area was no longer an issue of dispute; and this alone should have resulted in a substantial relaxation of the genocidal sanctions policy. On 4 December the Security Council adopted Resolution 1143 (see Appendix V), reaffirming 986/1111 and welcoming the aim of the Secretary-General 'to find ways of improving the implementation of the humanitarian programme and to take such action over additional resources as needed to meet priority humanitarian requirements of the Iraqi people ...' (Paragraph 6). It is significant that 1143 was essentially a humanitarian resolution, nominally designed to ensure the equitable distribution of food and medical supplies, and to improve the overall situation of the civilian population. It need hardly be noted that the resolution was vacuous, in the context of the unbending sanctions regime, but at least the Security Council was beginning to acknowledge that perhaps it should no longer be a conscious architect of genocide. The slowly shifting mood was further reinforced when Benon Sevan, Executive Director at the UN Office of the Iraq Programme, said at a press conference that the humanitarian situation in Iraq would get 'worse and worse' unless urgent measures were taken. Some observers were beginning to ask whether 1998 would see the final lifting of the punitive sanctions regime.

Now the Security Council was blocking an Iraqi aid distribution plan – which in turn caused Iraq to halt the pumping of oil (allowed under the 986/1111 terms) via the Turkish pipeline. An Iraqi foreign ministry official declared: 'Iraq deeply regrets that the Security Council renewed the oil-for-food accord without taking into consideration the need for simultaneous oil sales and distribution of food and medicines'.[37] It was not difficult to understand Iraqi frustration. While much of the revenue from Iraqi oil was being speedily transferred to Kuwait and other pro-US claimants, Washington and London were constantly blocking contract approvals under the programme. On 4 December the Council had renewed the deal with Iraq for another six months but delayed a possible expansion of the scheme. The following day Iraq severely criticised the United States for ignoring Israel's weaponry while insisting on the removal of Iraqi weapons of mass destruction: 'The UN Security Council Resolution 687 demanding the elimination of Iraqi weapons of mass destruction includes a clause stipulating without equivoca-

tion the destruction of all mass-destruction weapons in the Middle East'*
(daily *al-Thawra*).[38]

There were now ample signs that the crisis was again escalating, with the
principal issue being UNSCOM access to sensitive sites. Richard Butler was
proclaiming that he would seek 'full access ... but in a way that shows respect
for Iraqi national sovereignty and for some of the palaces where the president and his entourage live'. And again the prospect of military action was
being openly considered: the British foreign minister Robin Cook, knowing
that he could rely on US belligerence, declared that military strikes would be
an appropriate response if UN inspectors were banned from any Iraqi sites:
'Iraq must fully comply with its obligations to give UNSCOM ... unrestricted
access to all sites, including the so-called sensitive sites'. In response the
Iraqi oil minister Amir Mohammed Rasheed asserted that the presidential
sites were 'totally forbidden ... Absolutely. It's a red line ...'; such sites were
'a symbol of sovereignty, and there is absolutely no justification ... to warrant
such an action'; and Rasheed repeated the familiar Iraqi charge that the UN
inspectors were following an agenda set by the CIA.[39] Again the impasse
seemed fraught with hazard. The Iraqi position was uncompromising, and
the United States, already irritated at the useful consequences of Russian
diplomacy, was in no mood to suffer another slight to its hegemonic pride.
War, seemingly averted a short time before, now appeared to be increasingly
likely.

Richard Butler, having talked in London with Robin Cook, was again
emphasising the UNSCOM need to inspect the Iraqi presidential palaces
and denouncing the Iraqi refusal of access: 'We can't work that way if we are
to help the Iraqi people' – as if such an aim were ever an UNSCOM priority.
In Baghdad, where Butler was described as a 'mad dog', the Iraqi media were
predicting that his mission was 'doomed to fail'; and a street party was being
organised to mark the first anniversary of the failed assassination attempt on
Uday, Saddam's eldest son. The United States was yet again advertising the
military option as a means of achieving Iraqi compliance with UN resolutions, while Iraq itself seemed oblivious to the need to cultivate the support
of its closest neighbours: four Jordanians were executed for smuggling $400-
worth of car spare parts, whereupon Jordan denounced the Iraqi 'betrayal'
and retaliated by recalling its chargé d'affaires from Baghdad and sharply
cutting the Iraqi diplomatic presence in Amman. King Hussein of Jordan
had personally intervened in a vain attempt to stop the executions, widely
perceived as a gratuitous insult to a sympathetic neighbour. An Arab diplomat in Amman said: 'Saddam must be trying to send some sort of message to

---

* See preamble to Security Council Resolution 687 (3 April 1991): 'Conscious of the
threat ...' (Appendix II of the present book, pp. 193–200).

Jordan, but God knows what. What is clear is that he thrives on a state of crisis. It keeps the regime alert and the people in fear'.[40] Throughout this period the larger crisis, stimulated by the growing tensions between Washington and Baghdad, was gathering pace.

In the United States Louis Farrakhan, leader of the Chicago-based Nation of Islam, was calling on Washington to allow the lifting of the sanctions regime ('Lift the sanctions; this is not the way the greatest superpower in the history of the world should behave. I think that the President needs better advice'); and he called on the Organisation of the Islamic Conference, which had recently concluded its eighth summit (held in Tehran), to ignore US policy, to *'defy these sanctions and begin to look after their brothers and sisters who are dying in what I call mass form of terrorism, because it is killing innocent men, women and children for political purposes'*. The 54 Member States of the Conference should make an appeal to the UN Secretary-General Kofi Annan. The US State Department, with its own agenda, had expressed its opposition to Farrakhan visiting particular States in the Middle East, including Iraq; and now had an interest in exacerbating the crisis.

On 12 December 1997 the Iraqi authorities again insisted that the UNSCOM teams must keep away from 'sensitive sites' used by Saddam Hussein; while the Baghdad media continued to brand Butler as an American agent who would not be allowed free access to designated locations in the country (Butler: 'UNSCOM must be allowed to go anywhere and see any document or interview any person'). Commented Baghdad's daily *al-Thawra*: 'Mr Butler acts like any secretary or advisor in Clinton's administration … He lies as they do … speaks with a clear hate for Iraq as they do – to the point that he has forgotten that he is the head of the Special Commission and not an American envoy'. As the military option was receiving increasingly overt attention, the possible assassination of Saddam Hussein was being openly discussed as a realistic possibility: in Britain, for example, the Reverend Ian Duncan cleared an article (*A Holy War!*) published in the Hereford Methodist Church magazine, suggesting that the 'best solution' to the Iraq problem was for the British SAS to assassinate Saddam (Duncan, defending the piece, commented in true Christian spirit: 'It is an opportunity for people to get things off their chest').

The American military build-up in the Gulf was continuing apace, in Britain the Labour Prime Minister Tony Blair was taking foreign-policy advice from the arch anti-Labour former premier Margaret Thatcher,[41] and in Baghdad Richard Butler was making 'some progress' in talks with Tariq Aziz on the inspection issue (Butler: 'The Iraqi side gave a report on where it thought the missile and warheads issue stood. It seems to me that some progress is being made … We must have access if we're to find those weapons, get rid of them, and help Iraq out of this hole in which it has put itself'). Fresh Butler/Aziz talks were planned but now there was growing concern that diplomatic progress was too slow to satisfy the Washington strategists. On 15 December, after a third round of talks, Butler commented that the Iraqis were insisting that UNSCOM would never be allowed to inspect the presidential sites; nor was Iraq prepared to provide a list of such locations, because 'it might help those who want to bomb Iraq to do so more precisely'.

Richard Butler was now conceding failure at the end of his four-day mission to Baghdad to gain unrestricted UNSCOM access to all the suspected weapons sites. He was now set to report the Iraqi 'derogation' to the Security Council (that is, to the US war planners), declaring that he 'gravely doubted' that Baghdad's arguments – as presented by Butler to the Council – would be accepted. He had not heard 'anything that was terribly new', and in fact the Iraqis had been 'rather defiant'. A measure of agreement had been reached on the submission of certain technical issues to an international panel of experts under UNSCOM supervision, but this seemed no more than a minor concession unlikely to deter Washington from preparations for military strikes. Now US Defense Secretary William Cohen was announcing that all America's 2.4 million active and reserve troops were to be vaccinated against the lethal anthrax biological agent. This seemed to be a somewhat absurd piece of hyperbole, designed to reinforce fears about Saddam's plans to kill every human being on earth. On 16 December President Clinton was again hinting at the likelihood of military action ('other options'), and declaring 'that we have to be very firm'. At the United Nations the US mood was confirmed by Bill Richardson: 'We think there is enough authority in previous Security Council resolutions – if we choose to have military action, we can proceed'. Few observers believed that the United States would be able to win international support for a fresh war: if Washington decided to bomb Iraq it would be a unilateral decision. Iraq seemed resigned to the prospect of war, with the Iraqi media knowing exactly what it thought of Clinton: 'The ugly adolescent is treating his dog like a human being, while his people are drowning in a hell of drugs, unemployment and crime' (*al-Iraq* newspaper). The likelihood of a peaceful solution to the crisis seemed more remote by the day.

On 19 December the Iraqi authorities allowed Western journalists into the presidential sites, though inspectors were still not welcome 'for reasons of dignity and sovereignty' (Aziz). Then, with a hint of the ludicrous that sometimes characterised UNSCOM proceedings, Richard Butler disclosed that his team had found a significant chemical precursor known to be used in the creation of toxic weapons. So what was it that the diligent inspectors had located? Nothing less than a trace of moisture: 'We took a sample from a barrel which should have been dry. It wasn't. It was moist, and the sample we took seems to be consistent with a precursor to a chemical weapon' (Butler).[42] *Seems to be consistent*? Was this really the hard evidence that US propagandists were constantly implying was sufficient to justify the endless misery of the Iraqi people under sanctions? A moist barrel? UNSCOM inspectors crawling over dozens of sites, and then a hint of moisture in a barrel is cited as a 'clue to Saddam weapons'. Was this the sort of evidence that would justify the launching of Gulf War II? Now Washington was becoming increasingly irritated at the constraints of the Security Council, what James Baker, Secretary of State under President Bush, had called 'getting wrapped around the UN axle'.[43] A spokesman for Jesse Helms, the chairman of the Senate Foreign Relations Committee, was denouncing the United Nations as 'an institution built to slow things down'; and Joshua Muravchik, a fellow of the American Enterprise Institute think-tank, was commenting that the UN had become a danger to American foreign policy: 'We have a great deal of experience of the UN behaving irresponsibly and there is a very big problem for us in the current circumstances and the longer term. There's some hindrance to Saddam in building weapons of mass destruction, but not prevention. I wouldn't say he's won but he's winning.'[44] The emerging message was a simple one: Saddam was expected to obey the United Nations but American pundits were suggesting that US interests might require that Washington ignore UN constraints in determining American foreign policy. The moist barrel might be enough to justify another war.

The Iraqis, like the Americans, knew where they stood. While *al-Iraq* was dubbing Clinton 'a despicable adolescent' who had 'turned the "Black House" into a cabaret', the Baath newspaper *al-Thawra* declared that the US president was 'seeking an escalation and a renewal of tension'; *Babel*, run by Uday Hussein, observed that 'writers, analysts and journalists' were talking about Clinton's 'moral perversions' and describing him as 'a liar'. Clinton, for his part, was well prepared to reiterate the existence of the military option in American thinking. Now he was declaring without ambiguity that the United States would retaliate if UNSCOM teams were not given full access to sites suspected of containing weapons of mass destruction. There was no hint in either the Iraqi or the American rhetoric to suggest that the much-hyped 'diplomatic solution' was on any practical agenda. On 21 December Bill Richardson expressed the almost universal US attitude: 'Patience is eventually going to run out'.

Now Iraq was submitting a new food-distribution plan to the United Nations, as a prelude to selling oil for humanitarian supplies under the third phase of the 986/1111 programme. At the same time a three-day summit in Kuwait was expected to generate sympathy for the plight of the Iraqi civilian population among the leaders of Saudi Arabia, Kuwait, United Arab Emirates, Qatar, Oman and Bahrain (though with the caveat that Baghdad should comply with UN resolutions). And with Christmas not far away there were signs that a festive humanitarian gesture would be made to the suffering Iraqi children. Thor Magnusson, founder of the Icelandic Peace 2000 group, having persuaded the United Nations that he was a 'non-political figure', was set to deliver medicines, food and toys to Iraqi children (the plane landed on 26 December, the second such flight in two days). But such matters could not be allowed to disturb the mounting American propaganda against the Iraqi regime. Perhaps Saddam would provoke a new crisis, or intensify the existing one, before long. He knew that Christmas was not the best public-relations time for US bombers to kill innocent Iraqi civilians; and the holy month of Ramadan, beginning on New Year's Eve, might delay the expected military strikes for a few more weeks. The Western media gave little publicity to the Iraqi decision to reduce the baby milk rations by a third in January. According to the Iraqis, Washington and London were deliberately delaying these and other supplies ('When children of the world gather to celebrate the New Year, they [the United States and Britain] are intentionally punishing the Iraqi children').

It seemed plain to Baghdad that Christmas and Ramadan would not long delay the military strikes being planned by the Washington strategists. In a letter (30 December 1997) from the Iraqi foreign minister Mohammed Said Al-Sahaf, addressed to both the UN Secretary-General and the President of the Security Council, emphasis was given to the 'continuing military preparations' being made by America in the Gulf region: *These include the stockpiling of various types of materiél and weapons, even internationally prohibited weapons, with a view to carrying out wide-ranging acts of aggression against Iraq ... Iraq expects that this prodigious military mobilisation in the region and the political and media escalation will lead to ... military strikes. ...'*[45] An enclosure with the letter suggested that the United States intended to use chemical and biological weapons against Iraq 'with a view to enabling' Washington to claim, once the strikes had been carried out, 'that its allegations were well founded'. Here it was emphasised that the United States had already used prohibited weapons, 'such as depleted uranium', during the 1991 Gulf War (26 December 1997). There is no dispute today about the accuracy of this last Iraqi accusation (depleted-uranium ordnance is widely regarded as a principal cause of the soaring incidence of cancers in post-war Iraq).

On 3 January 1998 a rocket-propelled grenade struck the UN headquarters of the arms inspectors in Baghdad. The Iraqi authorities quickly tightened security around the compound and blamed the raid on 'hostile parties who do not want stable relations between Iraq and UN weapons inspectors'. Denis Halliday, a representative in Baghdad of the UN Secretary-General, commented that the raid was 'some sort of isolated incident'; and President Clinton demanded a 'thorough and swift investigation' to determine who was responsible. This attack was not the first of its kind; in October a group of men had hurled grenades and fired at the offices of the World Health Organisation in Baghdad, destroying one vehicle and damaging two others.

In Amman a gunman fired at the Iraqi commercial attaché in an obvious assassination attempt. Such events, relatively minor, seemed symbolic of the wider conflict yet to come. No-one doubted that the Americans were preparing for war: the military build-up was continuing, as was the propaganda. Now the West was asserting that Iraqi scientists working in Libya were helping to develop weapons of mass destruction, including biological systems.[46] In Washington nearly 200 army, police, fire and medical experts, as well as federal and city emergency planners, were gathering for a crash course on how to respond to a chemical attack.[47] Commented Defense Secretary William Cohen: *'With advanced technology and a smaller world of porous borders, the ability to unleash mass sickness, death and destruction has reached a new magnitude.'* In these dire circumstances what reasonable person could object if a prudent Washington decided to take preventive military action against a demonised Iraq?

On 11 January 1998 a new team of UNSCOM staff arrived in Baghdad – and was immediately denounced by the Iraqi authorities as being dominated by American and British officials, so providing 'clear proof' of UN bias. The Iraqis were happy to exploit the fact that the new UN Special Commission was led by Scott Ritter, a US marine and Gulf War veteran, scarcely likely to be wholly objective in his sensitive talks with Iraqi officials. In a letter (12 January) to the President of the Security Council, Richard Butler recorded Scott Ritter's arrival in Iraq, noting that the UNSCOM team comprised 44 persons drawn from 17 nations: 'the team to be deployed to any given site would be drawn up on the basis of the nature of the site, the objective of the inspection at the site, the expertise required for the successful conduct of an inspection and the expertise held by individual inspectors'. What could be more reasonable? An Iraqi response (12 January) to the new UNSCOM team, appended to the Butler communication, included the words: 'The Americans who control the Special Commission centre and its activities in Iraq falsify facts and fabricate lies. Their intention is to prolong matters and they submit fallacious reports to the Security Council ... We cannot accept the continuation of this situation ... It has therefore been decided to halt the work of this team with effect from tomorrow. It will not be permitted to undertake any activity in Iraq until such time as its composition is reviewed and made more balanced by the equal participation of the permanent members of the Security Council'. With this new confrontation, set against Iraqi accusations that Scott Ritter was a US spy, the overall crisis was set to escalate.

The US/UK response to the new situation was predictable. Washington was not prepared to let Baghdad determine the composition of the UNSCOM teams, and British diplomats expressed their 'grave concern' at the new developments. With Scott Ritter branded as a CIA spy by the Iraqi authorities there seemed no clear route out of the impasse. George

Robertson, the British Defence Secretary, knew what to say: 'A country that has already used these dreadful instruments of war – chemical and biological weapons – and which continues to deceive and to hide its capabilities for the future is not one that can be trusted'. At the same time even the Western media were acknowledging that at least half the UNSCOM staff were American or British, a clearly disproportionate composition in view of official claims that the inspectors were acting in the interests of the United Nations as a whole. On 13 January the Iraqi authorities declared that Baghdad 'would not bow' to American threats, that it would 'remain committed' to protecting 'sovereignty, rights and national interest'. As for Bill Richardson, 'patience is running out ... The Iraqis are really pushing this to the brink'; and other US officials were preparing the ground for a unilateral American initiative (Mike McCurry, White House spokesman: it was better to act in concert *with 'others when we can'* but there was *no 'reluctance' in Washington to 'act alone if we must'*. So much for observance of the UN Charter and compliance with international law.

The propaganda continued. Now Western publics were being told that the Iraqis had tested biological agents on human beings,[48] immediately denied by Baghdad (Tariq Aziz: 'This is one of the lies that is being used as a pretext for intruding into sites, such as the intelligence agency headquarters, that Iraq considers a violation of its sovereignty').[49] But Washington's public-relations campaign, whatever the proportion of truth it may have included, was having little effect on international opinion. There was still no Security Council consensus (or even a majority) for UN military action against Iraq. The belligerent intransigence of Prime Minister Benjamin Netanyahu of Israel continued to cause Washington problems which it chose not to address – and erstwhile US allies in the Gulf region had no appetite for advertising possible support for American policy. The crisis was having its predictable effect on the world oil market. On 12 January oil prices slumped to their lowest level for four years, but then rallied as US/Iraqi tensions again began to intensify (the Iraq issue was not the only relevant factor: Saudi policy, the Far East economic turmoil, high stocks and a mild winter were all having an impact on the condition of the market). With suggestions that Iraq might be allowed to double its oil exports under new UN-authorised terms, oil prices were again under threat.

As the propaganda was fed to gullible Western publics on a daily basis, and with the unhelpful turmoil in the oil markets, the US/UK military build-up in the Gulf continued. On 16 January Britain ordered the aircraft carrier *Invincible* to the region in close support of the American forces already deployed (Robertson, in a House of Commons statement, rehearsed the familiar mantra: diplomacy was the preferred option – 'But, if these efforts fail, we may need to consider other measures, including the use of force'). *Invincible*, we were told, carried six RAF Harrier bombers and eight Royal

Navy Sea Harrier fighters, politically significant but a puny irrelevance in comparison with the hundreds of American aircraft in the Gulf. The UNSCOM teams, now hunting for files that might provide evidence of Iraqi weapons tests on human beings, were happy to provide justification for the continuous military escalation. Scott Ritter, likely CIA spy, left for Bahrain: 'We have not been allowed to complete our mission, to do our work. There is no sense for the team to be staying here doing nothing' (he may as well be in Bahrain doing nothing). Richard Butler was reportedly on his way to Baghdad to negotiate a route out of the US/Iraqi confrontation. Clinton, as always, prevaricated, waiting for the outcome of the Butler mission; while Defence Secretary Robertson in Britain emphasised the importance of backing diplomacy by 'military strength and readiness' (exactly the posture condemned by British politicians when practised by the IRA): 'An attempt by him [Saddam] to pick and choose who will inspect these sites, to continue to hide his capability in biological and chemical weapons, is simply not acceptable to the world community and he poses a huge, dangerous threat to his neighbours and to the wider region'. (Not to the entire world? Were Saddam's ambitions slipping?)

On 17 January Saddam Hussein warned that all the UNSCOM inspections would stop within months unless an end to sanctions could be agreed (the Iraqi National Assembly had demanded that they be finished by the end of May 1998). Bill Richardson, US ambassador to the United Nations, contributed the observation that Saddam was now 'dreaming' and commented with singular originality that force 'is an option' (presumably for Washington rather than Baghdad). Now Iraq was also condemning the American rejection of a Russian offer to supply reconnaissance aircraft to replace the US U-2 planes supplying espionage data to Washington. Bill Richardson again informed a waiting world that he was running out of patience.

It was now clear, overtly conceded, that the United States was running a military 'countdown'.[50] Madeleine Albright, US Secretary of State, was speaking openly about the 'threat of military force'; Bill Richardson declared that 'a punitive military strike was getting more likely' ('We will not hesitate to exercise the military option' – having hesitated for months); and Baghdad was calling on men and women to volunteer for military training to wage a 'holy war' against UN sanctions and to defend their country against a further American aggression. A CIA report suggested that Iraq was winning the diplomatic battle,[51] so providing a further incentive for Washington to attempt a military solution in a deteriorating propaganda situation. Sir Edward Heath, former British premier, made the provocative suggestion on a GMTV broadcast that Britain did not have to follow the American lead into war: 'It's not going to produce the result that we want, which is to get a proper settlement of this problem'. The British Labour government, pursuing its 'ethical' foreign policy, was in no mood to listen to such pacific advice.

On 17 January Iraqi/Jordanian relations took another serious blow. A month before, the execution of four Jordanians in Iraq had outraged opinion in Jordan. (King Hussein had spoken of 'the ugly and unpleasant picture' revealed in Iraq). Now, at a Saturday night dinner party, seven Iraqis were murdered in Amman in what commentators dubbed a mafia-style execution (the victims included a senior embassy official and two wealthy businessmen). Hikmet al-Hajou, the murdered diplomat, was second-in-command at the Iraqi embassy, regarded by some Iraqi opposition sources as the Iraqis' top spy in Jordan. This was a gruesome business. The victims, including the diplomat's wife, were bound before being hacked to death with knives; the one survivor, a Greek woman in a critical condition, said that the killers had spoken in Arabic with Iraqi accents. A spokesman for the opposition Iraqi National Congress commented: 'Our sense is that this is feuding inside the regime, probably to do with money'. Some observers commented on the possibility of a revenge motive or of a US involvement. Again, whatever the cause, the lives of Iraqi citizens were brought to a bloody end.

Now the UN Secretary-General was reporting to the Security Council on the Iraq situation, as he was required to do by Paragraph 7 of Resolution 1143. Here he noted the 'severity of the problem' afflicting the electricity sector, the fact that 'the nutritional security of the Iraqi people had remained unsatisfactory, notwithstanding the implementation of resolution 986 (1995)', 'the prevalence of acute malnutrition of children under five years of age', 'the need to meet the emergency requirements of the severely malnourished', the inadequacy of medical stocks, and many other problems and difficulties. It was plain that 'humanitarian requirements' were not being met, a fact that was obvious to anyone who troubled to read the Secretary-General's report. In conclusion, Kofi Annan emphasised: '*In implementing the programme to meet the humanitarian needs of the Iraqi people, we must remember the human dimension*'. It was some reflection on the inadequacy of the 986/1111 provisions and on the cynical posture of the US-dominated UN Sanctions Committee that this needed to be said. The basic life needs of innocent Iraqi men, women and children were not being met. A basic theme of American policy was that this genocidal oppression be maintained as long as possible.

On 21 January the sanctions issue received one of its inconsequential airings in the British House of Commons. Here, as was the custom, various speakers raised a series of factual and humanitarian concerns which the British government then carefully ignored. This well-tried procedure created the impression that the Iraqi question was being openly discussed, but in fact did no more than consolidate the cruel status quo.

The Member of Parliament Harry Cohen began the Adjournment debate by reminding people of the 100,000 Iraqi soldiers killed in the 1991 'turkey shoot', a graphic consideration that was highly relevant to the possibility of any future military action against a largely defenceless Iraq. Was there to be another turkey shoot? Said Cohen: 'Perhaps the war aim would be to bomb Baghdad or even to raze it to the ground. As the *New York Times* has said, the targets would be difficult to choose without assuming enormous civilian casualties ... If the Government are travelling along with the Americans towards another war that could kill thousands of Iraqis and some of our people, they should spell out the war aim without blandness or obfuscation.' Then, talking of the UNSCOM teams, Cohen asked why the Americans had blocked offers by France and China to supply inspectors; cited the UNICEF estimate that some 960,000 children in Iraq were chronically malnourished; and quoted from the recent Kofi Annan report:

> The current food ration ... and, in particular, its composition fall far short of meeting the nutritional needs of the Iraqi population. This is particularly valid since nutritional security is contingent upon a host of interrelated factors, such as safe water and available medicine, which are grossly inadequate at the moment. The current ration, even if it is distributed completely and in a timely manner, cannot address the chronic malnutrition and energy deficiency in adults ... United Nations observers regularly report an exceptionally serious deterioration in the health infrastructure: a high infant mortality rate and high rates of morbidity and mortality in general ...

After a brief factually inaccurate and insensitive comment from Ann Clwyd, Cohen quoted a letter received from the highly authoritative journalist Felicity Arbuthnot, just returned from her 10th post-war visit to Iraq. Here there is factual reference to the chronically malnourished, hugely bloated 'sugar babies', denied adequate nutrition by the US-sustained sanctions policy; and to the scale of child mortality comparable to

> *the genocide of Pol Pot ... Does Britain's new 'ethical' foreign policy really include supporting genocide?*

Cohen quoted also Mary Robinson, the new UN High Commissioner (speaking on 15 November at Oxford University):

> How can you expect me to condemn Human Rights abuses in Algeria and China and elsewhere when the United Nations themselves are responsible for the worst situation in Iraq. It's part of my job to bring to public consciousness the incredible suffering of Iraqi society.

And, after analysing the inadequacy of the 986/1111 provisions, Cohen concluded by declaring: '*It is time that the West stopped its war on Iraqi children.*'

The response of the Foreign Office minister Derek Fatchett is easily encapsulated: *Saddam Hussein is an evil dictator and so we must continue to starve and poison to death the helpless people of Iraq.* The argument was embellished, but only with factual error and special pleading. There was (is, mid-1998) a *de facto* embargo on food and medicine because Iraq's assets are frozen and the scale of oil sales is limited by 986/1111 (so drastically limiting all humanitarian purchases); the evil Iraqi dictator is *not* able to spend oil money on his palaces instead of on his people because all the revenues are fed to an escrow account administered by UN staff; and UNSCOM has produced no evidence that Iraq has diverted humanitarian resources to the development and production of weapons. The question is not whether US/UK-sustained sanctions are killing thousands of innocent Iraqis (there is virtual consensus on this fact) but whether public officials like Fatchett, Cook and Blair are acting through ignorance, malice or political cynicism.

On 20 January Richard Butler held further talks with Iraqi officials over the issue of UNSCOM access to sensitive sites, while limited progress was reported on an agreement to establish an independent body of experts to discuss UN monitoring of Iraq's weapons programmes. Butler, describing the talks as 'direct and tough', predictably ruled out any compromise on the question of access to presidential palaces and other sensitive sites ('I have come here to make it very clear to the Iraqis that those places cannot be off limits'). During the talks some 5000 demonstrators on the streets of Baghdad were echoing Saddam's call for a 'holy war' against sanctions and threats of a new American aggression. Yet again Washington and its London echo were warning that if diplomacy failed there would have to be resort to the military option.

It was not long before Richard Butler was again accusing the Iraqis of failing to observe their obligations to the UN inspectors, declaring that there were 'grave instances' of Iraqi attempts to mislead the Security Council and the UNSCOM teams. John Weston, the British ambassador to the United Nations, was declaring that there was 'no chance' of the UN inspectors completing their mission and urged the Council to reject Iraq's proposals: 'This is a very serious and direct challenge to the Security Council because ... it amounts to a definitive rejection of the UN Security Council's resolutions on which this whole operation is based. I do not see how the Security Council can acquiesce in such a situation while wishing to retain any credibility.' The message was clear. Baghdad was refusing to comply, with the stark implication for the Council that force was now the only option. But again this was a conclusion drawn by Washington and London only: there was still no prospect of a consensus among the Permanent Members of the Security Council, much less among the fifteen Members as a whole. Nizar Hamdoon, Iraq's UN ambassador, called Butler's comments 'biased and unfair'.

The Butler talks in Baghdad had accomplished nothing, except to exacerbate the tensions. In one account the exchanges had been 'bitter, brutal and bad-tempered'. In this version Aziz and the other Iraqi delegates made long statements 'that the inspectors knew were untrue'; moreover they were 'personally abusive', blaming the United Nations for what seemed to be an indefinite prolongation of the inspection regime. If the United Nations could not accept Iraqi assurances then 'the government of Iraq has no intention of continuing to work with the commission. Iraq was ready to face the consequences, including war.' In this account *relations were now at breaking point*: 'An assault by American and British forces seems more likely by the day'.[52] Saddam's alleged biological weapons were said to be feared the most, since just one tumbler of anthrax spore 'could kill tens of thousands of people'.[53] Not millions? No doubt here was a reason for cautious optimism. Of course little mention was given of the uncongenial fact that one of the principal architects of Iraq's biological warfare programme was educated in part at the British government's chemical and biological research centre at Porton Down, Wiltshire. As early as 1988, among 80 scientists attending an important workshop in Winchester were Dr Nasser el-Hindawi and his assistant Dr Thamer Abdel Rahman, both microbiologists working for Iraq's secret biological-weapons programme. A principal aim of the programme was to develop weapons to spread anthrax, gas gangrene, botulism toxin, brucellosis, rabbit foot and tetanus. A pupil of Hindawi, Dr Rihab el-Taha, was in charge of the Al-Hakam biological weapons factory blown up in 1996 by UNSCOM staff.[54]

It was this education and research support supplied to Iraqi scientists hosted in Britain that helped Saddam to develop his biological-weapons capability; and the United States had been equally assiduous in supporting Iraq's military plans. Thus the germ culture to grow anthrax was freely imported from the US military's centre for chemical and biological research at Fort Detrick, Maryland, via the extensive civilian laboratories operated by the American Type Culture Collection (ATCC).[55] Such details were given little exposure in the propaganda preparing the world for yet another US/UK military onslaught on Iraq to destroy the weapons systems that the Americans and British had helped the Iraqis to develop.

On 24 January the United States was reportedly discussing specific military moves against Iraq 'amid signs that the escalating crisis between Iraq and the United Nations security council will lead to conflict'.[56] Now it was widely assumed that Richard Butler had convinced Washington that force was the only way to make Saddam comply with Security Council resolutions. Again there was talk of a military 'countdown'; and it was useful to learn from Bill Richardson that 'we are not ruling any option out'. The next step was expected to be a US/UK approach to the Security Council to secure a ruling that Iraq was in 'material breach' of the 1991 ceasefire terms. Such a ruling – like the vague terms of Resolution 678 (1990) – would then be taken by

Washington as authorisation for military action, which of course implied that the United States was not really confident that existing resolutions were sufficient to authorise war. Nonetheless, with or without legal authorisation, Washington now seemed irrevocably committed to military action. On 24 January 1998 a member of Clinton's National Security Council declared: *'There'll be one final round of diplomacy, and then an ultimatum, and then we act'*. It was assumed that the sex scandal increasingly engulfing the US president would not distract the Washington strategists from the important matters of foreign policy.

The Iraqi authorities were now claiming that thousands of civilians were joining a million-strong 'volunteer' force to help counter the threatened military strikes by America and Britain. No independent observers imagined that such a force would have much value against US/UK bombing attacks, but doubtless there was a morale factor involved for the Iraqi people. We were again being regaled with the sheer scale of the anti-Iraq military build-up: USS *Nimitz*, USS *George Washington*, HMS *Invincible*, USS *Bunker Hill*, USS *O'Brien*, USS *John S. McCain*, hundreds of aircraft (including Stealth fighters, B52s, other strategic bombers), the USS *Olympia* submarine, RAF Tornados, and so on. There seemed to be no doubt that the armada would soon be called into action: unfortunately a devious Saddam Hussein had probably dispersed his alleged weapons and so bombing would necessarily have to be comprehensive, with the inevitable civilian casualties. It was in such terms that Washington and London contemplated the mass slaughter of innocent Iraqi men, women and children.

In the British House of Commons the growing awareness of imminent war stimulated another largely futile debate. Tony Lloyd, a minister of state in the Foreign Office, paraded the usual government platitudes (*'We are actively pursuing a diplomatic solution ... but we cannot rule out military action if the diplomatic approach fails to shift Saddam Hussein's stance ... The Government remains very conscious of the sufferings of the Iraqi people, with whom we have no quarrel'*). Then the Member of Parliament Tam Dalyell, an indefatigable opponent of military action against Iraq, asked a number of key questions:

What does Mr Primakov have to say about military action?

What do the Chinese say about military action?

What do the French say about it?

My hon. Friend the Minister refers to Scott Ritter's distinguished record, but is it really necessary to have a former captain of the US Marine Corps as the leader of this very delicate [UNSCOM] operation in the Arab world?

How can there be United Nations military action without the unambiguous support of the Security Council?

Can the Minister name just one Arab country that is in favour of military action?[57]

Tony Lloyd made no attempt to address any of these questions (instead the familiar platitude, repeated *ad nauseam*: '... this country is looking to every diplomatic avenue ... if that does not have the required impact, we ... would not be in a position ... to rule out a military option'). The veteran peace activist Tony Benn then reminded the minister that the bombing raids during the 1991 Gulf War equalled in force seven Hiroshimas, that a million children were starving in Iraq, that 500,000 had already died, that 54 Catholic bishops in the United States had appealed to President Clinton to end the sanctions, and that Iraq's alleged anthrax capability had been supplied by the United States. Furthermore: *'Is the Minister aware that, despite the fact that the United Nations Security Council has demanded compliance by Iraq, there is absolutely no United Nations authority for military action by the United States or Britain?'*[58] Again the minister refused to address such important considerations; Lloyd concluded the debate in characteristic fashion ('the military option exists and will not be discounted or discarded').

The British Royal Navy carrier task group was now reportedly preparing to launch bombing missions on Iraq using RAF Harrier GR7s, 'integrated with an awesome array of American aircraft'.[59] On 26 January, highlighting the serious divisions in the UN Security Council, Russia denounced the planned US/UK use of force as 'unacceptable and counterproductive', and dispatched a further peace envoy to Baghdad. James Rubin, White House spokesman, commented in response that the time was running out for a diplomatic solution. In Baghdad *al-Thawra* declared: 'The Clinton administration is trying to make its aggressive madness louder, and give its threats ... a dramatic clamour ... this does not frighten our people.' (Again there were hints that the sexual allegations against Clinton in Washington might affect the course of the crisis. Said a European diplomat: 'It will clearly cast doubt on Clinton's motives and it's likely to make him more risk averse'.) Now there were suggestions that Iraq faced the possibility of a sustained bombing campaign lasting three or four days, but that this threat was not eroding Baghdad's resolve (Humam Abdel Khaleq, information minister: 'The Iraqi leadership can no longer accept the humiliations inflicted on it [by UNSCOM inspectors] that treat its security and sovereignty as if it was an occupied country').[60] The Russian envoy, deputy foreign minister Viktor Posuvalyuk, had now arrived in the Gulf, but the chances of a peaceful solution to the crisis were seeming increasingly remote. In Britain Premier Tony Blair contributed the usual banality to the London-based *al-Hayat* periodical: 'We hope that diplomatic efforts to end the crisis will succeed, but we are not willing to rule out any option. We cannot and will not rule out the use of military force.' On 28 January Russia was joined by France in opposition to the use of bombing strikes against Iraq (Hubert Vedrine, France's foreign minister: 'Resorting to force is not desirable ... and would not solve the problems ...'). It was now plain that UNSCOM had in fact destroyed the bulk of the Iraq military arsenal that had survived the 1991 Gulf War (Figure 5.1). But despite this the US/UK pressure for *in-perpetuity* sanctions and an early resort to military action was unambiguous. If Washington and London were allowed to have their way the Iraqi people would be granted no relief. Now the CIA was spreading alarmist propaganda that Baghdad would be likely to fire Scud missiles at Israel in the event of a combined US/UK bombing campaign against Iraq, whereupon Israeli officials warned Saddam Hussein that subsequently he could expect a nuclear response. Said David Bar-Illan,

---

Missiles

- over 140 SCUD-variant missiles (exact inventory not verifiable)
- over 15 SCUD launchers (exact inventory not verifiable)
- 30 chemical warheads for SCUD variants (exact inventory not verifiable)
- 28 Al Hussein (SCUD variant) fixed launch pads (operational)
- 32 Al Hussein fixed launch pads (under construction in 1991)
- a variety of long-range missile production equipment

Chemical

- 38,537 filled and empty chemical munitions
- 690 tonnes of chemical weapons agent
- more than 3000 tonnes of precursor chemicals
- 426 pieces of chemical weapons production equipment and 90 pieces of related analytical instruments

Biological

- the entire Al Hakam custom-built biological weapon production factory complex
- a variety of biological weapons production equipment and materials

Other

- a variety of assembled and non-assembled 'super-gun' components

---

Figure 5.1 Destruction of Iraqi weapons conducted or verified by UNSCOM
Source: UNSCOM.

Premier Netanyahu's communications director: 'Surely Iraq must know that it will not pay to attack Israel, and that Israel has all the means necessary to make such an attack very, very dangerous for Iraq – much more dangerous for Iraq than it is for Israel.'[61] Western security sources were now saying that the likely Israeli response to an Iraqi chemical or biological attack would be the dropping of an Israeli neutron bomb on Baghdad.[62] At the same time the Israeli defence minister Yitzhak Mordechai was urging the Israelis to obtain gas masks. There was no evidence that Iraq had either the capacity or the inclination to launch a chemical or biological attack on Israel, but the Western and Israeli media persisted with their unremitting campaign of alarmist propaganda. There were no signs that Viktor Posuvalyuk was making any diplomatic progress in Baghdad by persuading Iraq to allow the UNSCOM inspectors into the off-limits presidential sites.

On 29 January the Russian foreign minister Yevgeny Primakov continued to express optimism about the possibility of a diplomatic solution to the crisis, but said he was not certain that Washington could be restrained from taking military action; at the same time US Secretary of State Madeleine Albright described the situation as 'very grave' – 'We have all but exhausted the real diplomatic options. The moment to make a decision is quickly approaching'. A senior British official reliably gave voice to the London echo ('The options are narrowing'), with Premier Blair continuing to emphasise that Britain stood firmly behind the United States. Baghdad was now again complaining of US-controlled U-2 espionage flights over Iraq, activities that few independent observers doubted were closely linked to the developing plans for bombing strikes against Iraqi targets. Thus a letter (28 January 1998) for Iraqi foreign minister Al-Sahaf noted that by 1998 the U-2 spy plane 'had carried out 390 overflights' of Iraq 'for a total flight time of 1716 hours and 4 minutes since its first overflight in August 1991'. The U-2's espionage activities were clearly quite unrelated to any UN requirements: *an aircraft was being employed by the United States 'in a coercive manner to violate Iraq's airspace and to spy on Iraq for purposes other than those of the Special Commission'.*[63]

The United States, for its part in creative diplomacy, was happy to publicise the development of a new 'bunker buster' bomb, able to create a 30-second inferno of several thousand degrees, for use against the flesh and fabric of Iraq. A Major Ken Ekernot related to *CBS News* that it had been several days before he could even set foot in the incinerated bunker where the new bomb was tested at the Eglin Air Force Base in north-west Florida. There was much publicity about 5000 lb laser-guided bombs fitted with hardened nose cones and able to scythe through layers of metal armour and reinforced concrete to a depth of well over 100 ft before producing an inferno. Weapons of mass destruction? Commented Frank Robbins, research director at Eglin: 'I don't believe a person can pour enough concrete to protect himself from the attack capabilities we're developing'. Albright was making her own contribution to creative diplomacy by touring the Middle East to drum up support for war.[64] The British Foreign Office was rehearsing a quick spin of the mantra (though 'we want to achieve a peaceful situation, the options are narrowing'), while commentators noted that no military action would be likely before the end of the Eid al-Fitr festival, which had begun (29 January) to mark the end of Ramadan.

It was now being reported that the United States was planning to attack Iraq in the second week of February.[65] Washington declared that President Clinton was continuing 'to attach urgency' to the situation, while Madeleine Albright worked hard but unsuccessfully to dragoon the Russians into support for a fresh bombing campaign. The Russian Premier Viktor Chernomyrdin was emphasising the importance of a peaceful solution to the crisis, and Qin Huason, China's UN ambassador, was noting Baghdad's 'legitimate concerns' about its sovereignty. Now the vast American armada in the region included 24 ships and 2 attack submarines, 325 aircraft and 26,300 personnel. A few observers commented that there was not much of a diplomatic argument in all this.

On 30 January the Iraqi authorities ordered all UN staff into secure hotels, which immediately encouraged speculation in the West about the possible use of 'human shields' to deter bombing raids on certain targets. Albright declared, in one of the other well-tried phrases, that 'patience is running out' (as it had been doing for some months); and British Foreign Secretary Robin Cook summoned up a comment of breathtaking originality: 'We have not ruled out the military option ... .' Chernomyrdin thought that bombing would make matters worse, 'not only in the Middle East but in the world at large'; and China repeated that it was 'firmly' opposed to force. Any pretence at consensus among the UN Permanent Members had long since disappeared; if Washington was to attack it would have to do so in the teeth of world opinion (a supine Britain apart). Albright, with patience running out, declared that 'the time for diplomacy is fast expiring'; the time was 'fast approaching' for fundamental decisions to be made. Sir Peter de la Billière, who had commanded the British forces during the 1991 Gulf War, was now expressing doubts that a bombing campaign against Iraq would be entirely effective.

A new report from the UN Secretary-General, pursuant to his obligations under the terms of Resolution 1143, continued to highlight the abysmal state of the Iraqi social infrastructure and the unrelieved suffering of the Iraqi civilian population.[66] The overall situation was unchanged; unless indeed there had been further deterioration. In particular, *the nutritional security of the Iraqi people has remained unsatisfactory, notwithstanding the implementation of resolution 986*,[67] which meant that innocent men, women and children were being condemned to a slow and remorseless starvation under the cruelties of the US-sustained sanctions policy. And again Secretary-General Kofi Annan concluded his report with the appeal: '*In implementing the programme to meet the humanitarian needs of the Iraqi people, we must remember the human dimension. I therefore urge the Security Council to bear this in mind ...*'.[68] But what the Council as a whole thought did not appear to weigh in the balance: with Washington seemingly wedded to a new and devastating bombing campaign, the media headlines conveyed the unambiguous mood:

Fuse burns to Gulf war II[69]

One last chance for diplomacy as air strikes are planned on Iraq[70]

Iraqis braced for airstrike[71]

American officials were emphasising that any strike against Iraq would be the most severe since the 1991 Gulf War. The 'pin-prick' bombing strikes since that time had accomplished nothing but to strengthen the position of Saddam Hussein. The forces were in place (one listing is shown in Figure 5.2); and Madeleine Albright, after two hours of talks in London with the British Foreign Secretary Robin Cook, declared: 'What has to be expected is that, if we do use force, it will be significant'; and Cook contributed his own remark, a piece of absurd posturing in the context of the grossly mismatched range of forces in the Gulf region: 'We want to leave Saddam Hussein with no doubt in our resolve to win this struggle and with no doubt that we will win this struggle'. In the same vein, Premier Tony Blair, having authorised a relatively minuscule supplement to the massive American forces in the region, announced that he would 'not shrink' from military action – presumably on the understanding that American forces would not want to be left out of any ensuing carnage and destruction. It was plain that a massive new military campaign was well into the planning stage: the forces had been assembled, a limited US/UK alliance had been agreed (with minor peripheral support offered by a few other states), and the targets had been selected. The only impediment to American military action was the transparent fact that the Washington strategists were ranged not only against Baghdad but against most of world opinion. Britain could be relied upon not to utter any constructive or independent word, but that was the sum total of the support for the new US campaign. Few observers doubted that a military countdown was in progress; and that in the event Iraq would suffer heavy and wide-ranging damage (when Albright said 'significant' she clearly meant 'substantial'). At the beginning of February 1998 there were few clues as to how the onset of a devastating Gulf War II might be averted.

In the midst of this mounting turmoil UN Secretary-General Kofi Annan continued to explore how the 'oil for food' scheme (986/1111) could be improved and expanded. At a press conference (2 February 1998) he

US ships
USS *Nimitz*, aircraft carrier
USS *George Washington*, aircraft carrier
USS *Normandy*, guided missile cruiser
USS *Barry*, destroyer
USS *Carney*, destroyer
USS *Ingersoll*, destroyer
USS *John Young*, destroyer
USS *Reuben James*, guided missile frigate
USS *Samuel B. Roberts*, guided missile frigate
USS *Annapolis*, attack submarine
USS *L. Mendel Rivers*, attack submarine
USS *Olympia*, attack submarine
USS *Seattle*, fast combat support ship
USS *Ardent*, minesweeper
USS *Dextrous*, minesweeper
En route: USS *Independence*, aircraft carrier
USS *Bunker Hill*, cruiser
USS *McCain*, destroyer
USS *O'Brien*, destroyer
USS *Charlotte*, submarine

US aircraft
279 total, including carrier aircraft, 6 F117 stealth fighters,
30 F15Cs, 30 F16CGs, 24 A10s, 4 Awacs, 8 B52 strategic,
bombers, 2 B1B strategic bombers

UK ships
HMS *Invincible*, aircraft carrier
HMS *Nottingham*, destroyer
HMS *Coventry*, frigate
RFA *Fort Victoria*, auxillary
En route: HMS *Illustrious*, aircraft carrier, to replace HMS
Invincible

UK aircraft
28 total, 14 Harriers, 12 Tornados and 2 VC10 tankers

Figure 5.2   US/UK forces in the Gulf
Source: *The Sunday Times*, 1 February 1998.

referred to his recent report on this issue and observed that 'the report is going to generate quite a lot of discussion, not only because of its import-ance, but also the timing and the projected expansion of the programme'. It was inevitable that the press conference would focus also on the imminence of military action against Iraq. Here the questions were direct, Kofi Annan's answers, if not evasive, characteristically diplomatic. Question: *Would such bombing be justified*? Answer: 'I think no one in the Council is pushing for the use of force in the first instance.' Question: *Would the United States have authorisation for bombing without further action by the Council*? Answer: '... consultations are going on, and I would not want to prejudge the outcome'. Question: *Would the United States have authorisation to act militarily*? Answer: 'The United States is talking to Council members ... it would be preferable to hold everyone together'. Question: *How would the United Nations react to an attack without Security Council approval*? Answer: 'I think first that it is an issue the Security Council is very much engaged in. They are in close touch with the United States ...'.[72]

The questions, carefully parried to avoid disturbing the central player in the Security Council, indicated a mounting concern. How could the United States even consider taking unilateral military action when there was no sem-blance of consensus in the Security Council? If Washington wanted to bomb Iraq the decision (Britain apart) would be unilateral. No-one doubted that the American forces in the region would be able to act with impunity: any Iraqi attempt at a military response would be instantly crushed. But at the same time Israel – unlike the situation with the 1991 Gulf War – was deter-mined to win the right to take its own action if Baghdad were to attack.[73] The prospect was looming of a direct US aggression outside all United Nations authorisation; Britain continuing to clutch the American coat-tails; and a possible Israeli nuclear strike against Baghdad if an Iraqi attack were to be attempted. This seemed far removed from any 'preferred diplomatic option'. The British House of Commons held a further spurious debate on the mounting crisis, with important questions routinely ignored.[74] A few British Members of Parliament were criticising the government's unquestioning acquiescence in America's belligerent posture, involving as it did a blatant indifference to the legal constraints of the UN Charter. Furthermore it was now obvious that Washington could not rely on the Arab support for the US action that had been manifest during the 1991 Gulf War. The United States was contemplating a course of action that would leave it almost totally isolated.[75]

Washington was continuing to insist that the diplomatic options were fast running out – which soon would leave the US strategists with only one choice; but even the Americans, keen for military conflict, were beginning to have doubts that a new bombing campaign would achieve all the required objectives. Defense Secretary Bill Cohen was suggesting that there should be no 'unreasonable expectations' of what might be accomplished by military attacks on Baghdad, and the US planners knew that it would be unhelpful in public-relations terms if Saddam were able to lay out the corpses of innocent civilians in front of the world's television cameras. Such matters had not been thought through. Albright had failed to shore up support among the Arab states of the region, and it seemed that Washington now had recourse only to bluster and threat:

Iraq warned as talks go on[76]

West set for air strikes on Iraq[77]

Washington seeks to keep Saddam guessing over choice of targets[78]

The Russian envoy, Viktor Posuvalyuk, had failed to reach any sort of agreement with the Iraqi authorities. He suggested that fresh talks were needed, while the United States and Britain were predictably sceptical about any new diplomatic initiative. The British Foreign Secretary Robin Cook was now suggesting that a new UN resolution, condemning Iraq for flouting its international obligations, would be helpful – so implying that perhaps Washington and London were not confident that the existing resolutions provided sufficient authorisation for a further military campaign against Iraq. And again the Russians were warning against fresh bombing strikes, predicting heavy loss of civilian life and unpredictable consequences for the Middle East. In Israel preparations were made for the use of US Patriot anti-missile missiles against the possibility of incoming Scuds, while Yosef Goell, a *Jerusalem Post* columnist, tried to inject a dose of realism into the proceedings: 'Are our gas masks effective against anything, or are they and the recommended plastic-wrapped and Scotch-taped safe rooms merely a modern form of voodoo medicine, comparable to the American Patriot anti-missile missiles which did not succeed in shooting down even one Scud in 1991?' Such comments did not stop Israelis flocking to the centres handing out gas masks and other kits. Israeli security officials continued to emphasise that the chances of an Iraqi germ warfare raid on Israel in retaliation for American bombing were 'quite low'. In an opinion poll published by the Tel Aviv daily *Yediot Aharonot* some 52 per cent of Israelis thought that Iraq would fire missiles at Israel in the event of US air strikes against Baghdad.

Madeleine Albright was pleased to report that the Saudi government agreed with the United States that Saddam would be responsible for the 'grave consequences' of any refusal to comply with UN resolutions (a televised Saudi statement urged diplomacy to solve the current problems but failure of this approach 'would entail grave consequences'). This was the best that Albright had managed to achieve: there was no suggestion that Riyadh would approve bombing strikes against Iraqi targets. None of America's Gulf allies had publicly pledged military co-operation with a fresh US bombing campaign. This was certainly one of the circumstances that was now encouraging Saddam Hussein not to bow to the mounting American threats of military strikes. On 17 January he had likened himself to Abraham. *Thus when Abraham 'decided, on God's orders, to move with his clan from Iraq, where he was born, he carried only a stick to ward off wolves and stray dogs ... he was neither timid nor afraid of the disparity in material resources. Without the leader's vision, no people or army in history achieved a collective heroic goal or immortal record ... Our righteous martyrs are high in heaven, with their God and those who are living will always be potential martyrs'. The Americans should be aware 'of the capability of great Iraq and how God cares for it'.*[79] God apart, Saddam knew that he could rely on substantial world opinion ranged against the option of Gulf War II. Thus Russia, France and China, as Permanent Members of the Security Council, were opposed to a fresh military campaign; President Mubarak of Egypt had declared that the time was not right for force; President Khatami of Iran had urged the head of the 55-member Islamic Conference to mediate to avoid military confrontation; Turkey opposed the prospect of a new bombing campaign; Kuwait had reluctantly acquiesced in American plans and Israel was happy to contemplate a further military strike against Arab civilians. It was scarcely a comprehensive coalition for another war.

On 4 February Egyptian foreign minister Amr Moussa declared that Baghdad had proposed an inspection compromise, offering to open eight of the 'presidential sites' to UNSCOM staff. The offer, immediately dismissed as a 'red herring' by UN personnel, had reportedly been made also to French and Arab League diplomats (and then dismissed by Baghdad). An UNSCOM official commented that the new proposal, even if agreed by the Iraqi authorities, 'does not address the question of unrestricted access to all sites'; a White House official commented predictably that the proposal was unacceptable. Now the Russians were raising the stakes: President Yeltsin warned that Clinton could *'stumble into a world war'* by attacking Iraq and that the American president was *'behaving too loudly'*. In response, Tony Blair told Yeltsin that there had to be *'a real threat of force and the use of force if necessary'*; and he added for good measure that Saddam Hussein was *'a nasty dictator, sitting on an awful lot of nasty stuff'*, and that people should be told *'about the evils of Saddam'*. (Had no-one mentioned them before?)

The crisis was now generating widespread anxiety in the region and beyond. Arab states, unwilling to support the American posture, were concerned that another military conflict would arouse public opinion and destabilise their regimes; in Turkey, already suffering the economic consequences of the years-long embargo on Iraq, internal tensions were being fuelled by the likelihood of a further American intervention; and Israel was worried by the thought of a new *intifada* fed in part by the collapse of the Arab–Israeli peace process and in part by the possibility of a fresh pro-Saddam upsurge of Arab passions in the occupied territories. Tony Blair in Britain was determined 'to stand absolutely firm ... it is abundantly clear that diplomacy with Iraq can work only if backed by a willingness to use force'.[80] Again we were being told that Saddam had the capacity to produce enough nerve gas *'to kill the world's population'*[81] (again it seemed that the demon king's ambitions knew no limit). At the same time it seemed that the likely Gulf War II would be a mere shadow of the 1991 conflict. Operation Desert Storm had relied on the four great 'military cities' built in Saudi Arabia to aid the projection of US military force in the region, but no longer available for any new onslaught on Iraq. The 1991 Coalition involved naval units from Argentina, Australia, Belgium, Canada, Denmark, Holland, Italy, Norway, Poland, Portugal and Spain, in addition to the British forces and the massive American presence; furthermore there were substantial Arab contingents, including divisions from Egypt and Syria. In February 1998, by contrast, the relative American isolation was plain. The United States continued to threaten and bluster (Cohen: '... the kind of campaign that would be undertaken would be ... far more than what has been experienced in the past, certainly since the Gulf war'), but there were obvious uncertainties among US war planners about the precise targets that should be selected (suspected weapons sites? the Iraqi security infrastructure? factories?). The cruise missile 'pinpricks' had accomplished nothing in the past. What were the alternatives?

Now further doubts were being raised about the likely effectiveness of further air strikes against Iraq. Sir Peter de la Billière, who commanded British forces in the 1991 Gulf War, was commenting that various matters should be thought through:

> Therefore, before launching into irrevocable and, of necessity, limited military action, it is wise to address the consequences should, as is probable, Saddam remain alive and in power after it is over. His immediate response is likely to result in the permanent expulsion of all the inspectors, and it is difficult to see how the UN will re-establish them. No amount of further military action, short of a full-scale invasion, is likely to do more than enhance his personal prestige at the expense of the UN, and of the forces of America and Britain in particular.[82]

Such doubts, and many others, were continuing to underline American isolation during what seemed the preamble to inevitable military conflict. Robin Cook, visiting Riyadh to drum up Saudi support, had obviously studied his brief: 'If diplomacy fails, it will not be our fault. If there is military action it will be serious action'. But Cook's plea for Saudi support achieved little ('If he [Saddam] can see that the UK and the US are not isolated, then that will become another factor in whether or not he recognises that he has to back down before something worse happens to him'). Russia, France and China were now warning Washington that they would use their vetoes in the Security Council to block any new military strike against Iraq. Again President Yeltsin was threatening that 'a world war' might be the result of US bombing raids; China's Qian Qichen declared that Beijing was 'extremely and definitely opposed to the use of military force'; and the French foreign minister Hubert Vedrine declared that France had 'no intention of associating itself' with the threat of military action. Such comments appeared to be having little effect in Washington and London (Blair, visiting the White House, remarked that Saddam knew 'that the threat of force is there'; and should perhaps have read Article 2(4) of the UN Charter). Netanyahu in Israel was claiming the right to retaliate in the event of an Iraqi attack, while on 5 February Yeltsin was declaring in Moscow that the worst was over: 'The peak of tension has gone down a little. We cannot yet say with confidence that the situation is all right and no upsurge is possible. But tension is down'. Saddam seemed unconvinced. To the Turkish foreign minister Ismail Cem he commented: 'We accept our fate. If God puts us at harm today, he will surely compensate for it tomorrow. We are complying with the UN resolutions, but America is distorting this. We are prepared for anything'. The United States and Britain were now warning of huge air strikes, which some commentators were suggesting might cause the national disintegration of Iraq – an increasingly alarming prospect to such regional powers as Turkey and Saudi Arabia.

It was now being reported that the targets in Iraq had been selected by the war planners in Washington, and that Tony Blair had agreed with the outline battle plan (Blair: 'There will undoubtedly be military action unless there is a diplomatic solution'). Commentators thought it likely that Saddam would survive the fresh bombing campaign, and that air strikes would probably mean an end to all the UNSCOM inspections.[83] There were still tensions between the White House and the Pentagon on what should be the scale of the war,[84] with great scope for miscalculation and a further erosion of American influence in the Middle East. Washington, as much as Baghdad, appeared trapped in an irrevocable drift to war that would have entirely unpredictable consequences. The television and other media were gearing up for a new spectacular ('CNN emerged the winner last time but the others are determined not to be beaten again'). In Saudi Arabia Robin Cook had failed to elicit support for US/UK air strikes, but speculation continued about the scale of the coming military onslaught. Said one defence source in Washington:

In the past, attacks have been mainly at night to minimise casualties. *What is being considered are attacks during working hours with the explicit goal of killing people as they work* and raising questions among Saddam's supporters as to whether their continued support is worthwhile [my italics].[85]

Now it appeared that the deliberate slaughter of civilians, far from being a poor public-relations option, was being actively evaluated as a realistic tactical goal. In such cynical calculation such entities as the UN Charter and the Geneva Conventions seemed nothing more than trivial irrelevancies. Even General Norman Schwarzkopf, the victorious US commander in the 1991 Gulf War, was voicing doubts about the wisdom of American policy. Was there a danger of a new Vietnam predicament? On NBC television Schwarzkopf declared: 'We run the risk of doing the same thing we did to North Vietnam'. Here the bombing was massively escalated without the United States being able to achieve military or other goals: 'It's definitely a risk. What after that?' It might also be the case that 'a big strike' would help Saddam to fracture international opinion still further, so making it more likely that the embargo would end. And again it was not hard to find international commentary hostile to American war policy: on 8 February Saudi Arabia, Iran, Egypt, Morocco and Russia were all declaring against military strikes (Tony Blair continued to threaten military action). On 8 February two senior ministers in the French Socialist-led government said that they would resign if France gave any logistical or diplomatic support for US air strikes on Baghdad. Now the increasingly frustrated Americans, including the Defense Secretary William Cohen, were querying European willingness to play a coherent role as allies in the crisis. Britain could be taken for granted, but the rest?

A February (1998) *Guardian*/ICM poll showed that the British public rejected by a ratio of two to one the idea that Britain was in some way America's 51st state, always doing as bidden by Washington. Some 61 per cent believed that Britain had more in common with the United States than with Europe, with a clear majority then prepared to back Blair's unconditional support for Clinton's strategy on Iraq; but a significant minority (one in three) judged that diplomatic pressure on Iraq should not be accompanied by military action. Now the US/UK posture was facing significant opposition in the North Atlantic Treaty Organisation (NATO), with France vehemently warning against air strikes and Russia continuing to exert pressure from outside the Organisation. On 9 February thousands of Turkish troops poured into northern Iraq to establish a so-called 'security belt' in the Kurdish-controlled enclave. This renewed violation of a US/UK-established 'safe haven' did not only ignore a range of American guarantees but constituted serious infringement of the UN Charter and international law. As always it was plain that Turkey, an important strategic US ally, would be allowed to invade sovereign Iraqi territory with no objection from the war planners in Washington and London. The West always finds illegal acts congenial if they support perceived strategic objectives.[86]

On 9 February Esmat Abdel Meguid, the secretary-general of the Arab League, said that Russia, France and the Arab League were drawing up a compromise plan to avert a new bombing campaign against Iraq. Eight presidential sites would be opened to an UNSCOM team accompanied by diplomatic personnel; other sites would be open for inspection for a limited period, perhaps between 30 and 60 days. Observers doubted that Washington and London would be prepared to tolerate any such compromise. Now some 3000 more ground troops were being sent to Kuwait, coinciding with the arrival of the first of eight RAF Tornado GR1 bombers, bringing the British presence to some 2500 personnel. Such moves were doing nothing to quell the growing anxieties throughout the region. For example, Egyptian officials were now warning that new air strikes against Iraq could trigger a shock wave of Islamic militancy and Arab nationalism that would destabilise Arab governments and end finally any residual chances of agreement in the Arab–Israeli peace process. The Egyptian government was now keen to express its support for the peace proposals being advertised following the talks between Russia, France and the Arab League. The UN Secretary-General Kofi Annan, having so far kept a relatively low profile, was appealing for cool heads to prevail: Iraq, he suggested, had painted itself into a corner but should be helped to extricate itself gracefully. *For the first time it emerged that Annan was holding himself in readiness for a possible mission to Baghdad as a way of defusing the mounting tensions.* Later this option would be seen as a pivotal detail in the evolving crisis.

The world was pleased to learn on 10 February that the responsibility faced by British premier Tony Blair of sanctioning military strikes that could kill innocent Iraqis 'weighs seriously' upon him, but not sufficiently seriously to heed an appeal made by ten Anglican bishops. The bishops of Monmouth, Kingston, Bangor, Croydon, Aston, Manchester, St German, Truro, Sheffield and Worcester together signed a letter, distributed at the General Synod, declaring that it would not be a 'just war' if the United States and Britain were to bomb Iraq. It would be morally weak and would 'reinforce the already deep Muslim mistrust of the West': 'We do not write from a pacifist position but from a common concern to urge the Government to search for alternatives to violence'; efforts should be directed towards achieving an 'international consensus' rather than allowing a 'superpower mentality to make the running'; the points were raised 'on the basis of the Christian conviction that innocent citizens have the right not to become the target of threats'. But Tony Blair, with the support of former British premier John Major, saw nothing wrong in bombing (and starving) innocent Arab men, women and children if this was part of a genocidal campaign against a regional dictator over whom they had no control. The appeal of the bishops for a peaceful resolution of the crisis was ignored: Blair's much vaunted Christian commitment was of an altogether different type.

There were signs that Baghdad was prepared to heed the Russian proposal for some degree of access to the presidential sites, though the proposals fell short of the 'full and unfettered access' demanded by Washington and London. The United States at once rejected the hint of an Iraqi compromise (Clinton: 'Saddam Hussein must let the weapons inspectors back with full and free access to all suspect sites. If he will not act, we must be prepared to do so'). Now General Anthony Zinni, the US commander in the Middle East, was declaring that his forces were 'within a week or so' of readiness to bomb Iraq. Spain, Portugal, Italy, Belgium and Germany were now prepared to offer the use of their bases to US aircraft, but European governments, like the bulk of the regimes in the Middle East, appeared reluctant to show significant support for the gathering US/UK forces in the Gulf (the disaster of the US warplane that had torn through cable-car wires in the Dolomites, killing 20 people, had done little to encourage Italian co-operation).

The US/UK propaganda continued to mount, along with the military preparations: the Iraqis had struggled to preserve their weapons of mass destruction while at the same time consistently deceiving the UNSCOM teams: 'It is what remains unfound, undetected and undestroyed that is the worry'.[87] This of course was the perennial Catch-22 faced by the Iraqis all the time: if weapons were found, the UNSCOM worries were confirmed, just as, if weapons were not found, then they must have been hidden 'in a tissue of lies'. No-one doubted that the Iraqis had lied. Was this really a justification for a years-long genocide of an innocent civilian population? The new compromise deal suggested by the Iraqi authorities had been routinely rejected by a Washington and a London more interested in launching a bombing strike as soon as possible. The British government, though currently holding the European Union (EU) presidency, had no interest in securing a European consensus on action. London had its sights constantly set on Washington, and scarcely disguised its contempt for European misgivings: for Blair the US/UK connection was what mattered and New Labour's role 'at the heart of Europe' was a pathetic sham.

A few independent observers continued to question the rationale behind the US/UK commitment to an ill-defined but substantial bombing campaign; some were prepared to remind people that the United States itself was insisting on weapons inspection conditions (for example, regarding the Chemical Weapons Convention) that were very similar to those demanded by Saddam Hussein ('Who will inspect the inspectors?').[88] There were some signs that the failure of the US/UK campaign to win an international consensus for military action was even now encouraging the search for some sort of peaceful resolution of the crisis. Perhaps, following the Russian proposals, diplomats could be allowed to accompany the UNSCOM teams; perhaps such an arrangement would finally induce Saddam to climb down and permit Washington and London to claim that 'diplomacy backed by the threat of force' had won the day. Again there was talk that Kofi Annan might be willing to take specific face-saving proposals to Baghdad; but that

Washington would oppose any suggestion that the UN Secretary-General *negotiate* with Saddam. The Iraqi dictator was required to 'climb down': in the *realpolitik* realm of American hegemonic vanity, nothing less would satisfy the Washington strategists.

On 13 February Kofi Annan made a statement on Iraq to correspondents and answered their questions. On this occasion he confirmed that he was 'prepared to go to Baghdad, and the work I am doing now with the Permanent five is in preparation for that visit'. There was a willingness, declared Annan, for the Permanent Members of the Security Council to work together 'and find a common ground that will permit me to move on to Baghdad'; and he confirmed also that a technical team would be sent to Baghdad to work with the Iraqi authorities on the mapping of the presidential sites ('I expect them to conclude this task within three or four days'). Staffan de Mistura, the Swedish Director of the United Nations Information Centre in Rome and a former UN Humanitarian Co-ordinator for Iraq, had been appointed to lead the team. Answering questions from UNTV Kofi Annan commented: '*I hope that in the next few days things would clarify, and positions would be brought closer, and that a trip to Baghdad would be meaningful and at that point I will be ready to go to Baghdad.*' Such developments were seen as little more than an irritation to Washington, pressed by many politicians and pundits to run an American foreign policy unencumbered by unhelpful UN bureaucrats. Throughout the Middle East any efforts by United Nations officials to resolve the crisis were seen was at worst irrelevant and as at best inconsequential. It was assumed that in the last resort the Washington strategists would determine the subsequent course of events. In Jordan and elsewhere there was manifest public feeling in support of Iraq, despite government attempts to ban pro-Saddam demonstrations.[89]

The British Cabinet had now come out in unambiguous support for Premier Tony Blair's unquestioning support for the Clinton policy, though influential Labour Members of Parliament (Tony Benn, Tam Dalyell and others) were expressing dissent, and criticism of the British position was expected in the European Parliament for Britain's failure to consult its EU partners. Marshal Igor Sergeyev, the Russian defence minister, publicly rebuked US Defense Secretary William Cohen in front of television cameras, accusing the Americans of rushing into battle and endangering world security: 'I would like to relay to you our deep concern over the possible prospects for Russia–US relations in the military sphere if military action takes place ... Is the extremely tough and uncompromising position of the United States on the Iraq issue conducive to stability?'; and Sergeyev then quoted Abraham Lincoln: 'Force is all-conquering but its victories are short-lived.' Cohen, evidently shaken by this rebuke, commented that Washington was not rushing into battle but 'proceeding cautiously and with great prudence'. The American congress was divided over the prospects of a new war with Iraq, and there were growing criticisms of the proposed visit by Kofi Annan to Baghdad. Said one source: 'If the Secretary-General goes to Baghdad, he must do so with a mandate constrained by the sharp red lines set down by those parties with forces on the ground.' Now it was plain that all the American diplomacy in the Middle East had failed to coerce or persuade Arab governments into support for a new US-led war. What Washington had feared most of all had happened: *Iraq had become a victim.*

The American public, as the British public, both bombarded with unremitting bogus propaganda, were prepared for war; though US military spokesmen conceding that 'we will lose some people, and that weighs heavily' (General Henry Shelton, chairman of the Joint Chiefs of Staff), and that despite a new generation of 'smart' weapons Iraqi civilians were likely to be hurt (Shelton). President Clinton continued to encourage the idea that war was likely, with little attention given to what the proposed Annan trip might accomplish. Some observers (for example, Harold Walker, a former British ambassador to Baghdad) were suggesting that Baghdad be shown a 'light at the end of the tunnel': sanctions would be lifted if genuine compliance with UN resolutions were shown (such suggestions were superfluous since they were already stipulated in Paragraph 22 of Resolution 687). Tony Blair, with Clinton, was emphasising that people must be prepared to face up to the use of the military option.[90] In Baghdad there appeared to be a mood of resignation, with many civilians, remembering the hundreds of women and children killed in the 1991 bombing of Amiriya, determined to avoid public shelters (Iman Ali Hussein, who lost four of his relatives at Amiriya, said: *'I cannot imagine any Iraqi will enter a shelter again. It's better for them to die in their homes'*).

By mid-February 1998 the US/UK forces massed in the Gulf region were ready to strike against Iraq in a prolonged campaign dubbed Operation Desert Thunder. Expectations were growing that the missiles and bombers would be unleashed soon after 18 February.[91] Some spurious debate was continuing on the terms of the new humanitarian provisions under Resolution 986 and the associated Memorandum of Understanding between Iraq and the United Nations (with Iraq complaining that it could not be expected to accept a formula consolidating the scheme as a permanent alternative to the lifting of sanctions); but most attention was being focused on the assumed imminence of war. General Henry Shelton was warning that the planned 'devastating' strike against Iraq could kill 1500 civilians and soldiers, since war was 'a dirty thing'.[92] The arrival in Baghdad of a technical team to survey eight of the so-called presidential palaces was doing nothing to arrest the seemingly irrevocable countdown to military strikes. A pressing fear in Washington was that a high Iraqi death toll on the first night of bombing might force the US strategists 'to scale back the later phases of the operation'[93] because of the unwelcome publicity that would be afforded by televised rows of Iraqi corpses. In one report the planned air strikes might cause more civilian deaths than occurred in the 1991 Gulf War.[94]

In Britain a senior military source declared that the British forces in the Gulf were 'ready to go now', just as American forces would reportedly be at peak readiness in a few days' time. The British MI5 was targeting hundreds of Arabs living in Britain, now facing the prospect of detention in the event of air strikes against Iraq; some would be detained, some deported and some merely warned (a list of Arab individuals, said to be in the 'lower hundreds',[95] had been drawn up); commentators remembered the fiasco during the 1991 Gulf War when some fifty innocent Arabs were interned as terrorists and 167 more were deported. The Member of Parliament Tony Benn stated that all MPs who supported the British government would be 'voting consciously and deliberately for the deaths of innocent people if war begins, as I believe it will'; the MP George Galloway commented that to bomb a stockpile of biological or chemical weapons would 'choke the very Iraqi people we are told we have no quarrel with'; and now the war planners were facing further problems. It was being suggested that a US/UK attack on Iraq could inflame the Middle East into turmoil that might quickly run out of control; on 17 February Bahrain, a former staunch US ally, declared its opposition to air strikes; and on the following day Secretary of State Albright, Defense Secretary Cohen and National Security Advisor Berger were loudly heckled by anti-war protesters (shades of Vietnam) in an Ohio 'town meeting' staged to rally support for war. The US and UK publics were happy to support the slaughter of more Arabs, but the rest of the world (the Arab states, the Non-aligned Movement, a majority in the UN Security Council, a majority in the UN General Assembly, most of European opinion *inter alia*) was bitterly opposed to the launching of Gulf War II.

The media were delighted at the prospect of a fresh news spectacular ('Oh what a lovely TV ratings war!'). Chris Hampson, a senior NBC producer, boasted: 'CNN has a handful of top reporters but NBC has a stableful.' The Turner Cable News Network had dominated the television news coverage in 1991, but this time 'ABC, NBC and BBC's News24 are determined to offer an alternative.' In 1991 the US Defense Secretary Richard Cheney had opined that he thought the bombing raids had been successful because that was what he had heard on CNN. In mid-February 1998 the US/UK military forces were well prepared to wreak fresh destruction and slaughter; the media were happy to boast that they too were ready to convey the glad news to American and British audiences demanding constant entertainment.

In the Middle East, the United States, Britain, Europe and elsewhere protests were staged against what everyone assumed was the imminent war. In the European Parliament the Dutch foreign minister Hans van Mierlo delivered a stinging personal attack on Tony Blair for his uncritical support for American policy. The British posture was seen as hampering EU efforts to forge a common foreign and security policy; the White House (Albright/ Cohen/Berger) public-relations disaster was stimulating further tensions in Washington;[96] and in Britain Whitehall was reportedly 'in spin over lack of public support' for war.[97] Large number of Israelis were said to be leaving the country for safer locations (while mystical rabbis circled Israel seven times in a chartered plane, blowing the *shofar* ram's horn, in an attempt to replicate the biblical Joshua's magical seven flights around Jericho to bring down its walls); Jordanians and other Arabs were now resigned to the coming cataclysm; and American GIs, remembering the 1991 war, were confident that they could do it again.

In the journalistic accounts the 'moment of truth was dawning for Saddam',[98] but 'cracks were beginning to show' in the Washington/London alliance.[99] The expected bombing campaign had not yet begun, but now the 'day of reckoning' had arrived ('It's no bluff ... the United States and Britain could start bombing Iraqi targets within days').[100] The war plans had been comprehensively developed. The massive US forces had been given their detailed orders; the role of the RAF in support of the American military power was well defined; and detailed target lists had been agreed. There were hints of tension in the British Cabinet, with suggestions that Foreign Secretary Robin Cook was more concerned about international law than was Premier Tony Blair,[101] but such minor details were doing nothing to erode the gathering war clouds. A London-based counselling service, Exploring Parenthood, was offering guidance on how to calm (British) children apparently tormented by the endless war propaganda, while hundreds of thousands of diseased and starving (Iraqi) children waited for the inferno incendiaries, the atomic-scale fuel–air explosives, the earthquake bombs and the 'flesh-shredding' cluster explosives to fall on their homes and hospitals.

Few observers doubted that Gulf War II was about to begin. *Time* magazine (23 February 1998) published multicoloured graphics to illustrate in detail the 'Order of Battle' (there would be four waves of bombing that in all were 'scheduled to go on for about a week ... war is just around the corner'[102]); and the television media barons were excited at the prospect of a fresh entertainment spectacular. It seemed that now nothing could stop another massive military onslaught, with all the vast destruction and human suffering that would be caused.

Part III
End Game?

6 The Annan Deal

PREAMBLE

Through February 1998 the crisis had continued to escalate. Iraq, seemingly faced by the prospect of cruel economic sanctions in perpetuity, appeared desperate to bring matters to a head; while Washington, enthusiastic for a new phase of military activity, was doing nothing constructive to aid the 'diplomatic solution' that the Clinton Administration professed to want. It was plain that American 'diplomacy' had one central purpose: to brace erstwhile military allies and the rest of the world for a comprehensive bombing campaign that would range promiscuously over much of Iraq. Gulf War II was not designed to be a 'pin-prick'. With all the genuinely pacific diplomatic channels constantly decried or ignored by Washington, it seemed that war was inevitable. Critical observers suggested that, as in 1990/1, the United States would use a quasi-UN authorisation firstly to propagate a pretext for war and secondly to clear away all UN impediments before launching a unilateral and illegal military campaign. Through February it seemed increasingly unlikely that Washington would permit a peaceful solution to the crisis.

A NEW SECRETARY-GENERAL

By December 1996 the United States had made it plain that in no circumstances would it approve the re-appointment of UN Secretary-General Boutros Boutros-Ghali, formerly an Egyptian career politician, for a second term in office. Boutros-Ghali had been thought sufficiently pliable by Washington at the start of his first term in 1992 but subsequently demonstrated an abrasive independence that the United States, alone among the fifteen members of the Security Council, found themselves unable to tolerate. The Secretary-General had shown a stubborn unwillingness merely to echo US foreign policy on such issues as Iraq, Bosnia and Somalia, and on the persistent question of reform of the UN Secretariat. The final US/Boutros-Ghali rupture came with the Secretary-General's insistence on the publication of the UN report showing Israeli culpability in the massacre at the Qana refugee camp in Lebanon: Washington did not want further publicity to be given to Israeli lies about its deliberate plan to target innocent men, women and children. The publication of this report was a principal reason why the United States was determined to veto what would have been the normal second term of office for the incumbent Secretary-General.

Fourteen members of the 15-strong Security Council voted in favour of Boutros Boutros-Ghali but were defeated by the American veto. There then began a series of wrangles around the selection of a new Secretary-General. In early December, time was pressing since the Council had only until the end of the month to find a successor to Boutros-Ghali who would be acceptable to Washington. It soon emerged that Kofi Annan, a veteran UN diplomat and currently head of peace-keeping, was the strongest candidate. Eleven members, including the United States, voted to 'encourage' him; and four, including France, voted to 'discourage' him (France was making it plain that it would prefer Amara Essy, the Ivory Coast foreign minister). Diplomats were now criticising Paris for blocking the Ghanaian Kofi Annan simply to retaliate against Washington for opposing Boutros-Ghali, a French protégé. Said one source: 'France has no objections to Annan's personal qualifications. It is motivated by a sense of political pique. It's saying to the Americans, "You're not the only people who can play this game".' President Jacques Chirac had also commented that he would veto Tanzania's Salim Ahmed Salim, the Secretary-General of the Organisation of African Unity (OAU), because he was not fluent in French (on this point Annan, as a fluent French speaker, met Chirac's requirement).

Since Washington was supporting Kofi Annan there were suspicions that he would inevitably be too close to the United States, further consolidating the American grip on the Security Council. There had been some minor Albright/Annan arguments over Bosnia, but the bureaucratic Annan was 'not at all confrontational' and the Americans seemed confident that they could handle a pleasant man thought by many observers not to be tough enough for the job. A member of a family of traditional Fante tribal chiefs, Annan had worked for the United Nations since 1962, serving in Addis Ababa and Geneva, and with the High Commission for Refugees and the World Health Organisation, before becoming the assistant secretary-general for budget and finance in New York and in 1993 being appointed by Boutros-Ghali to the post of Under-Secretary General for the peacekeeping department. His office on the 37th floor of the UN building in New York was stuffed with African carvings, medals and plaques.

For a candidate to be put to the General Assembly for confirmation of the Security Council decision, he has to receive at least nine votes with none of the five Permanent Members exercising their veto. In mid-December 1996 there seemed every likelihood of a 'tit for tat' veto battle between France and the United States in formal voting. African candidates were necessarily favoured because of the tradition that a person from the same continent should serve two consecutive terms, a custom that put both Kofi Annan and Amara Essy in strong positions (some observers were even speculating that Boutros-Ghali, still not resigned to defeat, might re-enter the contest). In the event, France dropped its opposition to Kofi Annan and declared that it would be prepared to accept the candidate from Ghana, a non-Francophone nation. Sir John Weston, the British UN envoy, applauded Annan's appointment ('This is a good result for Africa and the UN organisation'), and Boutrous-Ghali expressed his pleasure that Africa would have a second five-year term at the UN helm. Annan himself had commented that he had not set out with the intention of working for the United Nations ('I was presented with the opportunity of working with the World Health Organisation … and here I am today'), and was now suggesting that he would work hard to improve staff morale and to reform the UN organisation ('People talk of the failings of the UN, forgetting that we have had many success stories'). It now seemed likely that Washington had secured a mild-mannered Secretary-General that it could push around, and that Annan's intended financial reforms would lead to a reduction in the level of the US contribution (a constant Republican bone of contention on Capitol Hill). In common perception, Boutros-Ghali had emerged as no push-over. Was Kofi Annan Washington's man?

It was obvious that Annan had many American connections. At the end of the 1950s he had won a Ford Foundation scholarship to Macalester College, Minnesota; and later earned a master of science degree at the Massachusetts Institute of Technology. As soon as he was elected as the new Secretary-General, Annan was emphasising the need for UN reform, a requirement close to the US heart (Washington owed $1.4 billion and was unlikely to settle its debts without substantial changes to the UN structure and operations). Britain had quickly acquiesced in the US veto of Boutros-Ghali but was reluctant to advertise that Annan was the 'Anglo-American choice', a ploy that could well have damaged his candidacy. Said one British source: 'It was our view that the best approach was to allow the innate weight of Annan's case and his qualifications to bear down on everyone gradually. Once everyone looked seriously at Annan he was always going to measure up to expectations.' Annan *was* the Anglo-American choice, achieved in part surreptitiously and through backstairs manoeuvring. British diplomats had reportedly begun a campaign of corridor murmurs: the French had 'cocked up', and African UN delegates were warned that unless a choice were made soon the Council might consider a non-African candidate: 'There is probably much more we do not yet know – of trial balloons popped before they ever took flight and of dastardly schemes buried as quickly as they were conceived … score up a big win for Britain and the United States and an embarrassing defeat for France'.[1] Now it was obvious that Annan was Washington's candidate; was it true to say that 'he is not its poodle'.[2] Already it was being charged that Annan would be 'too accommodating to the United States',[3] though one analyst suggested that 'he can be very tough on the Americans' (after the Somali episode Annan criticised the Americans for giving the impression of cowardice).[4] Had the Americans really got what they wanted?

At least Kofi Annan was in a position to learn from the experience of Boutros Boutros-Ghali. Soon after the Americans had made plain their opposition to Annan's predecessor, Boutros-Ghali asked Madeleine Albright, then chosen by Clinton to be Secretary of State, why Washington had opposed his second term: 'What went wrong? Why this campaign against me for six months?' She offered no explanation but then, according to Boutros-Ghali, quickly requested his assistance in connection with the Arab–Israeli peace process ('She knew that because she was against my re-election the Arab world was not happy'). Administration officials were prepared to say that US opposition to Boutros-Ghali derived from policy differences, rather than from any personal animosity – as if it must be assumed that a UN Secretary-General was under obligation to accept US foreign policy. Boutros-Ghali himself declared that for six months Washington had been ordering American embassies to drum up opposition to his candidacy; that, after the Republican capture of Congress, he was sacrificed for domestic political gain.

On 23 January 1997 Secretary-General Kofi Annan declared in Washington that he accepted the need for financial cuts and other reforms at the United Nations: 'If we do not change, we may lose our relevance ... What the UN wants is what the US wants – to be effective, efficient, leaner and relevant'. President Clinton, well prepared to acknowledge American blackmail of the United Nations, commented that the United States had to pay its debts 'as long as the UN does its part' (in short: do as we say or we will not meet our obligations under the UN Charter). At the same time there was a clue that Annan was not prepared merely to echo American rhetoric ('A country cannot be a delinquent and a good leader,' referring to US debts to the United Nations). Washington was now advertising its enthusiasm for the new Secretary-General: 'The welcome it gave the American-educated Ghanaian was almost cloying.'[5] On the same day Madeleine Albright was sworn in as Secretary of State, now keen to celebrate her first official act as Secretary by meeting the US president and the UN Secretary-General ('It is a very good sign of the support that the US is going to give the UN').[6] In one view Annan was in Washington '*to pay discreet fealty to the country which appointed him, and to hear the terms of the financial deal between Washington's political factions which will shape the UN's future*'.[7] For example, the Congress was pressing for a cut in the American share of the UN budget from 25 per cent to 21.7 per cent, which arguably represented more accurately the US share of the global economy.

Kofi Annan knew that he was under pressure to reform the United Nations in the interest of the American Republican Congress. Britain, on cue, was urging rapid reform, and now it seemed likely that the US/UK pressure for a slimmed-down United Nations organisation with reduced American financial dues would have effect. In February 1997 Kofi Annan sacked two officials of the UN's Rwandan war crimes tribunal after reports of waste and incompetence. At the same time he was ready to joke when criticised for not reforming quickly enough (told by the Russian ambassador that he had had more time than God, Annan replied: 'God had a great advantage that he could start from scratch. He didn't have to work with any committees and 185 member states'); and to rebut any suggestion that, promoted by Washington, he was America's poodle: 'A Secretary-General's ability to work cohesively ... with the only superpower we have today – should be an asset and not a handicap'. In March, Annan announced plans for the cutting of 1000 UN jobs and the slashing of £76.8 million from the planned UN administrative budget of just over £625 million for 1998/9.

The United States was maintaining the pressure for reform. In June 1997 US Representative Rick Lazio introduced a bill for America to withhold $10 million in UN funding until UN employees, hiding behind diplomatic immunity or behind international agreements that protect UN salaries and pensions, paid up the millions of dollars due in parking fines and made due payments for their abandoned families in America: 'The UN has been touted as the symbol of international justice and human rights. Ironically, the organisation's own restrictive salary and pensions policies deny families of their own staff such basic rights as spousal and child support'. As one example, Irene Philippi, an Argentinian formerly married to a senior UN official, said that she and her two children had been abandoned in the United States four years ago and that she had since spent $100,000 in legal fees attempting to get her ex-husband to pay child support.[8] Kofi Annan was reportedly urging officials to speed up the search for a remedy to such problems.

On 16 July Kofi Annan announced the 'most extensive and far-reaching' reform in the UN's 52-year history. In one interpretation no radical restructuring was on offer, but improved co-ordination was expected to bring cost savings. The planned UN reforms included:

- Setting up a development fund for poor countries, financed by the elimination of 1000 jobs and other administrative cuts;

- Creating a deputy secretary-general in charge of collaboration among UN organs;

- Establishing a cabinet-style structure for the UN;

- Co-ordinating aid agencies in two groups – humanitarian affairs, and development;

- Consolidating programmes for drugs, crime, terrorism and drug trafficking;

- Giving the High Commissioner for Human Rights control of the Centre for Human Rights.

Annan was also suggesting a revolving voluntary credit fund of up to $1 billion, allowing States to earn interest in return for pledging funds to plug financial gaps. Significantly enough, the Secretary-General had not so far responded to US congressional pressure for a reduction in the American share of the UN budget. In Annan's own words 'a quiet revolution' had begun, with reforms that were 'bold but not suicidal'. In December 1997 the UN General Assembly largely approved his list of reforms (said a top aide: 'People don't like to say no to him'). At the same time the perception remained among the Group of 77 developing countries that Kofi Annan was 'the United States' creature'.[9] There were suspicions that the proposed deputy secretary-general, Annan's Number Two, would be a US watchdog, peering over his shoulder; already it seemed that some of the G77 fears were well-founded, with reforms to the budgeting process shifting substantial areas of financial control from the South to the North.[10]

By 1998 the image of Kofi Annan was already a mixed one. It seemed unlikely that he would act to disturb Washington in any important area of policy, though he had publicly criticised the United States for failing to pay its obligatory UN dues. His reforms, with significant effects in important organisational and financial areas, did not slavishly echo the prejudices of the US Republican Congress; but it still seemed unlikely that Annan, as a seemingly diffident career diplomat, would seriously upset the Washington strategists as they developed their global plans. Now the 1997/8 US/Iraqi crisis was coming to a head. Baghdad was refusing to bow to American demands, and few observers doubted that Washington was managing a tight military countdown. It remained to be seen whether Secretary-General Kofi Annan, having had no substantial impact on international affairs through 1997, would be able to intercede in 1998 according to the preamble of the UN Charter *'to save succeeding generations from the scourge of war ... '*. In mid-February 1998 most international observers assumed that a fresh US bombing campaign against Iraq was now imminent, and that the scale of the air strikes would be substantial and prolonged. It seemed highly improbably that one softly-spoken diplomat would be able to arrest the growing momentum of the American military Establishment.

THE ANNAN DEAL

The imminence of war had done nothing to define the precise purpose of a bombing campaign. Would it be intended to destroy weapons stockpiles (what stockpiles?), to destroy weapons-making capacity (factories in general?), to decimate the Republican Guard (air attacks on personnel?), to destroy any rebuilt social infrastructure that might be held to serve the regime, or to serve as a purely punitive gesture with little practical purpose?

And what of civilian casualties? What would rows of civilian corpses do to an already badly-bruised American image in the world community? Some Western pundits were prepared to argue that the Iraqi civilian population deserved all it got. Thus an editorial in *The Daily Telegraph* (London, 10 November 1997), while acknowledging the 'pitiable' plight of the Iraqi people, declared that *'they should not expect to be exonerated from responsibility for those who lead them'*; if the people wanted an improvement in their situation then Saddam had to be removed from power, 'and that only they can achieve'.

The Iraqi authorities were continuing to complain about the nationality imbalance of the UNSCOM teams, often engaged in scrutiny of highly sensitive sites. Thus inspections were carried out on a General Security facilities complex and the Directorate of General Security headquarters, key organisations at the heart of the Iraqi regime; and inspections were being carried out on such buildings as the Tourism and Hotels Institute, the Ibn al-Quff Hospital and the Air Force Medical Centre – 'to ascertain the presence of any means of spying on the BMVC (Baghdad Monitoring and Verification Centre)'. For this last purpose radar and other sensor devices were used but allegations of Iraqi spying activities were never supported with any evidence. Now it was also being alleged that suspect Iraqi vehicles were being moved around at certain alleged weapons sites, and that UNSCOM had U-2 spy photographs to support the charges. When the Iraqi authorities asked to see the photographs in order to assess their significance they were denied access, while one of them was broadcast on the CNN television network to support the accusations of concealment. Richard Butler, as UNSCOM head, was making it plain that the Iraqi authorities had no right to see any espionage information collected by the teams of inspectors or by U-2 spy planes, and he said more: *'It is not the practice of UNSCOM to provide to the members of the Security Council ... materials which it has compiled from a variety of sources for use as a basis for the conduct and the evaluation of the results of particular inspections'*. So the American spy planes, flown by American pilots over Iraq and with communication links to Washington, were collecting espionage information which the Permanent Members of the Security Council were not allowed to see. Washington, not UNSCOM, would decide what information was made available to the Security Council – yet it was on the basis of precisely this information that the Council was being asked to support the genocidal sanctions regime with no hint of 'light at the end of the tunnel'. In short, American spies collected data, Washington made selective presentations to the Security Council, and on this basis the Council was urged to underwrite American policy.[11]

Such practices were helping to escalate the crisis, as were fresh allegations that the Iraqis 'may have' tested chemical and biological weapons on human beings. With this in mind the UNSCOM personnel were investigating the

Abu Ghraib jail in Baghdad in a vain attempt to find evidence that prisoners had been used as human guinea pigs (Aziz called the allegations 'sheer lies used as a pretext' to obtain espionage information: 'When you have a situation where an adversary is the judge, this is unfair'). While the crisis continued to escalate, there were still many calls for a diplomatic solution. In an interview with Swiss television on 30 January 1998 UN Secretary-General Kofi Annan commented that 'all of us would prefer ... a political and diplomatic solution', adding that 'the Iraqi people have suffered enough; they have been through major tragic events and they don't need another one and therefore, for the sake of the people, the sake of humanity, they [the country's leaders] should work with the international community and avoid a confrontation'; at the same time the Chinese UN ambassador was urging restraint in the handling of the current crisis. For his part, Richard Butler continued to contribute to the worsening atmosphere, suggesting the absurd proposition that Baghdad had enough weapons and missiles 'to blow away Tel Aviv' (these words appeared in the *New York Times* on 27 January 1998 and a correction was published three days later). Butler decried the 'fuss' made over the inaccurate article and commented that UNSCOM had a 'fairly good idea' of what weapons remained, although it did not have details (a typical Butler ploy – bland assertion unsupported by evidence). No progress was being made to resolve the crisis. Washington, London, Richard Butler and others continued to make general allegations while doing nothing to discourage the countdown to war.

The Iraqi people were being exhorted by Baghdad to prepare for an American bombing campaign and to wage a 'holy war' (*jihad*) against the punitive years-long sanctions regime. Butler continued to fan the flames, calling the situation 'dire'. Relations between the Iraqi authorities and UNSCOM were continuing to worsen, with no sign that diplomatic accommodations might be negotiated. Butler's current report[12] was serving to confirm the mutual and growing hostility that existed between his teams and the Iraqi authorities. Thus Butler commented on the recent talks held with the Iraqis (Tariq Aziz supported by ministers and senior military and civilian officials):

> The talks were characterised ... by: extended statements by the Iraqi side to which no even remotely equal reply was invited, accepted or apparently wanted; moments of abuse and denigration of UNSCOM and its professional officers; an attempt literally to apportion all blame to UNSCOM, past and present, for the fact that the disarmament task had not been completed and sanctions on Iraq remained in force. UNSCOM representatives ... found Iraq's decision to conduct its participation in the meeting in this manner disturbing and disappointing.[13]

Again Butler emphasised UNSCOM's need to inspect all the 'presidential and sovereign sites'; and concluded the report with the charge that certain Iraqi claims were 'utterly untrue and distasteful'.[14] There was nothing here – on either the UNSCOM or the Iraqi side – to suggest the likelihood of a peaceful resolution of the mounting crisis.

On 25 January 1998 it was reported in Washington that the countdown to US-led military action against Iraq had already begun.[15] US officials were telling journalists that a punitive raid against Iraq would take place 'within weeks' if Iraq continued to block UN weapons inspectors from sensitive sites; and that, although various governments would be informed about the impending bombing campaign, it was possible that the United States would act with only British support. The British aircraft carrier HMS *Invincible*, escorted by the guided-missile destroyer *Nottingham* and the anti-submarine frigate *Coventry*, had arrived in the Gulf (*Invincible* was now reportedly carrying 19 Harrier jump-jets and five sea King helicopters – a paltry contribution compared with the hundreds of US aircraft in the region). The United States had now assembled the vast carriers *Nimitz* and *Washington*, nearly two dozen other warships and 350 aircraft; B52 bombers and support aircraft were in readiness on the British Indian Ocean island of Diego Garcia. After considering the typically hostile Butler report,[16] Secretary of State Madeleine Albright told a press conference: 'This is not something that can last much longer'. The Iraqis had announced their intention to give weapons-training to a million defence volunteers – a feeble response to imminent attack by cruise missiles; and Iraqi propaganda had no hesitation in linking the US policy on Iraq with the sex scandals faced by President Clinton (*Babel*, owned by Saddam's eldest son Uday, said in an editorial: 'To turn attention away from his personal scandal, it is not far fetched that the American President Clinton would undertake a military stupidity against Iraq'). In Britain (31 January), protesters picketed the Foreign Office during the meeting between Madeleine Albright and the British Foreign Secretary, Robin Cook. Placards carried the slogans 'HANDS OFF IRAQ' and 'LIFT THE SANCTIONS', with the protesters angrily demanding that the UNSCOM teams leave Iraq immediately. Hugh Stephens, the Secretary of the Hands Off Iraq Committee, declared: '*The people of Britain do not want war in the Gulf. The British government will face a storm of protest if it backs a US attack on Iraq. This small protest aims to give a foretaste of the wave of public anger that the government would face if such an attack takes place.*' Now it was assumed that a new bombing onslaught on Iraq was only days away.

As Madeleine Albright and other American leaders were using all their diplomatic tools (that is, black propaganda, bribery, intimidation, etc.) to gather support for a fresh military attack on Iraq, some anti-Saddam initiatives achieved risible proportions.* Now the Iraqi authorities were objecting to the terms being developed by the United Nations for an expansion of the 986 'oil for food' agreement. One general objection from Baghdad was that new proposals from the UN Secretary-General took 'no account of the Iraqi Government's role and responsibilities'. Again, from the Baghdad perspective, the United Nations was attempting to erode yet further the sovereignty of the Iraqi nation: 'The Iraqi Government will not endorse any plan for the distribution of increased income if it is prepared by any party other than Iraq'. The new proposals suggested an ongoing and permanent arrangement, clearly violating the principle (specified in Paragraph 22 of Resolution 687) that sanctions would be lifted in certain well-defined circumstances. Other Iraqi objections, all documented in detail, related to the use of the supplementary resources for purposes other than humanitarian relief, the limited scope of certain proposals, general erosions of Iraqi autonomy, and various other matters.[17] It seemed clear to Baghdad that the new proposals were nothing more than a consolidation of the harsh sanctions regime, to the point that earlier agreements (including Resolution 986 and the Memorandum of Understanding) would be violated. Concluding comments in the 7-page Iraqi document convey the flavour of the many objections: '... the goal of the resolution [986] is humanitarian. It is intended to meet the basic needs of the Iraqi people, not to provide additional sums to pay compensation or for administrative and other expenses ... We reaffirm ... the need to comply with paragraph 6 of the Memorandum of Understanding, which gave the Government of the Republic of Iraq exclusive responsibility for preparing the purchase and distribution plan'.[18] Such matters are important: the much-hyped claims made in the United States and Britain that efforts were being made to help the Iraqi people were generally bogus, the real purposes behind 986 expansions being to increase financial compensation to US-friendly claimants and to further erode the sovereignty of the Iraqi state.

There were now hints that UN Secretary-General Kofi Annan was planning to fly to Iraq, though he was still insisting that he would only visit Baghdad if a clear deal was in the offing. In Cairo the Arab League announced that in co-operation with France and Russia a compromise plan

---

* Greg Mitchell, a Denver-based effigy-maker, was marketing Saddam voodoo dolls: 'They make great collectors' items and look just like Saddam Hussein, with black mustache and beret. I make them with rope and paint them in army green. The three stick pins that come with the dolls have American flags attached. They also come with a suction cup to hang on your car window and show your patriotic support. He looks fearsome. He's Saddam, you know'. The dolls were selling like hot cakes.

was being developed to defuse the crisis. Thus Esmat Abdel Meguid, the secretary-general of the League, was outlining a scheme for a new UN panel to inspect the eight presidential palaces at the heart of the dispute, while sixty more sensitive sites could be opened for a limited period. Such a plan was bad news from Washington and London, keen only to arouse international opinion against Baghdad as a prelude to a new military onslaught. In Kuwait, William Cohen was keen to assert, as everyone knew, that 'the window of opportunity is getting narrower'. King Hussein of Jordan, having met Premier Tony Blair in London, said that he would not support action 'that would affect the people of Iraq ... The people have suffered enough.'

On 10 February a joint declaration issued by President Boris Yeltsin and Romano Prodi, President of the Italian Council of Ministers, noted that the situation regarding Iraq was becoming 'increasingly tense' but suggested that a diplomatic solution might be possible. Iraq must obey UN resolutions but military action could have 'unforeseen consequences'; and again there was the suggestion that Kofi Annan might be the catalyst for a peaceful solution: 'There is reason to believe that the United Nations Secretary-General, Kofi Annan, can play a coordinating role in resolving the issue of how to end the current crisis. In these circumstances, it is of crucial importance that he travel to Baghdad'. Others were now also proposing that Kofi Annan visit Baghdad with a view to preventing the American military action that was already under countdown. Thus Fernando Naranjo Villalobos, the foreign minister of Costa Rica, was with others urging Secretary-General Annan to make a personal initiative to resolve the crisis: '... the time has come for the Secretary-General to undertake a personal mission to Iraq, with the objective of conveying to President Saddam Hussein the grave concern of the international community in relation to this very serious crisis ... the Secretary-General, according to his mandate and the Charter of the United Nations, could exercise his good offices to promote and facilitate a diplomatic solution ... Costa Rica attributes extraordinary priority to your personal involvement at this time'.[19] On 10 February Kofi Annan, doubtless sensitive to these and other appeals, appealed for 'courage' and 'wisdom' on Iraq and urged all sides to abandon 'purist or fundamentalist positions', otherwise 'we will not find a solution'.

These developments were deeply alarming to Washington and London. The US/UK war planners wanted no confusions or ambiguities, and now they were disturbed that the UN Secretary-General was signalling his readiness to be flexible in demanding access for UNSCOM personnel in Iraq (Annan: *'I think that full compliance is the position now and the position today. It does not mean that, depending on what can be worked out, that would be the position tomorrow.'* Iraq's leaders had *'painted themselves into a corner and we need to work with them to get them to back down, but I think we should not insist on humiliating them'*). Any Annan 'flexibility' would clearly have represented a departure from the simple US/UK obduracy that was fuelling the pace of the military countdown. The Washington strategists wanted no UN bureaucrat to mess up their carefully laid bombing plans, but now UN sources were indicating that Annan might go to Baghdad if a credible deal could be accomplished. Washington and London were keen to insist that in no way could the relevant UN resolutions, at the centre of the crisis, be watered down: it was essential that Kofi Annan, with his alarming talk of a negotiated deal, be kept 'on message'. Britain, acting as so often as a US-directed messenger boy, was busy drafting a resolution for submission to the Security Council as a means of preparing the way for military action. From the US/UK perspective it was becoming increasingly important to block any initiative from Annan or elsewhere for a peaceful solution; hopefully, the military countdown was now sufficiently advanced to block an Annan visit to Baghdad, with all the unwelcome consequences that might flow from such a move. On 13 February Kofi Annan spoke of a possible personal initiative to solve the crisis, declaring that there were moves among the five Permanent Members of the Security Council that would allow him to go to Baghdad to talk with Saddam Hussein. There was, he said, 'a willingness for us to work together' towards a visit, but he emphasised that he would only go if there were 'a reasonable chance of success'. At the same time he was sending two map-makers to survey the eight presidential palaces at the heart of the escalating crisis.

Now Washington and London were putting pressure on Kofi Annan to maintain a firm stance if he were to visit Baghdad. In one view the Secretary-General had often undermined the US/UK insistence that Iraq comply fully with all the relevant UN resolutions, and now Kofi Annan was increasingly perceived as likely to yet further undermine the tenuous case for war against Iraq. Britain was reportedly prepared to support a French plan that would allow diplomats to accompany the UNSCOM teams if they were allowed to visit all the sensitive sites, but this scheme was provoking a fresh bout of dismay in Washington, now concerned that the British may be losing their nerve in the face of mounting international opposition to war. Britain still favoured a new Security Council resolution, to provide some sort of justification for military strikes, but the immediate priority was to ensure that Kofi Annan did not betray the US/UK resolve. Thus the British Foreign Secretary Robin Cook commented: 'Before he goes, we need to be clear that Baghdad is willing to enter into a serious discussion and that the objective of any visit is to make sure that the outcome is the inspectors going back to work with no restrictions and no areas out of bounds'.

The Americans, declared one Western diplomat, 'appear to have lost faith in a diplomatic solution' (as if they ever had it); the British were supposedly trying to work out a peaceful solution but, said one UN ambassador, 'they are Krazy-clued to the Americans'; and another ambassador was hinting at

British hypocrisy: 'There is a slight element of psychological strategy by the British here, with a view to hindsight – being able to say that everything was tried.' Increasing attention was being given to the possible role of the Secretary-General; said one UN source: 'He believes that Iraq has been painted into a corner, and needs to be given a rope to get out with ... What if Iraq has in fact painted the Americans into the corner, that Saddam is thinking "I want you to hit me – and at the end of this I will have got the inspectors off my back, and can develop my weapons"?' Perhaps Annan would prove able to negotiate an agreement to save Saddam's face: UNSCOM-plus was the favoured candidate, whereby the usual inspectors could be accompanied by diplomats during visits to sensitive sites; and perhaps the presidential palaces, the *most* sensitive sites, could be treated in a special way. But would the Americans tolerate *any* of the new proposals? In one quoted diplomatic view the British were supporting 'whatever the Americans do, while the Americans try to figure out what they are doing'. In reality the US posture was transparent: the military countdown was running and all the diplomatic efforts were no more than unwelcome distractions from the issue in hand. Now it was obvious that other members of the Security Council, and not just other *Permanent* members, were resenting the US/UK rush to war. Thus Hans Dahlgren, the Swedish UN ambassador, expressed a widespread view when he criticised the US/UK assumption that time was running out: there were several 'diplomatic options' still to be tried and it was right that the Secretary-General was trying to find the basis for a solution. Dahlgren, with others, was insisting that force would not be justified without a new Security Council resolution: 'This is not a conflict between the US and Iraq or even between the coalition and Iraq. It is between the Security Council and Iraq.' It was plain that Washington was exerting massive pressure on Security Council members to agree a new 'force' resolution. The posture of the Permanent Members was well known, but US ambassador Bill Richardson had also approached all ten of the non-permanent members to request (demand?) their support in the Council. Said one diplomatic source: 'There is enormous pressure to toe the line. Every country in the world has a bilateral relationship to worry with the only superpower, the USA.' Again Washington was using blatant coercion in support of its own foreign policy on Iraq. It remained to be seen whether Kofi Annan would be able to counter the momentum of the American juggernaut.

At the height of the crisis the debate over the shape of any 986 enlargement was allowed to continue, with Iraqi complaints over sovereignty and other considerations repeatedly expressed.[20] Turkish violations of Iraqi territory were being repeatedly brought to the attention of the Security Council,[21] and routinely ignored by the United States and other Council members allegedly opposed to violations of national sovereignty. The principal US interest remained the military build-up in the Gulf and the associated 'diplomatic' coercion on other countries to tolerate or support a new bombing campaign against a largely defenceless country. With Kofi Annan now scheduled to visit Baghdad within a few days, the US National Security Advisor Sandy Berger was threatening *'repeated attacks on Iraq'*, declaring that *'the international community is not gonna go away – and what's most important is – the United States is not gonna go away'*.

On 16 February 1998 a statement issued by Secretary-General Kofi Annan noted his talks with the Permanent Members of the Security Council ('We had very constructive discussions for about an hour ... the permanent five are engaged in intensive consultations and have told me they need a little more time to arrive at a conclusion'). On the following day Kofi Annan reported:

> I have had a very constructive meeting this afternoon with Permanent Representatives of the permanent members of the Security Council and subsequently with those of the non-permanent members. I believe I now have a clear basis on which to brief the Security Council tomorrow and prepare to proceed to Baghdad.
>
> An advance team will leave tonight to prepare the ground for my visit. I expect to arrive in Baghdad on Friday, with the support of the entire Security Council, and to conduct discussions this weekend to attempt to resolve the crisis.
>
> It is my hope that we can achieve a diplomatic solution that will ensure the full implementation of all Security Council resolutions.

Any US/UK support for the Annan visit was grudging; despite the optimistic Annan statement it was emerging that the Security Council had not yet achieved a consensual position on the Secretary-General's initiative. While some Council members were prepared to countenance 'negotiation' with Saddam Hussein, Washington and London saw Annan's task as being nothing more than to deliver a final ultimatum: show total compliance, as we two define it, or we bomb.

Kofi Annan had secured Council agreement that he visit Baghdad but the American and British threats continued unabated. President Clinton emphasised yet again that military action was sometimes 'the only answer', while the British Foreign Office was stressing that the planned bombing would be 'devastating'. Polls showed that about two-thirds of Britons and three-quarters of Americans favoured the bombing of Iraq, hardly surprising in view of the endless stream of propaganda in support of 'resolute', 'firm' or 'robust' action against the demonised Saddam. On 17 February the British government won a House of Commons vote backing the use of 'all necessary means' against Iraq with a majority of 468 (some 21 Labour MPs decided to vote against): there was of course no attempt to define 'necessary' and no attempt to define the specific military objectives, rendering the vote a totally absurd charade.

The UN team sent to map the eight 'presidential sites' had now completed its work and would quickly submit a report to Kofi Annan. It seemed clear that in trying to avert the impending war the Secretary-General was facing the toughest task of his diplomatic career. Few observers thought that Saddam Hussein would be likely to back down, and the Americans were plainly hostile to the entire Annan initiative for peace, believing that a military option was now inevitable. Annan was (is) a decent man, thoroughly liked by his staff and with (in one account) ' a surfeit of decency' (in a recent interview he declared himself a natural conciliator, 'but I can be firm when it is necessary ... I'm not one of those who believe that you have to pound the table or shout to be tough'). Was this the man to cajole the Demon King into compliance with humiliating UN resolutions with no real prospect of an end to the genocidal sanctions regime? He had dealt with Baghdad before, having negotiated the repatriation of 900 international staff after the Iraqi invasion of Kuwait in 1990; but in February 1998 few observers doubted that the soft-spoken international diplomat was 'going up against one of the world's wiliest dictators'.[22] The US-led attack on Iraq had been halted, at least for a matter of days, and already Washington was preparing the ground for a rejection of any Annan deal that failed to meet US foreign policy objectives. Thus Bill Richardson, interviewed on ABC Television, declared:

We reserve the right to oppose a potential deal that would harm our national interests ... If Iraq does not comply there are going to be some very, very serious consequences.

Now Washington and London appeared to be working on the assumption that the Annan initiative would fail. Britain, under US tutelage, was preparing a resolution for submission to the Security Council for military authorisation should Saddam fail to comply with all US/UK demands; and the military preparations, despite the delay in the countdown, continued to advertise the imminence of war. By now, some sort of coalition for military strikes had been constructed, with at least an element of support for the United States and Britain being offered by various countries: Kuwait, Turkey, Germany, Spain, Portugal, Czechoslovakia, Italy, Australia, Canada, Denmark, Poland, Argentina, New Zealand, Romania, Norway, Belgium and the Netherlands. Most of the proffered support was trivial but the propagandists of the US/UK axis were keen to stress the political significance of any positive gesture in the international community. This was the thrust of American and British diplomacy throughout this period – not to seek a peaceful solution but to garner as much international support as possible for Gulf War II. Doubtless Iraq was impressed to learn that Tony Blair judged his own posture to be 'right' and 'immovable'; and that the British Defence Secretary George Robertson was again threatening 'very considerable damage' to Saddam Hussein and his military structure. This was the atmosphere being deliberately cultivated by Washington and London as the UN Secretary-General prepared to embark on his peace mission to Baghdad.

On 19 February the Security Council, without the agreement of Iraq, passed a new resolution (1153), designed to expand the terms of Resolution 986. Again there was token acknowledgement of the 'very serious nutritional and health situation' that continued to afflict the civilian population of Iraq, but no hint that the cruel sanctions regime would be terminated in the near future. On the same day, Kofi Annan gave a press conference prior to his departure for Baghdad via Paris. He hoped that Saddam would listen, 'because the alternative is too serious to contemplate'. Would there be room to negotiate? – 'I think I have what I need to undertake these discussions in Baghdad'. Would diplomats accompanying UNSCOM officials be acceptable to the United Nations? – 'I don't want to get into those kinds of details'. And did Kofi Annan feel that he was up to the job? – 'That's a strange question'. When he arrived in Baghdad on 20 February 1998 he declared:

> The last time I was in Baghdad was October 1991, and so it's been a long time. And I am now back in Baghdad on a very important mission. In fact I describe it as a 'sacred duty', and I am here in search of a peaceful solution. I hope that my talks in the next few days will permit me and the Iraqi leadership and President Saddam Hussein, to find a way out of this crisis.
>
> As the Secretary-General, I have an obligation, a juridical and moral obligation, to try and reduce international tensions wherever I can. And this is the purpose of my mission here, and I hope I will leave Baghdad with a package that will be acceptable to all.

Finally Kofi Annan declared himself 'reasonably optimistic' that a peaceful solution would be found.

President Clinton, now on the defensive, continued to insist that the United States would take action if Saddam failed to comply; and he hinted at divisions in American opinion ('I believe it will unite, just as we did in 1991'). British Premier Tony Blair, well aware of the US preference for military action, insisted to Kofi Annan that 'the threat of force is real', and stressed – as if the Secretary-General were a junior message carrier – that there should be no 'fudging' in Baghdad. Both Washington and London were insisting that Kofi Annan would be given the narrowest of briefs with no latitude to negotiate. And after meeting Annan in Paris, President Chirac appeared willing to reflect the US/UK posture: 'I call upon Iraq to accept the proposals of the Secretary-General ... because these are the proposals of the whole international community ... I hope that wisdom and reason will prevail'. But in the midst of all this pressure it seemed that Kofi Annan remained determined to protect his own diplomatic autonomy. He was not going to Baghdad to present Saddam Hussein with an ultimatum – which is what the US/UK axis wanted – but to propose ideas that could block the military option: 'I think I have ideas that I think can get us off the hook if they are accepted'. In Baghdad, vice-president Taha Yassin Ramadan declared that Iraq would work 'very positively' with the Secretary-General, while at the same time some 29 UN staff crossed into Jordan as a precaution against the imminent US bombing campaign.

The US/UK propaganda continued, even on occasions to the point of word-for-word iterations. Saddam was not to be trusted; diplomacy had to be backed by the threat of force; if Saddam did not comply he would be making a 'big mistake'; now the entire international community was in agreement that UN resolutions should be observed (though no mention was made about how little support there was for the use of force); time was running out; all diplomatic avenues had been explored (a manifest lie), etc. When two white supremacists were being held in Las Vegas on 19 February on suspicion of plotting an anthrax-based terrorist attack, efforts were made to link them to Saddam Hussein. (It was later found that the men did not possess anthrax.)[23] The main US/UK ploy, apart from trying to exert maximum pressure on Kofi Annan, was to create a belligerent political atmosphere in which a resort to war would surprise no-one. It seemed clear that Washington and London regarded the Annan visit to Baghdad as an irritating hiccup in the military countdown. Once Annan, having failed in his mission, had left Iraq the preferred American agenda of comprehensive and sustained air strikes could be implemented.

The UN-appointed map-makers had now completed their work and submitted their comprehensive findings (report, 20 February 1998). In a short time the survey had covered eight 'presidential sites' specified by the Iraqi authorities: Republican Palace (Baghdad), Radwaniyah (Baghdad), Sijood (Baghdad), Tikrit, Thartar, Jabal Makhul, Mosul and Basra. Most of the sites were 'extensively over flown' by helicopter and then visited on the ground. Identified buildings included offices for government staff, a headquarters building for the Presidential Battalion, a helicopter pad, two medium-sized helicopter sheds, sentry towers, guard rooms, guesthouses, villas for dignitaries, artificial lakes with small decorative islands, and other items. The surveying team reported total co-operation by the Iraqi authorities: '*The team experienced undisturbed access to all buildings they wished to survey and unrestricted authorization to take photos*'. Both Iraqi and UNSCOM helicopters were used as necessary. It was obvious that the Iraqi authorities had co-operated with the UN surveyors and placed no obstacles in their way; and it was equally plain that Washington now had fresh espionage data concerning Iraqi administrative structures and systems for suitable targeting in the event of war. Washington was still assuming that the Annan initiative could be decried or circumvented once his irritating intervention was at an end.

Even with the hopeful prospect of the Annan talks, the United States was doing nothing to dispel the accumulating war clouds. Now Washington was encouraging the dependants of its diplomats in Kuwait and Israel to leave the region, so fuelling fears that Iraqi attacks with biological and chemical weapons were likely. A senior Western diplomat in Kuwait acknowledged that the US move 'might cause panic', and speculated that other embassies might follow suit. The American families were not being ordered to leave but, once the US authorities had raised the option, 'the government pays their way' if they decided to return home. Other embassies, doubtless influenced by the American move, were already taking steps: for example, the German embassy in Kuwait was offering to ship its families home, while the Spanish and Swiss embassies were distributing gas masks. At the same time much publicity was being given to the 'armada of doom' lying in wait for Saddam in the Gulf.[24] It was clear that Washington was doing everything possible to escalate the crisis and to prepare the international community for the coming conflict.

On 20 February 1998 Kofi Annan, prepared to fulfil what he had called his 'sacred duty', arrived in Baghdad. Thirty more UN aid workers were leaving Iraq as the talks between Annan and the Iraqi authorities began. Later, a UN spokesman declared that the discussions had got off 'to a good start' and that the Secretary-General would be in Baghdad for a few days. In Jordan, Crown Prince Hassan, having held preliminary talks with Annan, expressed his optimism about the final outcome ('We are delighted that the Secretary-General has been able to find the necessary agreement in the Security Council for this mission to be made possible and I echo ... this general hope ... that agreement is possible in Baghdad ...').[25] The Jordanians were now also declaring that a US-led military strike on Iraq would have a devastating effect on the Kingdom's fragile economy. Thus Jawad Anani, deputy prime minister and foreign minister, commented that the direct losses resulting from the launch of Operation Desert Thunder would be 'no less than $600 million per annum, considering only the interruption of Iraqi oil supplies and trade flows'.[26] Richard Butler, the UNSCOM head, continued to foment the mounting tensions by reporting his fears that Iraq still harboured a huge potential armoury of chemical and biological weapons; and if it did not have such frightening stockpiles it would be able to produce them. Again, the well-rehearsed Catch-22: Iraq either had vast numbers of dreadful weapons or, if not, it was able to produce them. President Clinton, for his part, gave every indication that he expected the Annan/Iraqi talks in Baghdad to fail, but pledged that he would kill as few Iraqis as possible: 'If force proves necessary to resolve this crisis, we will do everything we can to prevent innocent people from getting hurt. We have no quarrel with the Iraqi people ...'. In Minneapolis the American UN ambassador Bill Richardson was jeered with chants of 'no blood for oil' as dozens of opponents of military action heckled him at the University of Minnesota (he suggested that the protesters were 'wrong' about Iraq).

In Britain, at the commencement of Kofi Annan's Baghdad talks, security was being tightened at ports to prevent the imagined infiltration of Islamic 'extremists', while some one hundred 'fundamentalists' in Britain reportedly faced detention or deportation.[27] On 20 February British Members of Parliament (Tony Benn and Jeremy Corbyn) were among a number of speakers who addressed a crowd of around two thousand demonstrators in London demanding an end to the US/UK war threats. An English-Iraqi family in Manchester had collected 1000 signatures on a petition for peace, and the parents and their three children presented it to the door of Number 10, Downing Street. Hugh Stephens, the organiser of the protest, stressed the need for further demonstrations in the days ahead.

On 22 February a statement by F. Eckhard, a spokesman for the UN Secretary-General, reported that, following talks with Saddam Hussein, Kofi Annan was 'on the verge of a breakthrough ... The Secretary-General is authorised to enter into an agreement with any Member State which he has done in this case. He has carefully tried to build Security Council support for the parameters within which he feels he has stayed in his talks with the Iraqi authorities these last couple of days. He expects that when he emerges from these talks he will be able to sell them to the Security Council.' Eckhard emphasised that *'substantial progress' had been made and that a deal was 'within reach'*. One can only imagine the bitter frustration in Washington at this news. The vast armada had been assembled and a military countdown begun. Now a UN diplomat was working with evident success to abort American plans involving tens of thousands of personnel and billions of dollars. There was much at stake here. The US strategists, bored by the years-long genocidal sanctions regime, had become excited at the prospect of supplementary modes of destruction and carnage – in the interests of US hegemony, war games, macho posturing, command of Gulf oil, and all the other usual suspects beloved of armchair war planners.[28] All the military hardware was in place, US and UK military personnel were hyped up, Clinton was urging all American citizens to leave Iraq – and now the efforts of the soft-spoken Kofi Annan were puncturing all the macho posturing.

There were hints also that the Baghdad talks were generating tensions in the US/UK axis. The Americans were opposed to the so-called 'UNSCOM-plus-suits' plan, whereby UNSCOM teams would be supplemented by diplomatic personnel when the Iraqi dictator's palaces were inspected: all that interested Washington was a total climbdown by Saddam, unqualified compliance with all the relevant Security Council resolutions. The British, it seemed, were prepared to consider the 'UNSCOM-plus' scheme as a possible route to ending the crisis. And in another area also there seemed to be differences between the American and British positions. Washington saw no need for any further Security Council resolution to justify the substantial bombing campaign that was already planned and under countdown; Britain, by contrast, seemed more interested in the need to secure another resolution and thereby a more impressive demonstration of international support for military strikes on Iraq. It remained highly unlikely that any British reservations would lead to a rupture in the US/UK axis: the British forces in the Gulf, under *de facto* American control, were ready for action.

The United States was now virtually isolated on the world scene. The international support that Washington had managed to garner in no way resembled the Coalition of 1991; a majority (France, China and Russia) of the Permanent Members of the Security Council were opposed to military action; the Arab world refused to be dragooned into support for more bombing; and even Britain was hinting that Annan's plans and a new Council resolution should be considered. Increasingly, it seemed that President Clinton and the Washington war planners were ranged not only against Saddam Hussein but also against the world. In one summary: 'The coalition of 1991 is non-existent; the UN is sceptical and there are even deep misgivings on the British side ... The Arab frontline states are reticent. The usually foursquare Secretary of State, Madeleine Albright, faltered visibly at last week's global "town meeting" when asked by a lowly student: "Why are we preparing to hit Iraq, when Iraq's neighbours don't want it?"' And Clinton himself, beset by sexual scandal, seemed increasingly isolated in Washington: *'White House aides spoke last week of a President who is ever more aloof, even from his own inner sanctum – a man setting out to war from what increasingly resembles a stockade of his own.'*[29]

In the early hours of 22 February a third round of talks ended in Baghdad, with no final agreement and the Annan team now saying that it was 'not confident' that the differences between the two sides could be resolved. The official Iraqi News Agency was describing the talks as difficult, and uncertainties remained whether Kofi Annan would have a chance to talk directly to Saddam Hussein. Reports were now emerging of the offers that Annan had been making to the Iraqi negotiators. The formula included three principal elements:

- An explicit public pledge that sanctions would be lifted once the UN inspectors were satisfied that the country had been cleared of weapons of mass destruction;

- Concessions to Saddam's demand that diplomats might join inspection teams when 'sensitive sites' such as presidential palaces were examined (but with the 'once-only' inspection demand rejected);

• Agreement to a wider range of nationalities on the inspection teams, while not conceding any right to Iraq to veto the ultimate UNSCOM right to choose personnel.

It was also being suggested that the United Nations would be prepared to elaborate on a far more specific timetable than hitherto offered for concluding the inspections and the sanctions regime. In addition, the UNSCOM inspectors would be prepared to 'check off' each of the four sectors (missiles, nuclear, biological and chemical) one by one, once they were completed. And a distinction would be made, for purposes of inspection, between the large presidential compounds and the palace residential areas. Already it seemed that Kofi Annan had won from the Security Council a degree of scope for negotiation that went far beyond what Washington had declared it was prepared to accept. In the event, the final agreement, insofar as it was placed in the public domain, lacked many of the features that had seemingly induced Iraq to compromise.

On 23 February 1998 Secretary-General Kofi Annan and the Iraqi deputy prime minister Tariq Aziz gave a joint press conference in Baghdad. Here Kofi Annan claimed to 'have concluded an agreement with the Government of Iraq on the issue of the United Nations weapons inspections' (see *Press Conference – Extracts*, Appendix VI). It seemed that Kofi Annan had achieved a 'diplomatic coup' in Baghdad:[30] 'If he has done so, the United Nations Secretary-General, who appears to have played his hand firmly, will deserve congratulations. It is what one would expect from an impressive public servant who has the confidence of both the Americans and the Iraqis. His last-ditch mission would seem to have saved the Gulf from an immediate prospect of renewed fighting'.[31] There would nonetheless be 'other crises'; it would still be necessary for the allies to curb 'Saddam's murderous ambitions'. The talks had lasted for three days, culminating in a three-hour session between Kofi Annan and Saddam Hussein. Clinton and Blair, manifestly frustrated by Annan's seeming triumph, signalled that they were withholding judgement until they had seen the details of the proposals; and already Madeleine Albright was preparing the ground for a rejection of Kofi Annan's wishes and recommendations: 'It is possible that he will come back with something we do not like, in which case we will proceed in the national interest' (it was, she declared, 'really premature' to talk about what Annan had negotiated). All that interested Washington was that Saddam be seen to back down (that is, he be publicly humiliated in the face of US military threats that violated the UN Charter).

The American discomfiture at what seemed like an agreed peace deal was manifest. Senior politicians in Congress, quick to denigrate Annan's efforts, were soon calling not for an end to the American military threats but for an escalation of them and for the overthrow of the Iraqi dictator; and, in such a view, a comprehensive bombing campaign might need to be supplemented by the use of ground troops. All the efforts of the UN Secretary-General in Baghdad had served to infuriate senior US politicians from both the main parties. Even such respected 'moderates' as the Democrat Senator John Kerry and the Republican John McCain were calling for action, reflecting the widespread congressional view that President Clinton had surrendered American foreign policy to the United Nations. Declared Kerry: 'We've got to be prepared to go the full distance. I believe it is worth fighting for on the ground'; and McCain echoed the general congressional attitude: 'I'm very nervous about all this talk of Kofi Annan selling a deal to the Security Council. America is subordinating its power to the UN, but it is not the UN's young people whose life will be on the line'. At the same time, despite the misgivings, it seemed likely that the Congress, if asked by Clinton for a resolution on Iraq, would rally to the Commander-in-Chief.[32]

The American military build-up in the Gulf was still continuing, with commentators suggesting that Saddam had again found 'victory in defeat';[33] and that the United States was 'losing battle after winning war'.[34] The 1991 Coalition was in ruins; much of the world had openly declared against military action; massive publicity had been given to the suffering of the Iraqi people under US-led sanctions; and the United States had emerged as a blustering bully, with Iraq seen in the unlikely role of victim. In Washington, Madeleine Albright was heckled by protesters chanting: '1-2-3-4, we don't want no racist war', reminiscent of the Vietnam protests staged thirty years before. As Bill and Hillary Clinton left the Foundry United Methodist Church in Washington on 22 February, demonstrators chanted 'Bill Clinton, shame on you' and waved signs saying 'Drop the sanctions, not the bombs'. The Americans were continuing to hedge on the Annan deal; in the Gulf the dozens of US ships and hundreds of aircraft remained ready for action, doubtless tended by thousands of hyped-up and frustrated young Americans who had been told that they were about to strike a blow with 'the sword of freedom'.

Now US politicians and pundits were 'gnashing their teeth'[35] at the Annan deal with Saddam Hussein (Republican Trent Lott: *'This is another example of how the Administration's foreign policy is subcontracted to others. I told Defense Secretary William Cohen ... I was worried that this initiative by Annan was going to put the President in a box, and that's exactly what's happened ... He's in a very difficult position now to say: "Oh no! This is not good enough"'*.[36] In the same vein, Larry Korb, a former assistant defense secretary, commented with regret that the deal now made it impossible for Clinton to launch bombing strikes: *'That's why the US didn't want Annan to go, but Washington has been saying it's a UN dispute so there was no way to stop it. Once you do that, you have given up control of your destiny.'* The former CIA director James Woolsey dubbed Clinton's foreign policy 'flaccid' and said that Saddam 'lies and kills' and would 'almost certainly renege' on the deal. At the same time the *New York Post* was carrying the headline 'Deal With the Devil'; with the *Weekly Standard* magazine calling for a 'serious, substantial and sustained' attack on Iraq as a first step to ousting Saddam ('A fig-leaf compromise brokered by the UN would be disastrous'). Few in Washington believed that the Annan deal was to be applauded, assuming that it merely delayed the time when the United States would have to take military action. Already Clinton had spent an extra $1 billion enlarging the forces in the Gulf and expected to spend several billions more before the crisis was over. The common Washington perception was that Clinton had failed to build and sustain diplomatic and political support for a robust American foreign policy. The US forces remained on alert in the Gulf but the Clinton Administration seemed uncertain what to do with them: all the psychological preparation for war, all the macho posturing, was now deflated. On 23 February Clinton signalled that he would 'tentatively' accept the Annan agreement, while maintaining the military presence in the Gulf (in London the supine echo was soon heard). British and American forces would remain in the Gulf until ministers were '100 per cent sure' that Iraq was allowing free and unfettered access to all the suspect sites.

The main points of the agreement had now reached the public domain (Figure 6.1). There was little of substance in the agreement that Iraq could represent as a real improvement in its position. UNSCOM would be under pressure to be more sensitive to Iraqi feelings, and Kofi Annan had agreed to bring the issue of sanctions to the attention of the Security Council (as if this gesture would make any difference to American obduracy). For the rest, apart from the fig-leaf of a diplomatic accompaniment to the inspectors, UNSCOM had been granted free and unfettered access to all the sensitive sites. There was clearly enough in this for US/UK propagandists to represent the agreement as a complete climbdown by Saddam, but Washington's real concern was elsewhere: *the plans had been laid for war, and now the opportunity for war – at least in the immediate future – had been removed.* This was the stark fact that was causing such agitation and dismay in Washington. The military planners had begun their countdown, with Clinton, suitably distracted by sexual scandal, now converted into an effete bystander who could be pressured into authorising war at the proper time.

In Iraq an official day of celebration was declared to mark a historic victory over the United States; and again there was widespread speculation, in the Arab world and beyond, that the US/UK axis had succeeded in transforming Saddam Hussein into a new Gamal Abdul Nasser, the undefeated 'Leader of all the Arabs'. Was this the fruit of all the high-level political machinations in Washington and London? It seemed ironic that the vast American armada, supplemented by a puny British presence and designed to intimidate any potential foe, had succeeded in offering the Iraqi dictator a singular political

- Iraq reconfirmed its acceptance of all the relevant UN resolutions and reiterated its undertaking to co-operate fully with UNSCOM and the IAEA;

- The UN reiterated its commitment to respect the sovereignty and territorial integrity of Iraq;

- Iraq agreed to allow UNSCOM and the IAEA immediate, unconditional and unrestricted access. UNSCOM agreed to respect Iraq's national security, sovereignty and dignity;

- The UN and Iraq agreed that with respect to the eight presidential sites the inspection group will include UNSCOM and IAEA experts, and also diplomats appointed by the UN Secretary-General;

- The UN and Iraq agreed that all other areas, facilities, equipment, records and means of transportation shall be subject to existing UNSCOM procedures;

- The UN and Iraq agreed to improve co-operation and efficiency, effectiveness and transparency of work;

- The Secretary-General agreed to highlight the lifting of sanctions.

Figure 6.1   Main elements in the agreement between Kofi Annan and Iraq

victory. Kofi Annan had promised Iraq that there would be 'light at the end of the tunnel', but this was scarcely within his gift: the Americans, outraged at the frustration of their military designs, would now be even less likely to grant a reprieve to the suffering Iraqi civilians. Iraq had not achieved any promise that the cruel sanctions would be ended in the near future.

Kofi Annan returned to the UN headquarters in Washington on 24 February to be given a hero's welcome. Here, yet again, he showed himself to be a master of diplomacy. Addressing President Rosemarie Waters (of the UN Staff Union), colleagues and friends, he declared himself 'really touched by this warm and wonderful demonstration of your affection and faith in what I am trying to do', but emphasised that he had not done it alone ('Lots of people made contribution to this and made its success possible'). Annan began by thanking President Clinton and Prime Minister Blair 'for being perfect UN peacekeepers … in the sense that we taught our peacekeepers that the best way to use force is to show it in order not to use it' – an ironic comment in view of the bitter opposition shown in Washington to the entire Annan initiative and the final agreement. In an address frequently punctuated by applause the Secretary-General variously praised President Yeltsin, the Russian foreign minister Primakov, President Chirac, the President of

Qatar, the Canadian government, President Mubarak of Egypt, King Hussein of Jordan, the Qatari foreign minister, the Turkish foreign minister, and the many others who wrote to him. He noted that the Pope had pleaded with him 'to do something'; and there were of course 'you, my colleagues who were rooting and supporting me' (again, applause). He concluded by affirming the role and power of 'the United Nations of "We the Peoples"' (the opening words of the preamble to the UN Charter):

There were millions of people around the world rooting for a peaceful solution and praying for us – this is why in Baghdad I said you should never underestimate the power of prayer.

[*applause*]

This is a wonderful example of what the United Nations should be like.

[*applause*]

When I talk of the United Nations I am not talking only of the staff and those of us in this building. I am talking of the United Nations of 'We the Peoples'. When we pull together from across the world and work together to solve a problem, we almost always can do it.

[*applause*]

On these crises, when the world comes together, things happen. Together we are the ultimate power. If we pull our efforts together we can get almost everything done. All of us around the world – 'We the Peoples'.

So, I want to thank all those who supported, who rooted, who prayed for this to happen. I think we have a good agreement, an agreement that I will defend anywhere, and I am sure that the Member States would accept it.

About ten days ago in an interview with the BBC I said, to solve this problem we need courage, wisdom and flexibility. In the past few days these qualities have been very much on display.

I want to thank you. I am home and it is really wonderful to see you.

[*applause*]

Washington and London, less than impressed, were still threatening to use force: they had not assembled a massive armada for nothing. President Clinton was saying that force was still an option and Britain's Tony Blair, keen to demonstrate his toughness, was threatening 'the most severe consequences' for Iraq (presumably to be delivered by the United States) if Saddam failed to live up to the agreement: a 'piece of paper' signed by the Iraqi regime was not enough – 'The Saddam Hussein we face today is the same Saddam Hussein we faced yesterday. He has not changed. He remains an evil, brutal dictator … There will be no immediate change in the readiness of British or US armed forces in the Gulf …' Now there were suggestions that the American forces might have to stay camped around Iraq 'for good', watching for any signs that he was reneging on his promises or threatening his neighbours. It seemed ironic that Washington continued to voice the worries of Saddam's neighbours when the neighbours themselves seemed relatively unperturbed.

The US/UK axis was now working to win a Security Council commitment that rapid air strikes would follow any Iraqi reneging on the agreement. It seemed clear that Washington had been forced to abandon any pretence that it *already* had sufficient UN authorisation to launch air attacks whenever it felt like it. There was now general consensus that a new Security Council resolution would be necessary before the US/UK could legitimately go to war. But here there were fresh problems. If Russia, France and China, as the other three Permanent Members of the Council, had opposed a fresh war only a matter of days ago, would they be likely to sanction a new war if the manifestly anti-Iraq Richard Butler suddenly declared that an Iraqi official had been rude to him? Britain, with its great literary tradition, was busy as the usual US proxy drafting a suitable resolution. But precisely what words could at once win the acquiescence of all the Permanent Members and allow Washington to drop bombs if the mood took it. Many diplomats remembered how the 1990 Resolution 678, carrying the phrase 'all necessary means', had provided nominal UN sanction for a genocidal war. Were they prepared to agree another contrived phrase that would enable the United States to launch another war in 1998?

Soon the Western propagandists were beginning to suggest that Saddam Hussein was reneging on the agreement.[37] No emphasis was given to the massive degree of co-operation that the Iraqi authorities had shown to UNSCOM staff, despite many provocations, over years; or to such minor details as continuing American, British and Russian research into nuclear and biological weapons of mass destruction.[38] The new staffing structure for the UNSCOM inspections had been published (Figure 6.2) but had done little to assuage US/UK doubts about the value of the agreement. Pundits continued to speculate on whether Saddam was 'winning' and American critics lost no opportunity to decry Annan's work (he commented that the Security Council, rather than 'a few critics', would have the last word on the deal). Washington and Britain continued to press for a Council resolution that would open the way for a bombing campaign at the slightest excuse. Richard Butler continued to disparage the degree of Iraqi co-operation with the UNSCOM teams, citing technical evaluation reports indicating that there was still much to be discovered about the Iraqi weapons programme.[39] In turn, the Iraqis continued to criticise the fairness of the UNSCOM and technical reports.[40]

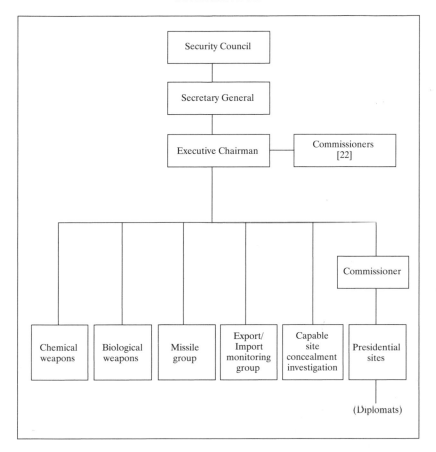

Figure 6.2   UNSCOM staffing structure deriving from UN/Iraqi agreement

King Hussein of Jordan was now suggesting that President Clinton should enter into direct talks with Saddam Hussein to end the differences between the two countries – a radical suggestion for a US president interested only in preparing the ground for a fresh war. On 27 February the Jordanian deputy prime minister Jawad Anani, attending a press conference with the Turkish foreign minister Ismail Cem, noted that Jordan and Turkey favoured lifting the sanctions on Iraq (it was time for 'a light at the end of the tunnel') and suggested that the degree of Iraqi compliance with UN resolutions should be measured. The United States, Anani implied, had no interest in a constructive solution to the continuing crisis: '*The US wants the Security Council to issue a resolution that gives them the automatic ability to strike Iraq in the name of the UN.*' But, he added, 'the world community does not believe in' that method: 'There must be clear-cut criteria, and an objective party which will determine whether there was a breach of the UN resolutions or not.' At the same time Anani welcomed a Turkish initiative aimed at enhancing Baghdad's ties with its neighbours in order to pave the way for a lifting of sanctions. The United States, with predictable British support, was now pressing for the specific Council resolution – to include a so-called 'material breach' clause that would authorise an instant American bombing campaign if any Iraqi derelictions were evident.[41] On 27 February Britain submitted a draft of the resolution in question, including words warning Iraq of 'very severe consequences' should it violate its commitment to allow UN arms inspectors to do their work in a free and unfettered way ('very severe...' was reportedly toned down from 'the severest...', under pressure from members outside the US/UK axis).

The pedantry or hidden agendas behind the new Security Council resolution were doing nothing to deflate the triumphalism now increasingly manifest in Iraq. The *al-Thawra* newspaper, the Baath Party mouthpiece in Baghdad, spoke of Iraq's '*historic political victory*', of how '*arrogant American imperialism had been vanquished*'. Washington was succeeding in uniting many disparate Arab elements into an increasingly vocal anti-US force: Saddam's picture was evident everywhere, with violent anti-US demonstrations taking place in the Palestinian territories, Jordan and many other parts of the Middle East. The US/Iraqi crisis, in conjunction with the stalled Arab/Israeli peace talks, was rapidly eroding any residual American influence in the region: the United States was nothing more than an alien bully pursuing its own perceived national interest. Said the US-educated lawyer Muhammad Aziz Shukri, head of international law at Damascus University: 'American policymakers are not aware of the state of uneasiness in the Middle East'; if America were to launch military attacks against Iraq now, the United States 'might as well wipe its name away as a superpower with any credibility in the Middle East'. Against this tumultuous background the purblind war planners in Washington and London continued to make their preparations for war, assuming that the rest of the international community could be persuaded to adopt their blinkered and callous view of the enduring crisis.

In early March 1998 it emerged that Richard Butler had almost been fired by Kofi Annan at the height of the UN confrontation with Baghdad. There were even suggestions that the Secretary-General was sympathetic to descriptions of some of UNSCOM staff as 'cowboys', intemperate and poorly disciplined. A senior diplomatic source was quoted: 'Butler is almost out of a job. He had better shape up or he will find himself tending municipal gardens in Perth.' The UNSCOM role was necessarily intrusive but Butler had often behaved in an unnecessarily provocative way. For example, when he wrongly asserted that Baghdad had biological weapons capable of 'blowing away Tel Aviv', he was reprimanded by Annan and forced to make a written apology to the Security Council.[42] Diplomats in Baghdad had themselves described the behaviour of some UNSCOM personnel as 'obnoxious and a disgrace', commenting: 'They behave like an occupation force, shouting in public, leering at women and drinking'. Furthermore they describe the humanitarian staff derogatively as 'bunny huggers' who help the SIPs ('starving Iraqi people'). Denis Halliday, the humanitarian co-ordinator, was sufficiently appalled by the attitudes of UNSCOM workers that he took the unusual step of removing all black UN identification stickers from the sides of his vehicles so that no-one would suspect his staff to be UNSCOM personnel.[43]

Washington and London were now making progress with the new UN resolution designed to authorise bombing strikes in the event of Iraqi derelictions. Amir Rasheed, the Iraqi oil minister, accused the United States and Britain of trying to sabotage the peace deal by introducing a new provocative resolution to the Security Council: 'This move by the British administration, supported by the American administration, is totally unnecessary. They are doing it for a purely political agenda which they have against Iraq ... They want to undermine the sovereignty of Iraq, they want to break Iraq, they want to control the oil fields.' In the event the Security Council passed Resolution 1154 on 2 March 1998, stressing the importance of Iraqi compliance and emphasising 'that any violation' of the agreement 'would have severest consequences for Iraq' (see Appendix VII). But even this resolution, giving Washington the option to punish Baghdad on American whim, was insufficient for many of the hawkish critics of the Annan deal. Senator McCain declared that the American goal should be to 'remove' Saddam from power, even though this might cause Iraq 'to fragment into three parts'; Senator Arlen Specter suggested that Saddam should be brought before the war crimes tribunal in The Hague; Senator Bob Kerry said that the UNSCOM teams were unlikely to work effectively as long as Saddam was in power ('We've got to try to replace this dictatorship with a democracy'); and Trent Lott, the Republican leader in the Senate, declared that it was not too late to reject the Annan deal 'if it leaves Saddam Hussein rejoicing'. Kofi Annan said that such scepticism about the agreement was 'unfortunate', and he accused Senate leaders of being ignorant of 'all the facts'. To *Time* magazine he commented: '*I don't know what is driving some of the statements coming out of Washington. I hope this agreement will hold, and we are going to test it ... it should become clear in the next three to six months whether it is going to work.*'

The agreement, whatever its merits, had done nothing in practical terms to address the issue of sanctions, the most pressing concern of the Iraqi people. Kofi Annan had pledged to raise the matter in the Security Council but the

American response to such an initiative was predictable: there would be no relief for a diseased and starving people. A slow parade of cars, each bearing the coffin of a dead baby, had given a graphic illustration in Baghdad of the anguish of the civilian population (*Time*, 2 March 1998). This grim 'Parade of the Dead Babies', involving 57 vehicles, was accompanied by weeping marchers, angry and bitter at what was being perpetrated by the United States. One woman shouted: 'Our babies die because of you. We need peace and milk, not war'; asked another: 'Why do Americans only want war? We have nothing left. We cannot hurt you. But you still want to kill us.'

The policy-makers in Washington and London knew the consequences of the economic embargo, and the fact that it was killing hundreds of thousands of innocent Iraqis without hitting the regime (said one Western official: 'It is a failure, but it's the best failure we have'). Denis Halliday, the UN human-itarian co-ordinator (one of what the UNSCOM staff called a 'bunny hugger'), commented: 'You have generations of young Iraqis coming up, some of whom have these nutritional difficulties, others are at schools where the system has collapsed. There's a huge potential for young people not being able to grow into useful citizens'; and even increased rations were no longer an adequate answer to the desperate needs of the children: 'That would require a significant focus on infants, on potable water, proper feeding techniques and so on.' A generation of young people, if they survived at all, was being conditioned by the horrendous deprivations imposed by the sanc-tions regime: 'There is a tremendous isolation of these people who are going to be the leaders of this country'. The United States was sowing the seeds of massive regional dislocations for future generations.

Washington and London, indifferent to the deliberately-induced plight of the Iraqi civilian population, was now mainly concerned to test the new agreement. Could any Baghdad dereliction be discerned that would allow 'the severest consequences' (as specified in Resolution 1154) to be inflicted on an already suffering population? The Security Council had reached its uneasy consensus on the resolution that again threatened Iraq; British troops in the Gulf were now being offered anthrax jabs – as a propaganda stunt rather than any practical precaution; and Clinton was insisting, against the interpretation offered by other Permanent Members of the Security Council, that Resolution 1154 gave the United States all the authority it needed to launch a new bombing campaign against Iraq: *'No promise of peace and no promise of patience can be without its limits'* (Bill Richardson, the United States UN ambassador, said *the resolution gave 'a green light'* for bombing if necessary). Washington had secured its 'force' resolution, just as the ambigu-ities of Resolution 678 had provided spurious justification for war in 1991. Thus James Rubin, a State Department spokesman, said that Washington interpreted the resolution as containing *'clear diplomatic code words for military action'* (Richardson: *'This is a victory for us'*).

The Annan agreement had succeeded in blocking the American count-down to military action (in the words of one satirical commentator: 'The bastard! He's nicked our war!'). But the United States had responded quickly by securing a unanimous vote in the Security Council for a resolution (Appendix VII) that gave Washington, against international opinion, the excuse for a fresh bombing campaign. Now the United States was bitter at what politicians and pundits saw as the suborning by the United Nations of American foreign policy. It remained to be seen just how long the Washington war planners would be able to tolerate the 'sell-out' by Kofi Annan and the 'triumph of Saddam' (*The Daily Telegraph*, London, 5 March 1998). The recent countdown to war had been aborted. How long before it was again set in train?

THE AFTERMATH

After the conclusion of the Annan deal the international political climate was uncertain: there were still obvious tensions but the sense of crisis was over. Few observers doubted that a new crisis might erupt at any time, fuelled by Iraqi machinations and the enduring belligerence of the United States. There was still no consensus in the international community on what action should follow obvious Iraqi derelictions regarding the new agreement. The UN Security Council remained deeply split: Washington and Britain continued to maintain that Resolution 1154 provided a UN authorisation for war, but France, China, Russia and other members of the Security Council disagreed. On 4 March 1998 France refused to endorse a North Atlantic Treaty Organisation (NATO) statement backing the new Security Council resolution: France had voted for 1154 but objected to NATO endorsement since the Iraq crisis clearly lay outside the alliance's theatre of operations. One diplomat commented: 'The French felt that the UN resolution spoke for itself and thus issuing this statement from NATO was inconsistent with NATO's position on Iraq.' Again the serious divisions in the international position on the Iraq Question were highlighted.

The Iraqi people continued to suffer. There had been no relaxation of the sanctions regime, with informed opinion acknowledging the ineffectiveness of Resolution 986 and the subsequent supporting decisions of the Security Council. As only one index among dozens, an oncologist's office in a Basra hospital displayed maps showing a massive increase of cancer incidence in southern Iraq.[44] Now thousands of children were dying in Iraqi hospitals because the sanctions regime was blocking their access to essential drugs.[45] The years-long genocide was continuing and Washington was ready to launch a bombing campaign if the Iraqis complained too loudly. A group of academics writing in *The Independent* (London, 6 March 1998) denounced the sanctions regime as 'indefensible' – '*Allowing the people of Iraq to suffer malnutrition and poor health is like refusing food and medicine to the passengers in a hijacked plane.*' Commented the celebrated English journalist Robert Fisk: 'Iraq's children are going through hell.' This was (is) the grim reality behind all the strategic pedantry of Clinton, Blair, Albright, Butler *inter alia*.

On 4 March the Campaign Against Sanctions and War on Iraq (CASWI) was launched in London with the support of academics, trades unionists, peace campaigners, youth representatives, and representatives of the Arab, Mauritian, Bangladeshi and Pakistani communities living in Britain; with messages of support received from campaigning groups in the United States, Italy, France, Spain and Greece. At the same time the Iraqi authorities were continuing to complain about the behaviour of UNSCOM staff. Thus Mohammed Said Al-Sahaf, the Iraqi foreign minister, declared in a letter addressed to the UN Secretary-General:

> ... we have, on many occasions ... reported ... the manner in which some officers and members of the Special Commission have contravened the legal and professional rules governing their conduct. They have behaved in a manner inconsistent with their professional duties by making public information that they had obtained while carrying out those duties, and by using such information in a selective manner in order to promote their personal views by revealing it to the press ... we have yet to see any disciplinary measures being taken ...'[46]

Material collected by UNSCOM staff was shown on a CNN programme ('High Noon in Baghdad – the Inspectors' Story', 1 March 1998), even though such material was the confidential property of the United Nations ('It should not be used without authorization for purposes of propaganda ... Was the use ... authorized? ... if so, by whom? ... Are [UNSCOM] officials permitted to behave in a manner which contravenes the legal agreements with the United Nations to which Iraq is bound, and which govern their legal position?'[47]). Despite such provocations Iraq was reportedly observing the stringent terms of the Annan deal. On 6 March Scott Ritter made 'surprise visits' to suspect sites without incident.[48] (In October 1998 Ritter confirmed Iraqi charges that he was a US spy by admitting he had visited Israel 'many times' for intelligence purposes – see Robert Fisk, *The Independent*, 6 November 1998.)

A press briefing (9 March) provided a few details about the activities of Prakesh Shah, the Secretary-General's special envoy for Iraq (he did not believe that his work would conflict with that of Richard Butler who 'had his own job as head of UNSCOM, which had been functioning for several years', but he avoided direct questions about his relationship with Butler). Soon, said Prakesh Shah, he would be setting up his own office in Baghdad. On the same day Kofi Annan published details of the procedures that had now been established in accordance with the Memorandum of Understanding signed on 23 February between the United Nations and the Iraqi government (these details represented an enlargement of the terms already set out, see Figure 6.1). The new provisions (see Appendix VIII) indicated, above all, Annan's view that Iraqi sensitivities should be considered, and that new checks and balances were required to improve the effectiveness of the UNSCOM work.

At the same time Madeleine Albright was facing angry protests on her arrival in London for talks with Foreign Secretary Robin Cook. Albright and Cook stood in embarrassed silence before the international press 'photo opportunity' while slogans were chanted against the US/UK war threats and support for sanctions. And then, in their clear hearing, they heard Hugh Stephens, the CASWI Co-ordinator, address them with a statement that included the words:

> Madeleine Albright first made her mark upon world public opinion by remarking that the death of more than half a million children in Iraq is 'worth it' to control the region. What irony that someone who utters such sentiments about children dying in their mothers' arms for lack of medicine and nutrition should arrive for talks on the day following International Women's Day![49]

The statement also emphasised the US/UK violations of international law and the willingness of Washington and London to perform criminal acts in furtherance of their 'national interests'.

The feeling of crisis had largely dissipated but no observer imagined that a new crisis could not flare up in a matter of hours: Washington was still waiting for its chance to bomb. The possibility of increased Iraqi oil production, under fresh UN terms, was predictably affecting the international markets; in London, CASWI was celebrating growing support; revelations that several Iraqis who had worked with the American CIA were probably double agents feeding information to Saddam were not improving US morale;[50] and Richard Butler was emphasising in a press briefing (13 March) that UNSCOM still 'had a long way to go' before Iraq could be pronounced clear of weapons of mass destruction. The inspections of the presidential palaces, under the terms of the Annan agreement, were expected to begin by the end of March; while the American and British deployments in the Gulf were being maintained in a state of readiness (there were reports of 'attempted self-harm' and suicide on HMS *Invincible*).[51] CASWI was continuing to emphasise the illegal posture adopted by Washington and London: *'The statements of Clinton, Blair and other US and British representatives that they would be prepared to attack Iraq without UN authorisation have amounted to statements of criminal intent to carry out aggression. Their claim that US and British "national interests" could justify such aggression challenges not only the authority of the United Nations but the entire conception of international legality.'* At the same time Washington was increasingly worried by the growing reputation of Kofi Annan. The UN Secretary-General was not supposed to pursue an independent line in the interest of world peace: he was supposed to function as a *de facto* minion in the US State Department, bowing to American pressure and always keenly sensitive to US national interest. Boutros Boutros-Ghali had bitterly learnt the penalty of straying 'off message'. Now Kofi Annan had the temerity to pursue an independent policy in the interest of global harmony. This was a very distressing development for the Washington strategists.

Richard Butler (acknowledged by one source to be 'a bit of a bull in a china shop')[52] was back in Baghdad – and determined not to sound optimistic. The Iraqi authorities, for their part, seemed prepared to contain their loathing for the man they had dubbed 'a mad dog' (though it appeared that they were not averse to spying on UNSCOM members).[53] But even Butler, now under unprecedented pressure from Kofi Annan, was being forced to admit the substantial degree of Iraqi co-operation following the new agreement: 'We are being shown a new degree of co-operation. I welcome it. I hope it continues. If it does we can do our part of this job ... without the passage of too much time'. And a Western source commented that while Butler was continuing to say that 'there are weapons there', the Iraqis were opening the door and saying, 'Be my guest'; so 'the race is on'. Now the UNSCOM inspectors would be accompanied by a 20-strong multinational panel appointed by Jayantha Dhanapala, a former Sri Lankan UN envoy and now Kofi Annan's representative. His involvement and that of Prakesh Shah pointed to a clear dilution in the authority of Richard Butler: the political partisanship and operational insensitivity of the UNSCOM teams over the years was now being advertised, even if only by implication. It was not long before Dhanapala was reporting that he had been given 'very strong assurances' that Iraq would honour the letter and spirit of the Annan agreement.

The Western propagandists, dismayed that the agreement seemed to be holding, then launched a fresh anthrax scare – anything to sour the political atmosphere and sabotage the Annan deal. We were suddenly informed by *The Sun* (24 March 1998), a London tabloid of poor repute, in a 'world exclusive', of a fiendish new Iraqi plot: 'SADDAM'S ANTHRAX IN OUR DUTY FREES' – 'Saddam Hussein is plotting to flood Britain with deadly anthrax disguised as duty-free goods'. What a 'chilling threat' this was, since a mere teaspoonful of anthrax, we were told, could wipe out 100 million people. A source 'believed to have access to intelligence in Baghdad' had unearthed the diabolical scheme: 'Iraq may launch a chemical and biological attack using material disguised as harmless fluids' (such as perfume sprays, cosmetics and bottles of spirits). It was heartening to learn that an 'all-ports alert' had gone out, presumably in the hope that our stalwart British customs officials, biochemists all, could immediately spot the dreaded anthrax spores (not to mention various toxic chemicals skilfully inserted into the perfume sprays).[54] The risible absurdity of this new piece of black propaganda (had Saddam now abandoned his 'doomsday' propeller-driven crop-sprayer?) struck even the British government. On 23 March Mike O'Brien, a Home Office minister, denied there was cause for alarm (what? with Britain confronted with a teaspoonful of anthrax that could kill 100 million people?): 'There is no specific threat so far as we can gather to Britain.' Home Secretary Jack Straw conceded that there was 'no evidence'.[55] And amused journalists were quick to talk about 'nonsense' and 'planted stories'.[56] Two respected journalists commented: 'There is no current information ... to suggest that Iraq is contemplating a terrorist campaign against western targets ... Defectors and Iraqi opposition groups have an interest in exaggerating the threat posed by Saddam. Ministers may share the same interest ... Exaggerated reports, more sceptical officials admitted yesterday, were self-defeating'.[57]*

The many smears and scares, planted in fertile ground in view of the undeniable brutality of the Saddam regime, had accumulated over the years and worked to aid the comprehensive demonisation of the Iraqi dictator and to feed the tensions in the region. Oil prices and the state of the arms industries continued to be affected by the vagaries of the Iraq Question; and Washington and London were doing what they could to keep alive the war option as a response to perceived Iraqi derelictions. But not all was going well with the efforts of the US/UK axis. On 26 March it was reported that HMS *Illustrious* would soon be withdrawn from the Gulf because its Harrier aircraft could not cope with the heat.[58] And it emerged also that the CIA had bungled an attempt to smuggle Nasser el-Hindawi, the founder of Iraq's germ warfare programme, out of the country. The practical efforts of the Americans and British to maintain control of the Iraq situation appeared fraught with problems: there was no international consensus for future action; and Iraq, seemingly in full compliance with the terms of the Annan agreement, was consolidating its emerging image as a victim of traditional

---

* Few commentators remembered or bothered to point out that the European Union (EU) had declared its intention to abolish duty-free shopping, a statement that had caused a 24-hour blockade of Calais and Boulogne by French ferry and dock workers If duty-free shopping could be artificially depressed, abolition might be easier. It is easy to see how the anti-Saddam anthrax scare could have been designed for a dual purpose. Paul Marston, 'Duty-free protest hits ferries', *The Daily Telegraph*, London, 20 March 1998; Stephen Bates and Keith Harper, 'Last orders', *The Guardian*, London, 19 March 1998).

American imperialism. UNSCOM inspectors, accompanied by foreign diplomats and Iraqi minders, were inspecting the first of the formerly-banned presidential compounds (without having given prior warning to the Iraqi authorities). Richard Butler was continuing to imply that there would be no early end to the inspections. In a letter dated 27 March 1998 he declared that he would visit Baghdad again in June 'in order to review the progress of the work in the various weapons areas'.[59] There was no urgency; the genocidal sanctions regime was still in place; the tens of thousands of Iraqi children would continue to starve to death.

The recent anthrax scare had died a natural death. The English journalist Auberon Waugh had well conveyed the derisory character of the government propaganda. How were 'these good Customs officers' going to detect the toxic germs? By squirting a perfume spray in the air' and having a sniff?' Waugh knew the score: 'Rage and frustration greeted the news that Saddam had agreed to inspection of the personal collection of weapons of mass destruction held in his private palaces. So it was necessary to raise a new scare, releasing this slightly preposterous document about duty-free anthrax bacteria'.[60] And the plausibility of the scare story had not been helped by reports that anthrax had been found in the walls and ceilings of London's King's Cross station.[61] The response of Felicity Arbuthnot, one of the foremost Western experts on Iraq, deserves to be quoted in full (*The Guardian*, 7 April 1998):

> Did I dream it, or did we nearly go to war with Iraq recently? And was not a reason for this that Iraq might have enough anthrax to wipe out whole cities? And were we not told by various Government spokespeople that a tiny vial of the substance could decimate the 'entire population' of London?
>
> Such anxiety was promoted despite the fact that the growth medium essential to produce anthrax was sold to Iraq by a British subsidiary of Unilever as recently as 1994.
>
> Now we hear that a large area of Kings Cross station is contaminated with anthrax. The substance has been lying around in the station's recesses for 150 years. But, we were told by a spokesman for the Health and Safety Executive on Radio Five on April 5 we need not worry; there is no immediate danger; it is very difficult to be infected with anthrax; and, in any case, anthrax infection can be treated with antibiotics.
>
> Heaven forbid that we nearly went to war – potentially a nuclear one – on the basis of disinformation.
>
> Or, is the Kings Cross anthrax, like the snow and leaves that fall on our railways, of the 'wrong kind'?

The pathetic British propaganda effort had drastically backfired, and no further effort was made to alarm the travelling public with tales of anthrax spores in their duty-free perfume sprays. Nor were US/UK spoiling tactics helped by Kofi Annan's praise (30 March) for Baghdad's co-operation with the UNSCOM teams investigating Saddam Hussein's palaces.[62] And even Butler, under unprecedented pressure, was forced to acknowledge the 'high degree of co-operation' being shown by the Iraqi authorities (without signalling that there would be any early end to the intrusive UNSCOM presence). The proper tone of UNSCOM scepticism was quickly re-established. In the comprehensive Annex to a Butler letter (8 April 1998) addressed to the President of the Security Council, it was affirmed that Iraq's disclosures about its weapons programmes were 'incomplete and inadequate'; there was 'little confidence' that the full scope of the biological-weapons programme had been revealed; the attitude of Iraq was 'disappointing'.[63] Nothing had changed. Again the scene was set for an UNSCOM presence in Iraq, and the continuation of the genocidal sanctions regime, in perpetuity.

The plight of the Iraqi civilian population was again highlighted when George Galloway, a British Member of Parliament, returned from Baghdad with the four-year-old Mariam Hamza, formerly unable to receive treatment for leukaemia because of the sanctions. Even with this desperate case, one of thousands in Iraq, it was necessary for the UN Sanctions Committee to relax the embargo so that the cancerous child could be flown out of Iraq. Inevitably, Galloway was attacked by the British media for giving Saddam Hussein a manifest propaganda *coup*. Replied Galloway: 'I don't see it that way. This child will die if she doesn't get treatment in Britain because of the cumulative effects of sanctions over seven years on the Iraqi health service, which is close to collapse.'[64] Here there was no doubt of the reasons for the girl's condition: '*Let us be clear, the responsibility for Mariam's condition lies with the sanctions policy, there is absolutely no doubt about that. She is a victim of the regime. Her parents never elected the Iraqi regime and they cannot remove it, however much we make her suffer.*'[65]

The British media swung into action to denigrate the humanitarian effort to save Mariam's life. She was just a 'pawn' of Saddam Hussein, with George Galloway, 'in Lenin's withering phrase' (*The Daily Telegraph*, 16 April 1998), one of Saddam's 'useful idiots', a politician 'prepared to be a part of Baghdad's game of exploiting physical suffering to divert attention' from Saddam's 'murderous ambitions'. Here it was: the callous Western outrage that ordinary people in Britain and elsewhere would hear about Mariam's plight and the hundreds of thousands of suffering Iraqi children. In London, *The Guardian* (15 April 1998) acknowledged the central fact: 'His [Galloway's] handling of this case seems to have been very sober. The argument over sanctions misses the central issue: they do not appear to hurt Saddam Hussein. Whoever is ultimately responsible, they do hurt the ordinary people of Iraq ... Something is seriously wrong with the policy'. And the indefatigable Felicity Arbuthnot, whose persistence and humanity are a constant rebuke to the disgusting Western leaders (Clinton, Albright, Blair, Cook *inter alia*) who support the genocidal sanctions regime, yet again drew attention to the misery being inflicted on thousands of helpless Iraqi children by the United States and Britain:

> In the 1930s Gertrude Bell wrote of the 'word which is the keynote of Iraq, it is romance. The huge Babylonian plains ... once a garden of the world, the great twin rivers gloriously named ... and last (to English ears not least) the enterprise, the rigours, the courage ...'
>
> Today the courage of the ordinary people of Iraq has been tested to the limit. More than an estimated 1,200,000 children are believed to have died since sanctions were first put into place: the equivalent of 10 silent Hiroshimas.
>
> That is why, when I was leaving Iraq just a day before George Galloway was arriving, I left him a message. Whatever you do, I said, go to Al Mansour Hospital and see the children. Mariam was the first child he visited ...[66]

Tell us now, Clinton and Blair (and Cook with your 'ethical' foreign policy), when you read of the tiny Ali Makfoud, cancerous and dying in the arms of his frantic and weeping mother, and of the dying Esra who weeps from her paralysed eyes, that your policies on Iraq are morally right. The 13-year-old Jassim from Basra, dying from leukaemia, wanted to be a poet when he grew up. The three cases are a minuscule example, a few among millions suffering in the horror that is 1998 Iraq. So the ordinary people of Iraq, especially the children, must be made to suffer because they are in the grip of a tyrant who offends Western vanity. Where, in the name of all decency and justice, is the logic in this obscenity?

On 15 April the UN Secretary-General submitted to the Security Council the report of the new Special Group on the visits to the presidential sites undertaken in the period from 26 March to 2 April 1998. The Group included 20 senior diplomats appointed by the Secretary-General, a group of UNSCOM experts, and IAEA staff. Visits to the eight presidential sites were described, prior to concluding observations that included the words: '*In general the senior diplomats observed that the relations between the UNSCOM and IAEA experts on the one hand and the Iraqi counterparts on the other were correct and both sides conducted themselves with professionalism and restraint.*'[67] Any misunderstanding 'was soon settled, often through the good offices of senior diplomats', though the Iraqi authorities 'expressed serious concerns about the confidentiality' of information being collected by UNSCOM and IAEA. The final conclusion of the report hinted at the possibility of future difficulties:

> On balance, the mission was successful, but it was apparent that some key issues will arise again in the not too distant future and the Council

should be prepared to face them when they arise. Certainly, the matter of continuing access is unsettled and will ultimately re-emerge as the Iraqi side clearly feels that the phrase in the 23 February Memorandum of Understanding referring to 'initial and subsequent visits' means for a limited period only.[68]

Despite the overall success of the mission there were still discernible tensions between the UN personnel and the Iraqi authorities. At the same time a United Nations report was claiming that Saddam Hussein was authorising mass executions in Iraqi jails as part of a 'prison cleansing operation', with relatives of the victims having to pay for the bullets used in the executions before being allowed to recover the bodies, some of which showed signs of torture. The 22-page report claimed that it was 'highly probable' that more than 1500 political executions had been carried out in the last year. The report, produced under the auspices of Max van der Stoel, the UN's special rapporteur on Iraq, was quickly cited in the West as yet a further reason why sanctions could not be relaxed: because Saddam Hussein was executing prisoners it was essential that the United States continue to starve Iraqi children. The Iraqi delegation at the UN Human Rights Commission denounced Max van der Stoel's charges as 'baseless lies', condemning the entire report as a 'mere repetition of the same allegations and false accusations' that had been made in the past.

Now fresh allegations were being made against the Iraqis. Charles Duelfer, the UNSCOM deputy head, was declaring that the Iraqi authorities were again planning to ban access to the presidential palaces. Trent Lott, the US Senate majority leader, had denounced the Annan deal as 'appeasement', and even that controversial deal had not removed all the tensions (Duelfer: the question of 'continuing access is by no means solved').[69] The Iraqis were quick to object to Duelfer's posture: his new statement to *The New York Times* (15 April 1998) included a quotation from a report which the Secretary-General had not yet transmitted to the Security Council. In speaking to the press in such a fashion, Duelfer had violated his undertaking to the United Nations (Annex to document S/1998/303): *'Unless specifically authorized by the Executive Chairman, I shall not accept speaking engagements or make statements to, or grant interviews with the press, radio, television or other agencies of public information during my assignment with UNSCOM.'*[70] Duelfer's manifest violation of a written pledge had done nothing to further the spirit and intention of the Annan agreement. Again a key UNSCOM official was knowingly eroding the accomplishments of the Secretary-General's diplomacy – and making war more likely. Commented Nizar Hamdoon, the Iraqi UN ambassador: 'The recent statements made by Mr Charles Duelfer, a United States national ... confirm the need for the United Nations to be more attentive to ensuring the impartiality of officials operating under its flag.'[71]

In a new report by Richard Butler, to be considered by the Security Council on 27 April, the UNSCOM head declared that his teams had made 'virtually no progress' since his last report six months ago. He criticised the Iraqi role in the recent crisis, speaking in particular of the disruptions to UNSCOM's work (*'If this is what Iraq intended by the crisis, then, in large measure, it could be said to have been successful. A major consequence of the four-month crisis authorised by Iraq has been that, in contrast with the prior reporting period, virtually no progress in verifying disarmament has been able to be reported'*). No weapons had been found in the palaces – which in all reasonable opinion should have strengthened the Iraqi claims, but here again the very *absence* of evidence was turned against Baghdad: the palaces had obviously been 'stripped bare' of anything suspicious.[72] If UNSCOM was able to find evidence of weapons then Iraq was damned; if it found nothing at all then Iraq was equally damned. Again the whole situation was deteriorating, giving every sign that soon Washington, unilaterally citing Resolution 1154, would at last have its chance to launch a devastating bombing campaign.

No publicity was given to the IAEA report (13 April 1998) that Iraq had complied with al the UN requirements to declare and destroy its nuclear weapons capacity. Instead Derek Fatchett, a British minister of state at the Foreign Office, was insisting that Saddam Hussein was exploiting the 'oil for food' programme to boost his military spending. Every effort was being made in Washington and London to cast doubt on the Annan deal, to ignore the scale of Iraqi co-operation with UNSCOM, and to re-establish the crisis atmosphere that had existed a few weeks before. There was nothing here to suggest that the punishing sanctions would be lifted in the short term, every reason to think that the Iraqi civilian population would be condemned to disease and starvation for months and years to come. The so-called 'light at the end of the tunnel' had been a mirage.

Iraq was now facing the virtual collapse of all social provision. The food ration, never adequate under sanctions, had been progressively cut; the hospitals were denuded of bandages, antiseptics, vaccines, sheets and working equipment; schools were without pencils, paper and books; emaciated children were dying at the rate of many thousands every month. One journalist noted the collapse of the immunisation programme, making polio, tuberculosis, meningitis, measles and other diseases common; with an increasing number of malnourished children forced to survive as beggars: 'as we drove into Baghdad, three girls, all beggars and all under eight, launched themselves at our moving car … allowing themselves to be dragged along the road until we could stop and pay them off'.[73]

On 20 April 1998 a two-day conference opened in Britain with the declared aim of improving the flow of humanitarian aid to Iraq. The event was a propaganda farce, boycotted by all Middle East countries except Kuwait, and doing nothing whatever to remove the sole cause of Iraqi civilian suffering – sanctions. Emma Bonino, the EU Commission for humanitarian affairs, declared at the conference that sanctions were causing 'unbearable hardships' for the Iraqi people, and that the policy should be urgently re-examined: 'We must remember that sanctions have humanitarian side-effects which affect innocent populations and which, if unchecked, can help to strengthen dictators'. Clare Short, the British Secretary for International Development, commented with monumental hypocrisy that *if children were suffering, they must be helped*. If? Was she so ignorant? And what of sanctions? Were children 'helped' by denying them food, clean water and medicines? Said Short, at one time allegedly a 'conscience' of the British Labour Party: 'We will not help the Iraqi people by wringing our hands at the extent of the problem, nor pointing the finger of blame ... People throughout the world are very concerned about the suffering of the people of Iraq. We are here today to explore whether we can help'. This – from the member of a government supporting genocidal policies in violation of Articles II and III of the 1948 UN Genocide Convention.[74]

The sanctions were continuing as a violation of the Geneva Convention (Article 54, Protocol 1 addition, 1977: 'Starvation of civilians as a method of warfare is prohibited') and countless UN Resolutions, Conventions, Declarations and Statements protecting civilian access to food.[75] In a letter (22 April 1998) addressed to the President of the Secretary Council, Tariq Aziz, Iraq's Deputy Prime Minister, again highlighted the suffering of the civilian population and urged a lifting of the genocidal sanctions regime. On the recent Butler report Aziz comments:

> This report blatantly fails to demonstrate objectivity and fairness, denies and misrepresents facts, and flouts the basic precepts of dealing with the issue of disarmament. The report tendentiously ignores everything that Iraq had done over the past seven years ... It is full of blatant falsehoods and lies and has been designed from the outset as a political document ... blaming Iraq and justifying continuation of the unjust embargo ...[76]

The Aziz document deals with specific disarmament issues (missiles, chemical, biological, etc.) in considerable detail and deserves to be examined in detail. As a plaintive conclusion Aziz declares: '*On this basis, the requirements of Security Council resolution 687 (1991), section C, have been fulfilled. Iraq requests the Security Council to implement paragraph 22 of resolution 687 (1991) forthwith, without any new restrictions or conditions. This implementation constitutes a legal and moral responsibility which the Security Council should meet without further delay. States which prevent such implementation must bear full responsibility for their unjust position and its consequences.*' In short, despite all UNSCOM's provocations, illegalities and intrusive belligerence; despite the unyielding 'double standards' of Washington in allowing

Israel to build up its arsenal of weapons of mass destruction (in violation of the preamble to Resolution 687); despite the illegal and genocidal sanctions regime that had already produced millions of Iraqi casualties – despite all the Iraq had substantially complied with the disarmament conditions, which in turn meant that (Resolution 687, Paragraph 22) the sanctions should be lifted.

The facts were now well known. Whatever else the 1997/8 crisis had achieved it had given worldwide publicity to the reality of the US-sustained sanctions against the Iraqi people. Now more and more people throughout the world knew about the deliberately contrived suffering that was afflicting an entire civilian population, and in particular the most vulnerable – the young, the sick, the old. But in mid-1998 the United States was in no mood to permit the lifting of sanctions, in no mood to assuage the misery of millions of helpless and innocent human beings. It remained essential to the Washington strategy, whatever the hidden agenda, that the Iraqi hospitals lacked swabs, syringes, bandages, disinfectants and vaccines; that the increasingly emaciated schoolchildren lacked pencils and books; that sick and underweight babies died on shriveled breasts; that an entire generation of children, to the extent that it survived at all, would be stunted, traumatised and diseased. It was essential that the Tigris continued to run brown with untreated raw sewage, that children went blind for want of insulin, that cancerous infants went untreated while dying in the arms of weeping and malnourished mothers. All of this was what Washington and the supine London echo continued to stand for through 1998.[77] Even the American 'hawks' were now being forced to admit that *'the sanctions are doing more harm to ordinary people than to the regime'.*[78]

Richard Butler, UNSCOM head, continued to procrastinate, giving no hint of an early lifting of sanctions: 'There is very good scientific and technical support for our difficulty in doing what we really want to do ... we need positive verification that what they created ... have all been used, destroyed and somehow accounted for ...'.[79] At an Iraqi press briefing on the same day (28 April 1998) the Iraqi foreign minister Al-Sahaf yet again reiterated the central fact: 'The people of Iraq have been subject to unprecedented injustice, through the application of a policy of continued starvation, and repeated military assaults ...'.[80] It was plain that Washington, humiliated by Kofi Annan's success in aborting the 1997/8 military countdown, was now struggling against international opinion to preserve the cruel sanctions regime in perpetuity: *a decimated Iraq would be unable to resist pro-US encroachments on the Iraqi oil resource.* And in mid-1998 Washington remained eager for an excuse to pronounce the failure of the Annan deal: both sides were 'now braced for the collapse of February's 11th-hour deal between President Saddam and the UN secretary-general, Kofi Annan'.[81] If

Washington were to have its way, the genocidal sanctions on the Iraqi people would be maintained on a permanent basis.

On 5 August 1998 Iraq imposed new restrictions on the UNSCOM inspectors. It was now increasingly obvious to Baghdad that on the sanctions issue there was no 'light at the end of the tunnel'. The United States quickly secured the unanimous adoption on UN Resolution 1194 (9 September 1998): 'The Security Council ... decides ... not to conduct any further such [sanctions] reviews ...' (1194, Paragraph 3). The genocidal sanctions regime was to be maintained *in perpetuity*.

The impact of sanctions was now plain. Denis Halliday, the UN humanitarian coordinator for Iraq, who resigned in protest, declared on 30 September: '*4000 to 5000 children are dying unnecessarily every month due to the impact of sanctions because of the breakdown of water and sanitation, inadequate diet and the bad internal health situation.*' At the same time the Iraqi health ministry was reporting that sanctions had killed at least 1.5 million people, mostly children. On 9 October the UN Committee on the Rights of the Child noted 'with grave concern' how sanctions were causing a deteriorating health situation for Iraqi citizens and children in particular. But even this remorseless use of biological warfare (i.e. starvation and disease) by the United States was deemed insufficient by the Washington planners.

On 31 October 1998 President Clinton signed into law the Iraq Liberation Act authorising $97 million to be spent on military equipment and military training for terrorist groups operating in Iraq. *Washington would do all it could to exterminate an innocent population while funding terrorist attacks on a sovereign member of the United Nations.* When, in mounting desperation, Baghdad decided to restrict further the activities of UNSCOM staff (widely acknowledged 'spies and agents'), the US-dominated Security Council unanimously condemned (5 November 1998) the Iraqi decision, and the scene was set for a new crisis (see Afterword, p. xviii)

Appendix I

Adverse Consequences of Economic Sanctions on the Enjoyment of Human Rights, UN Economic and Social Council

The Sub-Commission on Prevention of Discrimination and Protection of Minorities

Affirming the need to respect the principles of the Charter of the United Nations, the Universal Declaration of Human Rights, the International Covenants on Human Rights and the relevant provisions of the Geneva Conventions of 12 August 1949 and the two Additional Protocols thereto,

Concerned about the adverse consequences of economic sanctions, such as embargoes and blockades, on human rights,

Recognizing that such coercive measures should be adopted by or under the authority of the Security Council only in accordance with Article 24 and Chapter VII of the Charter of the United Nations,

Convinced that such measures should always be limited in time,

Aware, moreover, that such measures most seriously affect the innocent population, in particular the weak and the poor, especially women and children,

Concerned that such measures have a tendency to aggravate the imbalances in income distribution already present in the countries concerned,

Noting that in many cases they may give rise to smuggling and trafficking which greatly benefit mala fide business people often close to the oppressive government authorities which are insensitive to the suffering of their people,

1. *Appeals* to all States concerned to reconsider their adoption of or support for such measures, even if the legitimate goals pursued are not yet attained, if after a reasonable period they appear not to be bringing about the desired changes in policy, regardless of the nature of that policy;

2. *Decides* to consider the adverse consequences of economic sanctions on human rights at its fiftieth session under the agenda item entitled 'Implications of humanitarian activities on the enjoyment of human rights'.

37th meeting
20 August 1997

Appendix II

Security Council Resolution 687
(3 April 1991)

RESOLUTION 687 (1991)

The Security Council,

Recalling its resolutions 660 (1990), 661 (1990), 662 (1990), 664 (1990), 665 (1990), 666 (1990), 667 (1990), 669(1990), 670 (1990), 674 (1990), 677 (1990), 678 (1990) and 686 (1991),

Welcoming the restoration to Kuwait of its sovereignty, independence and territorial integrity and the return of its legitimate government,

Affirming the commitment of all Member States to the sovereignty, territorial integrity and political independence of Kuwait and Iraq, and noting the intention expressed by the Member States co-operating with Kuwait under paragraph 2 of resolution 678 (1990) to bring their military presence in Iraq to an end as soon as possible consistent with paragraph 8 of resolution 686 (1991),

Reaffirming the need to be assured of Iraq's peaceful intentions in light of its unlawful invasion and occupation of Kuwait,

Taking note of the letter sent by the Foreign Minister of Iraq on 27 February 1991 (S/22275) and those sent pursuant to resolution 686 (1991) (S/22273, S/22276, S/22320, S/22321, and S/22330),

Noting that Iraq and Kuwait, as independent sovereign States, signed at Baghdad on 4 October 1963 'Agreed Minutes Regarding the Restoration of Friendly Relations, Recognition and Related Matters', thereby recognizing formally the boundary between Iraq and Kuwait and the allocation of islands, which were registered with the United Nations in accordance with Article 102 of the Charter and in which Iraq recognized the independence and complete sovereignty of the State of Kuwait within its borders as specified and accepted in the letter of the Prime Minister of Iraq dated 21 July 1932, and as accepted by the Ruler of Kuwait in his letter dated 10 August 1932,

Conscious of the need for demarcation of the said boundary,

Conscious also of the statements by Iraq threatening to use weapons in violation of its obligations under the Geneva Protocol for the prohibition of the Use in War of Asphyxiating, Poisonous or Other Gases, and of Bacteriological Methods of Warfare, signed at Geneva on 17 June 1925, and of its prior use of chemical weapons and affirming that grave consequences would follow any further use by Iraq of such weapons,

Recalling that Iraq has subscribed to the Declaration adopted by all States participating in the Conference of States Parties to the 1925 Geneva Protocol and

Other Interested States, held at Paris from 7 to 11 January 1989, establishing the objective of universal elimination of chemical and biological weapons,

Recalling further that Iraq has signed the Convention on the Prohibition of the Development, Production and Stockpiling of Bacteriological (Biological) and Toxin Weapons and on Their Destruction, of 10 April 1972,

Noting the importance of Iraq ratifying this Convention,

Noting moreover the importance of all States adhering to this Convention and encouraging its forthcoming Review Conference to reinforce the authority, efficiency and universal scope of the Convention,

Stressing the importance of an early conclusion by the Conference on Disarmament of its work on a Convention on the Universal Prohibition of Chemical Weapons and of universal adherence thereto,

Aware of the use by Iraq of ballistic missiles in unprovoked attacks and therefore of the need to take specific measures in regard to such missiles located in Iraq,

Concerned by the reports in the hands of Member States that Iraq has attempted to acquire materials for a nuclear-weapons programme contrary to its obligations under the treaty on the Non-Proliferation of Nuclear Weapons of 1 July 1968,

Recalling the objective of the establishment of a nuclear-weapon-free zone in the region of the Middle East,

Conscious of the threat which all weapons of mass destruction pose to peace and security in the area and of the need to work towards the establishment in the Middle East of a zone free of such weapons,

Conscious also of the objective of achieving balanced and comprehensive control of armaments in the region,

Conscious further of the importance of achieving the objectives noted above using all available means, including a dialogue among the states of the region,

Noting that resolution 686 (1991) marked the lifting of the measures imposed by resolution 661 (1990) in so far as they applied to Kuwait,

Noting that despite the progress being made in fulfilling the obligations of resolution 686 (1991), many Kuwaiti and third country nationals are still not accounted for and property remains unreturned.

Recalling the International Convention against the taking of hostages, opened for signature at New York on 18 December 1979, which categorizes all acts of taking hostages as manifestations of international terrorism,

Deploring threats made by Iraq during the recent conflict to make use of terrorism against targets outside Iraq and the taking of hostages by Iraq,

Taking note with grave concern of the reports of the Secretary-General of 20 March 1991 (S/22366) and 28 March 1991 (S/22409), and conscious of the necessity to meet urgently the humanitarian needs in Kuwait and Iraq,

Bearing in mind its objective of restoring international peace and security in the area as set out in recent Council resolutions,

Conscious of the need to take the following measures acting under Chapter VII of the Charter,

1. Affirms all thirteen resolutions noted above, except as expressly changed below to achieve the goals of this resolution, including a formal ceasefire;

A

2. Demands that Iraq and Kuwait respect the inviolability of the international boundary and the allocation of islands set out in the 'Agreed Minutes Between the State of Kuwait and the Republic of Iraq Regarding the Restoration of Friendly Relations, Recognition and Related Matters', signed by them in the exercise of their sovereignty at Baghdad on 4 October 1963 and registered with the United Nations and published by the United Nations in document 7063, United Nations Treaty Series, 1964;

3. Calls on the Secretary-General to lend his assistance to make arrangements with Iraq and Kuwait to demarcate the boundary between Iraq and Kuwait, drawing on appropriate material including the map transmitted by Security Council document S/22412 and to report back to the Security Council within one month;

4. Decides to guarantee the inviolability of the above-mentioned international boundary and to take as appropriate all necessary measures to that end in accordance with the Charter;

B

5. Requests the Secretary-General, after consulting with Iraq and Kuwait, to submit within three days to the Security Council for its approval a plan for the immediate deployment of a United Nations observer unit to monitor the Khor Abdullah and a demilitarized zone, 10 kilometres into Iraq and 5 kilometres into Kuwait from the boundary referred to in the 'Agreed Minutes Between the State of Kuwait and the Republic of Iraq Regarding the Restoration of Friendly Relations, Recognition and Related Matters' of 4 October 1963; to deter violations of the boundary through its presence in and surveillance of the demilitarized zone; to observe any hostile or potentially hostile action mounted from the territory of one State to the other; and for the Secretary-General to report regularly to the Council on the operations of the unit, and immediately if there are any serious violations of the zone or potential threats to peace;

6. Notes that as soon as the Secretary-General notifies the Council of the completion of the deployment of the United Nations observer unit, the conditions will be established for the Member States co-operating with Kuwait in accordance with resolution 678 (1990) to bring their military presence in Iraq to an end consistent with resolution 686 (1991);

C

7. Invites Iraq to reaffirm unconditionally its obligations under the Geneva Protocol for the Prohibition of the Use in War of Asphyxiating, Poisonous or Other Gases, and of Bacteriological Methods of Warfare, signed at Geneva on 17 June 1925, and to ratify the Convention on the Prohibition of the Development, Production, and Stockpiling of Bacteriological (Biological) and Toxin Weapons and on Their Destruction, of 10 April 1972;

8. Decides that Iraq shall unconditionally accept the destruction, removal, or rendering harmless, under international supervision, of:

(*a*)   all chemical and biological weapons and all stocks of agents and all related subsystems and components and all research, development, support and manufacturing facilities;

(*b*)   all ballistic missiles with a range greater than 150 kilometres and related major parts, and repair and production facilities;

9.   Decides for the implementation of paragraph 8 above, the following:

(*a*)   Iraq shall submit to the Secretary-General, within fifteen days of the adoption of this resolution, a declaration of the locations, amounts, and types of all items specified in paragraph 8 and agree to urgent, on-site inspection as specified below;

(*b*)   the Secretary-General, in consultation with the appropriate Governments and, where appropriate, with the Director General of the World Health Organization (WHO), within 45 days of the passage of this resolution, shall develop, and submit to the Council for approval, a plan calling for the completion of the following acts within 45 days of such approval:

(i)   the forming of a Special Commission, which shall carry out immediate on-site inspection of Iraq's biological, chemical and missile capabilities, based on Iraq's declarations and the designation of any additional locations by the Special Commission itself;

(ii)   the yielding by Iraq of possession to the Special Commission for destruction, removal or rendering harmless, taking into account the requirements of public safety, of all items specified under paragraph 8 (*a*) above including items at the additional locations designated by the Special Commission under paragraph 9 (*b*) (i) above and the destruction by Iraq, under supervision of the Special Commission, of all its missile capabilities including launchers as specified under paragraph 8 (*b*) above;

(iii)   the provision by the Special Commission of the assistance and co-operation to the Director General of the International Atomic Energy Agency (IAEA) required in paragraphs 12 and 13 below;

10.   Decides that Iraq shall unconditionally undertake not to use, develop, construct or acquire any of the items specified in paragraphs 8 and 9 above and requests the Secretary-General, in consultation with the Special Commission, to develop a plan for the future ongoing monitoring and verification of Iraq's compliance with this paragraph, to be submitted to the Council for approval within 120 days of the passage of this resolution;

11.   Invites Iraq to reaffirm unconditionally its obligations under the treaty on the Non-Proliferation of Nuclear Weapons, of 1 July 1968;

12.   Decides that Iraq shall unconditionally agree not to acquire or develop nuclear weapons of nuclear-weapons-usable material or any subsystems of components or any research, development, support or manufacturing facilities, related to the above; to submit to the Secretary-General and the Director General of the International Atomic Energy Agency (IAEA) within 15 days of the adoption of this resolution a declaration of the locations, amounts and types of all items specified above; to place all of its nuclear-weapons-usable material under the exclusive control, for custody and removal, of the IAEA, with the assistance and co-operation of the Special Commission as provided for in the plan of the

Secretary-General discussed in paragraph 9 (*b*) above; to accept in accordance with the arrangements provided for in paragraph 13 below, urgent on-site inspection and the destruction, removal and rendering harmless as appropriate of all items specified above; and to accept the plan as discussed in paragraph 13 below for the future ongoing monitoring and verification of its compliance with these undertakings;

13. Requests the Director General of the International Atomic Energy Agency (IAEA) through the Secretary-General, with the assistance and co-operation of the Special Commission as provided for in the plan of the Secretary-General in paragraph 9 (*b*) above, to carry out immediate on-site inspection of Iraq's nuclear capabilities based on Iraq's declarations and the designation of any additional locations by the Special Commission; to develop a plan for submission to the Security Council within 45 days calling for the destruction, removal, or rendering harmless as appropriate of all items listed in paragraph 12 above; to carry out the plan within 45 days following approval by the Security Council; and to develop a plan, taking into account the rights and obligations of Iraq under the Treaty on the Non-Proliferation of Nuclear Weapons, of 1 July 1968, for the future ongoing monitoring and verification of Iraq's compliance with paragraph 12 above, including an inventory of all nuclear material in Iraq subject to the Agency's verification and inspections to confirm that IAEA safeguards cover all relevant nuclear activities in Iraq, to be submitted to the Council for approval within 120 days of the passage of this resolution;

14. Takes note that the actions to be taken by Iraq in paragraphs 8, 9, 10, 11, 12 and 13 of this resolution represent steps towards the goal of establishing in the Middle East a zone free from weapons of mass destruction and all missiles for their delivery and the objective of a global ban on chemical weapons;

D

15. Requests the Secretary-General to report to the Security Council on the steps taken to facilitate the return of all Kuwaiti property seized by Iraq, including a list of any property which Kuwait claims has not been returned or which has not been returned intact;

E

16. Reaffirms that Iraq, without prejudice to the debts and obligation of Iraq, arising prior to 2 August 1990, which will be addressed through the normal mechanisms, is liable under international law for any direct loss, damage, including environmental damage and the depletion of natural resources, or injury to foreign Governments, nationals and corporations, as a result of Iraq's unlawful invasion and occupation of Kuwait;

17. Decides that all Iraqi statements made since 2 August 1990, repudiating its foreign debt are null and void, and demands that Iraq scrupulously adhere to all of its obligations concerning servicing and repayment of its foreign debt;

18. Decides to create a Fund to pay compensation for claims that fall within paragraph 16 above and to establish a Commission that will administer the Fund;

19. Directs the Secretary-General to develop and present to the Council for decision, no later than 30 days following the adoption of this resolution, recommendations for the Fund to meet the requirement for the payment of claims

established in accordance with paragraph 18 above and for a programme to implement the decisions in paragraphs 16, 17, and 18 above, including: administration of the Fund; mechanisms for determining the appropriate level for Iraq's contribution to the Fund based on a percentage of the value of the exports of petroleum and petroleum products from Iraq not to exceed a figure to be suggested to the Council by the Secretary-General, taking into account the requirement of the people of Iraq, Iraq's payment capacity as assessed in conjunction with the international financial institutions taking into consideration external debt service, and the needs of the Iraqi economy; arrangements for ensuring that payments are made to the Fund; the process by which funds will be allocated and claims paid; appropriate procedures for evaluating losses, listing claims and verifying their validity and resolving disputed claims in respect of Iraq's liability as specified in paragraph 16 above; and the composition of the Commission designated above;

F

20. Decides, effective immediately, that the prohibitions against the sale or supply to Iraq of commodities or products, other than medicine and health supplies, and prohibitions against financial transactions related thereto, contained in resolution 661 (1990) shall not apply to foodstuffs notified to the Committee established by resolution 661 (1990) or, with the approval of that Committee, under the simplified and accelerated 'no-objection' procedure, to materials and supplies for essential civilian needs as identified in the report of the Secretary-General dated 20 March 1991 (S/22366), and in any further findings of humanitarian need by the Committee.

21. Decides that the Council shall review the provisions of paragraph 20 above every sixty days in light of the policies and practices of the Government of Iraq, including the implementation of all relevant resolutions of the Security Council, for the purposes of determining whether to reduce or lift the prohibitions referred to therein;

22. Decides that upon the approval by the Council of the programme called for in paragraph 19 above and upon Council agreement that Iraq has completed all actions contemplated in paragraphs 8, 9, 10, 11, 12 and 13 above, the prohibitions against the import of commodities and products originating in Iraq and the prohibitions against financial transactions related thereto contained in resolution 661 (1990) shall have no further force or effect;

23. Decides that, pending action by the Council under paragraph 22 above, the Committee established by resolution 661 (1990) shall be empowered to approve, when required to assure adequate financial resources on the part of Iraq to carry out the activities under paragraph 20 above, exceptions to the prohibition against the import of commodities and products originating in Iraq;

24. Decides that, in accordance with resolution 661 (1990) and subsequent related resolutions and until a further decision is taken by the Council, all States shall continue to prevent the sale or supply, or promotion or facilitation of such sale or supply to Iraq by their nationals, or from their territories or using their flag vessels or aircraft, of:

(*a*) arms and related material of all types, specifically including conventional military equipment, including for paramilitary forces, and spare parts and components and their means of production, for such equipment;

(b) items specified and defined in paragraph 8 and paragraph 12 above not otherwise covered above;

(c) technology under licensing or other transfer arrangements used in production, utilization or stockpiling of items specified in subparagraphs (a) and (b) above;

(d) personnel or materials for training or technical support services relating to the design, development, manufacture, use, maintenance or support of items specified in subparagraphs (a) and (b) above;

25. Calls upon all States and international organizations to act strictly in accordance with paragraph 24 above, notwithstanding the existence of any contracts, agreements, licences, or any other arrangements;

26. Requests the Secretary-General, in consultation with appropriate Governments, to develop within sixty days, for approval of the Council, guidelines to facilitate full international implementation of paragraphs 24 and 25 above and paragraph 27 below, and to make them available to all States and to establish a procedure for updating these guidelines periodically;

27. Calls upon all States to maintain such national controls and procedures and to take such other actions consistent with the guidelines to the established by the Security Council under paragraph 26 above as may be necessary to ensure compliance with the terms of paragraph 24 above, and calls upon international organizations to take all appropriate steps to assist in ensuring such full compliance;

28. Agrees to review its decisions in paragraphs 22, 23, 24 and 25 above, except for the items specified and defined in paragraphs 8 and 12 above, on a regular basis and in any case 120 days following passage of this resolution, taking into account Iraq's compliance with this resolution and general progress towards the control of armaments in the region;

29. Decides that all States, including Iraq, shall take the necessary measures to ensure that no claim shall lie at the instance of the Government of Iraq, or of any person or body in Iraq, or of any person claiming through or for the benefit of any such person or body, in connection with any contract or other transactions where its performance was affected by reason of the measures taken by the Security Council in resolution 661 (1990) and related resolutions;

G

30. Decides that, in furtherance of its commitment to facilitate the repatriation of all Kuwaiti and third country nationals, Iraq shall extend all necessary co-operation to the International Committee of the Red Cross, providing lists of such persons, facilitating the access of the International Committee of the Red Cross to all such persons wherever located or detained and facilitating the search by the International Committee of the Red Cross for those Kuwaiti and third country nationals still unaccounted for;

31. Invites the International Committee of the Red Cross to keep the Secretary-General apprised as appropriate of all activities undertaken in connection with

facilitating the repatriation or return of all Kuwaiti and third country nationals or their remains present in Iraq on or after 2 August 1990;

H

32. Requires Iraq to inform the Council that it will not commit or support any act of international terrorism or allow any organization directed towards commission of such acts to operate within its territory and to condemn unequivocally and renounce all acts, methods, and practices of terrorism;

I

33. Declares that, upon official notification by Iraq to the Secretary-General and to the Security Council of its acceptance of the provisions above, a formal ceasefire is effective between Iraq and Kuwait and the Member States co-operating with Kuwait in accordance with resolution 678 (1990);

34. Decides to remain seized of the matter and to take such further steps as may be required for the implementation of this resolution and to secure peace and security in the area.

Adopted by 12 votes to one (Cuba),
with two abstentions (Ecuador and Yemen)

Appendix III

Security Council Resolution 1134 (23 October 1997)

RESOLUTION 1134 (1997)

The Security Council,

Recalling all its previous relevant resolutions, and in particular its resolutions 687 (1991) of 3 April 1991, 707 (1991) of 15 August 1991, 715 (1991) of 11 October 1991, 1060 (1996) of 12 June 1996, and 1115 (1997) of 21 June 1997,

Having considered the report of the Executive Chairman of the Special Commission dated 6 October 1997 (S/1997/774),

Expressing grave concern at the report of additional incidents since the adoption of resolution 1115 (1997) in which access by the Special Commission inspection teams to sites in Iraq designated for inspection by the Commission was again denied by the Iraqi authorities,

Stressing the unacceptability of any attempts by Iraq to deny access to such sites,

Taking note of the progress nevertheless achieved by the Special Commission, as set out in the report of the Executive Chairman, towards the elimination of Iraq's programme of weapons of mass destruction.

Reaffirming its determination to ensure full compliance by Iraq with all its obligations under all previous relevant resolutions, and *reiterating* its demand that Iraq allow immediate, unconditional and unrestricted access to the Special Commission to any site which the Commission wishes to inspect, and in particular allow the Special Commission and its inspection teams to conduct both fixed wing and helicopter flights throughout Iraq for all relevant purposes including inspection, surveillance, aerial surveys, transportation and logistics without interferences of any kind and upon such terms and conditions as may be determined by the Special Commission, and to make use of their own aircraft and such airfields in Iraq as they may determine are most appropriate for the work of the Commission.

Recalling that resolution 1115 (1997) expresses the Council's firm intention, unless the Special Commission has advised the Council that Iraq is in substantial compliance with paragraphs 2 and 3 of that resolution, to impose additional measures on those categories of Iraqi officials responsible for the non-compliance,

Reiterating the commitment of all Member States to the sovereignty, territorial integrity and political independence of Kuwait and Iraq,

Acting under Chapter VII of the Charter of the United Nations,

1. *Condemns* the repeated refusal of the Iraqi authorities, as detailed in the report of the Executive Chairman of the Special Commission, to allow access to sites

designated by the Special Commission, and especially Iraqi actions endangering the safety of Special Commission personnel, the removal and destruction of documents of interest to the Special Commission and interference with the freedom of movement of Special Commission personnel;

2. *Decides* that such refusals to co-operate constitute a flagrant violation of Security Council resolutions 687 (1991), 707 (1991), 715 (1991) and 1060 (1996), and *notes* that the Special Commission in the report of the Executive Chairman was unable to advise that Iraq was in substantial compliance with paragraphs 2 and 3 of resolution 1115 (1997);

3. *Demands* that Iraq co-operate fully with the Special Commission in accordance with the relevant resolutions, which constitute the governing standard of Iraqi compliance;

4. *Demands* in particular that Iraq without delay allow the Special Commission inspection teams immediate, unconditional and unrestricted access to any and all areas, facilities, equipment, records and means of transportation which they wish to inspect in accordance with the mandate of the Special Commission, as well as to officials and other persons under the authority of the Iraqi Government whom the Special Commission wishes to interview so that the Special Commission may fully discharge its mandate;

5. *Requests* the Chairman of the Special Commission to include in all future con-solidated progress reports prepared under resolution 1051 (1996) an annex evaluating Iraq's compliance with paragraphs 2 and 3 of resolution 1115 (1997);

6. *Expresses* the firm intention – if the Special Commission reports that Iraq is not in compliance with paragraphs 2 and 3 of resolution 1115 (1997) or if the Special Commission does not advise the Council in the report of the Executive Chairman due on 11 April 1998 that Iraq is in compliance with paragraphs 2 and 3 of resolution 1115 (1997) – to adopt measures which would oblige all States to prevent without delay the entry into or transit through their territories of all Iraqi officials and members of the Iraqi armed forces who are responsible for or participate in instances of non-compliance with paragraphs 2 and 3 of resolution 1115 (1997), provided that the entry of a person into a particular State on a specified date may be authorized by the Committee established by resolution 661 (1990), and provided that nothing in this paragraph shall oblige a State to refuse entry into its own territory to its own nationals or persons carry-ing out bona fide diplomatic assignments or missions;

7. *Decides further*, on the basis of all incidents related to the implementation of paragraphs 2 and 3 of resolution 1115 (1997), to begin to designate, in consulta-tion with the Special Commission, individuals whose entry or transit would be prevented upon implementation of the measures set out in paragraph 6 above;

8. *Decides* not to conduct the reviews provided for in paragraphs 21 and 28 of res-olution 687 (1991) until after the next consolidated progress report of the Special Commission, due on 11 April 1998, after which those reviews will resume in accordance with resolution 687 (1991), beginning on 26 April 1998;

9. *Reaffirms* its full support for the authority of the Special Commission under its Executive Chairman to ensure the implementation of its mandate under the relevant resolutions of the Council;

10. *Decides* to remain seized of the matter.

Appendix IV

Security Council Resolution 1137 (12 November 1997)

RESOLUTION 1137 (1997)

The Security Council,

Recalling all its previous relevant resolutions, and in particular its resolutions 687 (1991) of 3 April 1991, 707 (1991) of 15 August 1991, 715 (1991) of 11 October 1991, 1060 (1996) of 12 June 1996, 1115 (1997) of 21 June 1997, and 1134 (1997) of 23 October 1997,

Taking note with grave concern of the letter of 29 October 1997 from the Deputy Prime Minister of Iraq to the President of the Security Council (S/1997/829) conveying the unacceptable decision of the Government of Iraq to seek to impose conditions on its co-operation with the Special Commission, of the letter of 2 November 1997 from the Permanent Representative of Iraq to the United Nations, to the Executive Chairman of the Special Commission (S/1997/837, annex), which reiterated the unacceptable demand that the reconnaissance aircraft operating on behalf of the Special Commission be withdrawn from use and which implicitly threatened the safety of such aircraft, and of, the letter of 6 November 1997 from the Minister of Foreign Affairs of Iraq to the President of the Security Council (S/1997/855) admitting that Iraq has moved dual-capable equipment which is subject to monitoring by the Special Commission,

Also taking note with grave concern of the letters of 30 October 1997 (S/1997/830) and 2 November 1997 (S/1997/836) from the Executive Chairman of the Special Commission to the President of the Security Council advising that the Government of Iraq had denied entry to Iraq to two Special Commission officials on 30 October 1997 and 2 November 1997 on the grounds of their nationality, and of the letters of 3 November 1997 (S/1997/837), 4 November 1997 (S/1997/843), 5 November 1997 (S/1997/851) and 7 November 1997 (S/1997/864) from the Executive Chairman of the Special Commission to the President of the Security Council advising that the Government of Iraq had denied entry to sites designated for inspection by the Special Commission on 3, 4, 5, 6 and 7 November 1997 to Special Commission inspectors on the grounds of their nationality, and of the additional information in the Executive Chairman's letter of 5 November 1997 to the President of the Security Council (S/1997/851) that the Government of Iraq has moved significant pieces of dual-capable equipment subject to monitoring by the Special Commission, and that monitoring cameras appear to have been tampered with or covered,

Welcoming the diplomatic initiatives, including that of the high-level mission of the Secretary-General, which have taken place in an effort to ensure that Iraq complies unconditionally with its obligations under the relevant resolutions,

Deeply concerned at the report of the high-level mission of the Secretary-General on the results of its meetings with the highest levels of the Government of Iraq,

Recalling that its resolution 1115 (1997) expressed its firm intention, unless the Special Commission advised the Council that Iraq is in substantial compliance with paragraphs 2 and 3 of that resolution, to impose additional measures on those categories of Iraqi officials responsible for the non-compliance,

Recalling also that its resolution 1134 (1997) reaffirmed its firm intention, if *inter alia* the Special Commission reports that Iraq is not in compliance with paragraphs 2 and 3 of resolution 1115 (1997), to adopt measures which would oblige States to refuse the entry into or transit through their territories of all Iraqi officials and members of the Iraqi armed forces who are responsible for or participate in instances of non-compliance with paragraphs 2 and 3 of resolution 1115 (1997),

Recalling further the Statement of its President of 29 October 1997 (S/PRST/1997/49) in which the Council condemned the decision of the Government of Iraq to try to dictate the terms of its compliance with its obligation to co-operate with the Special Commission, and warned of the serious consequences of Iraq's failure to comply immediately and fully and without conditions or restrictions with its obligations under the relevant resolutions,

Reiterating the commitment of all Member States to the sovereignty, territorial integrity and political independence of Kuwait and Iraq,

Determined to ensure immediate and full compliance without conditions or restrictions by Iraq with its obligations under the relevant resolutions,

Determining that this situation continues to constitute a threat to international peace and security,

Acting under Chapter VII of the Charter,

1. *Condemns* the continued violations by Iraq of its obligations under the relevant resolutions to co-operate fully and unconditionally with the Special Commission in the fulfilment of its mandate, including its unacceptable decision of 29 October 1997 to seek to impose conditions on co-operation with the Special Commission, its refusal on 30 October 1997 and 2 November 1997 to allow entry to Iraq to two Special Commission officials on the grounds of their nationality, its denial of entry on 3, 4, 5, 6 and 7 November 1997 to sites designated by the Special Commission for inspection to Special Commission inspectors on the grounds of their nationality, its implicit threat to the safety of the reconnaissance aircraft operating on behalf of the Special Commission, its removal of significant pieces of dual-use equipment from their previous sites, and its tampering with monitoring cameras of the Special Commission;

2. *Demands that* the Government of Iraq rescind immediately its decision of 29 October 1997;

3. *Demands also* that Iraq co-operate fully and immediately and without conditions or restrictions with the Special Commission in accordance with the relevant resolutions, which constitute the governing standard of Iraqi compliance;

4. *Decides*, in accordance with paragraph 6 of resolution 1134 (1997), that States shall without delay prevent the entry into or transit through their territories of all Iraqi officials and members of the Iraqi armed forces who were responsible for or participated in the instances of non-compliance detailed in paragraph 1

above, provided that the entry of a person into a particular State on a specified date may be authorized by the Committee established by resolution 661 (1990) of 6 August 1990, and provided that nothing in this paragraph shall oblige a State to refuse entry into its own territory to its own nationals, or to persons carrying out bona fide diplomatic assignments, or missions approved by the Committee established by resolution 661 (1990);

5. *Decides also*, in accordance with paragraph 7 of resolution 1134 (1997), to designate in consultation with the Special Commission a list of individuals whose entry or transit will be prevented under the provisions of paragraph 4 above, and *requests* the Committee established by resolution 661 (1990) to develop guidelines and procedures as appropriate for the implementation of the measures set out in paragraph 4 above, and to transmit copies of these guidelines and procedures, as well as a list of the individuals designated, to all Member States;

6. *Decides* that the provisions of paragraphs 4 and 5 above shall terminate one day after the Executive Chairman of the Special Commission reports to the Council that Iraq is allowing the Special Commission inspection teams immediate, unconditional and unrestricted access to any and all areas, facilities, equipment, records and means of transportation which they wish to inspect in accordance with the mandate of the Special Commission, as well as to officials and other persons under the authority of the Iraqi Government whom the Special Commission wishes to interview so that the Special Commission may fully discharge its mandate;

7. *Decides* that the reviews provided for in paragraphs 21 and 28 of resolution 687 (1991) shall resume in April 1998 in accordance with paragraph 8 of resolution 1134 (1997), provided that the Government of Iraq shall have complied with paragraph 2 above;

8. *Expresses* the firm intention to take further measures as may be required for the implementation of this resolution;

9. *Reaffirms* the responsibility of the Government of Iraq under the relevant resolutions to ensure the safety and security of the personnel and equipment of the Special Commission and its inspection teams;

10. *Reaffirms also* its full support for the authority of the Special Commission under its Executive Chairman to ensure the implementation of its mandate under the relevant resolutions of the Council;

11. *Decides* to remain seized of the matter.

Appendix V

Security Council Resolution 1143 (4 December 1997)

RESOLUTION 1143 (1997)

The Security Council,

Recalling its previous resolutions and in particular its resolutions 986 (1995) of 14 April 1995, 1111 (1997) of 4 June 1997 and 1129 (1997) of 12 September 1997,

Convinced of the need as a temporary measure to continue to provide for the humanitarian needs of the Iraqi people until the fulfilment by Iraq of the relevant resolutions, including notably resolution 687 (1991) of 3 April 1991, allows the Council to take further action with regard to the prohibitions referred to in resolution 661 (1990) of 6 August 1990, in accordance with the provisions of those resolutions.

Convinced also of the need for equitable distribution of humanitarian relief to all segments of the Iraqi population throughout the country,

Welcoming the report submitted by the Secretary-General in accordance with paragraph 3 of resolution 111 (1997) (S/1997/935) and his intention to submit a supplementary report, as well as the report submitted in accordance with paragraph 4 of resolution 1111 (1997) by the Committee established by resolution 661 (1990) of 6 August 1990 (S/1997/942).

Noting with concern that, despite the ongoing implementation of resolutions 986 (1995) and 1111 (1997), the population of Iraq continues to face a serious nutritional and health situation,

Determined to avoid any further deterioration of the current humanitarian situation,

Noting with appreciation the recommendation of the Secretary-General that the Council re-examine the adequacy of the revenues provided by resolution 986 (1995) and consider how best to meet the priority humanitarian requirements of the Iraqi people, including the possibility of increasing those revenues,

Noting also with appreciation the Secretary-General's intention to include in his supplementary report recommendations on ways to improve the processing and supply of humanitarian goods under resolution 986 (1995).

Welcoming the efforts made by the Committee established by resolution 661 (1990) to refine and clarify its working procedures, and *encouraging* the Committee to go further in that direction in order to expedite the approval process,

Reaffirming the commitment of all Member States to the sovereignty and territorial integrity of Iraq,

Acting under Chapter VII of the Charter of the United Nations,

1. *Decides* that the provisions of resolution 986 (1995), except those contained in paragraphs 4, 11 and 12, shall remain in force for another period of 180 days beginning at 00.01 hours, Eastern Standard Time, on 5 December 1997;

2. *Further decides* that the provisions of the distribution plan in respect of goods purchased in accordance with resolution 1111 (1997) shall continue to apply to foodstuffs, medicine and health supplies purchased in accordance with this resolution pending the Secretary-General's approval of a new distribution plan, to be submitted by the Government of Iraq before 5 January 1998;

3. *Further decides* to conduct a thorough review of all aspects of the implementation of this resolution 90 days after the entry into force of paragraph 1 above and again prior to the end of the 180-day period, on receipt of the reports referred to in paragraphs 4 and 5 below, and *expresses* its intention, prior to the end of the 180-day period, to consider favourably renewal of the provisions of this resolution, provided that the reports referred to in paragraphs 4 and 5 below indicate that those provisions are being satisfactorily implemented;

4. *Requests* the Secretary-General to report to the Council 90 days after the date of entry into force of paragraph 1 above, and again prior to the end of the 180-day period, on the basis of observation by United Nations personnel in Iraq, and on the basis of consultations with the Government of Iraq, on whether Iraq has ensured the equitable distribution of medicine, health supplies, foodstuffs, and materials and supplies for essential civilian needs, financed in accordance with paragraph 8 (a) of resolution 986 (1995), including in his reports any observations he may have on the adequacy of the revenues to meet Iraq's humanitarian needs, and on Iraq's capacity to export sufficient quantities of petroleum and petroleum products to produce the sum referred to in paragraph 1 of resolution 986 (1995);

5. *Requests* the Committee established by resolution 661 (1990), in close co-ordination with the Secretary General, to report to the Council 90 days after the date of entry into force of paragraph 1 above and again prior to the end of the 180-day period on the implementation of the arrangements in paragraphs 1, 2, 6, 8, 9 and 10 of resolution 986 (1995);

6. *Welcomes* the intention of the Secretary-General to submit a supplementary report, and *expresses* its willingness, in the light of his recommendations, to find ways of improving the implementation of the humanitarian programme and to take such action over additional resources as needed to meet priority humanitarian requirements of the Iraqi people, as well as to consider an extension of the time-frame for the implementation of this resolution;

7. *Requests* the Secretary-General to submit his supplementary report to the Council no later than 30 January 1998;

8. *Stresses the need* to ensure respect for the security and safety of all reasons appointed by the Secretary-General for the implementation of this resolution in Iraq;

9. *Requests* the Committee established by resolution 661 (1990) to continue, in close co-ordination with the Secretary-General, to refine and clarify working procedures in order to expedite the approval process and to report to the Council no later than 30 January 1998;

10. *Decides* to remain seized of the matter.

Appendix VI

Press Conference (Kofi Annan and Tariq Aziz, Baghdad, 23 February 1998) – Extracts

KA: I am pleased to announce that after detailed and intensive discussions with the Iraqi authorities culminating in a meeting with President Saddam Hussein on Sunday afternoon I have concluded an agreement with the Government of Iraq on the issue of the United Nations weapon inspections ... the terms of this agreement which have been concluded in writing are acceptable and remove a major obstacle to the full implementation of relevant Security Council Resolutions. I will soon report to the Security Council ... I would like to thank His Excellency President Saddam Hussein and the Government of Iraq for the good will, co-operation and courtesy extended to my delegation and myself during the last few days. The Deputy Prime Minister His Excellency Mr. Tariq Aziz and his senior colleagues have worked very hard ...

TA: ... we had constructive, intensive, objective discussions about the purpose of his mission. We highly appreciate the nature of the discussions we had, the understanding we reached and as His Excellency said, we have indeed reached a final agreement on the question we discussed. We also agreed that we will continue our co-operation with His Excellency the Secretary-General and with the United Nations in order to achieve the common objective and as far as Iraq is concerned ... the priority for the Iraqi people and the Iraq Government is an expeditious implementation of paragraph 22 of Resolution 687 and the lifting of all sanctions. We are going to work together in good faith and co-operation and we hope that this humanitarian, and legal objective of lifting of the sanctions will be done very soon.

Qu: Would you say that the threat of military force was a help or hindrance?

TA: When I was at the beginning of the crisis in New York in November, I made it quite clear that the military build up in the Gulf does not scare the people and the leadership of Iraq. What helped in reaching this agreement between the Secretary-General, my President and the Iraqi Government is the good will involved, not the American or the British build up in the Gulf and not the policy of sabre rattling. It was diplomacy, wise, balanced United Nations world diplomacy that enabled us to reach that agreement. Not the sabre rattling policy.

KA: ... You can do a lot with diplomacy but of course you can do a lot more with diplomacy backed up by fairness and force...

Qu: As the Secretary-General how can you give assurance that the [US] will comply with the agreement you have reached given that they have a history of not respecting UN resolutions?

KA: ... let me say that the agreement that I have reached with the Government of Iraq, I consider balanced and I consider that it is in conformity with the Security

Council Resolutions. It is in conformity in terms of spirit, and in terms of the intent and therefore I hope it will be acceptable to all members of the Council.

Qu: Is this a climb down by the Iraqi Government?

TA: No this is an agreement of reason and as the Secretary-General said, it's balanced and it is the conformity with UN Resolutions and as I have said and reiterated thousands of times that Iraq has no problem with the United Nations Resolutions, the problem is how they are implemented. If they are implemented in good faith, in a balanced manner along the spirit and the letter of the Charter of the United Nations, we have no problem with that...

Qu: Have you had telephone conversations with Mrs Albright and is the US reserving the right to accept the deal.

KA: Let me say that, the United States, or for that matter, other council members have neither accepted nor rejected this deal, they have not seen it, they will have it tomorrow and I will have discussions with them in New York.

Qu: What Iraq substantially has gained out of this crisis, and whether you feel that from a GOI perspective you can trust UNSCOM who have been mistrusted for so long?

TA: First of all, I think what we have achieved with the Secretary-General is a correct balanced manner to reach the truth. There were a lot of allegations and fabrications and dramatisations about the situation regarding Iraq on the question of disarmament ...

KA: Iraq and UNSCOM have had difficult relations at times. Those men and women working in UNSCOM have a difficult task. From Richard Butler right down. It is a task that regardless of whoever, there will be some difficulties. What is important for us is to work out practical, effective, instrumental relationships together. Mr Butler will continue to do his work but I think that what we are discussing here is better and enhanced co-operation between Iraq and the UNSCOM inspectors.

Qu: How close do you think we are from lifting sanctions?

KA: I am not sure I'm in a position to answer that question because that will be determined by the completion of the work of UNSCOM and the Atomic Agency. When and how soon they will complete it I cannot say, but I would hope that the way we have discussed this problem, our determination to improve relations, to enhance the work of UNSCOM and accelerate the process, we will be seeing light at the end of the tunnel.

Qu: What do you make about the possibility of war while there are US forces in the Gulf?

KA: I think a lot will depend on what happens when I get to New York after the Council has discussed my report. If they are convinced that we have a serious credible agreement, that is in conformity with all Security Council Resolutions I would hope that this will settle the issue.

Qu: Are there any time limits of future inspections to take place?

KA: I can say categorically that there are no time limits or deadlines in the agreement. Having said that, I think it is important that we try to do our work within a reasonable period.

Qu: Can Iraq see the light at the end of the tunnel?

TA: I think Iraq has achieved a great deal and it has had an opportunity to discuss its case, a just case before the whole world and the United Nations in the shape of the Secretary-General. We are not fearful of the truth. The agreement we have reached with the Secretary-General will prove the truth that has been previously presented by Iraq and will also show the lies and exaggeration regarding the situation ...

Qu: Could you tell us whether there will be any points in coming days, weeks that will demonstrate that Iraq will comply with the agreement. Iraq has, in the past Iraq signed agreement not carried out the contents. This concerns the US.

KA: We have negotiated this agreement in good faith. The Iraqi side was very serious and very frank in our discussions. I am hopeful, perhaps even confident, that this agreement will take us beyond the crisis and I would hope that the terms we have agreed on – questions of access, questions of inspections and all the things we are going to do are implemented respectfully and carefully. There will be no need for us to come back to this ...

I had a very good discussion with the President and we had good contact and the discussions were very very frank and at the end of it as you can see we did come to an agreement. The President was very well informed and was in full control of the facts. I was grateful to him that we were frank, constructive and at the end were determined to settle this issue diplomatically. My message to the young people around the world, is that in today's world which is rather inter-dependent, we need to be sensitive to the concerns of others, we need to understand other cultures ...

Qu: Does this accord cover the so called sovereign sites?

TA: Secretary-General and I agreed that we are not going to address details. We are only talking about the basic principles of the agreement and we all would prefer to leave the details until after the Secretary-General arrives in New York and briefs the Security Council.

Qu: Iraq had planned to open the Iraqi Presidential sites, this time you have waited for a long time. Is this diplomatic victory for Iraq?

TA: Since 26 November 1997, Iraq presented a proposal, a balanced proposal, to visit these Presidential sites by representatives of the international community. The principle is accepted by Iraq from the very beginning. We have nothing to hide in these sites, these are the sites of the Iraqi people and government ...

Qu: You spoke to Madelline Albright twice. What kind of encouragement do you have from her that this agreement will work?

KA: First of all, I did not seek encouragement or otherwise. We did talk about the status of the discussions and how we were likely to end up and then last time I spoke to her we do have a text that I'll be signing today. She did have some questions which I addressed and we will be talking further when I get back to New York ...

Qu: Can we say that the visit of the Secretary-General to Baghdad means the end of the crisis between Iraq and UN and US? How do you see the future relationship between Iraq and UNSCOM?

TA: In fact there was no crisis between Iraq and the UN. Evidenced by the fact of the agreement we have just reached by the Secretary-General and the positive atmosphere and constructive atmosphere which was the essence of this discussion. The crisis is with the US who is trying to impose its will on the UN. For Iraq this is not acceptable. The future relationship with UNSCOM will be determined by its behaviour. So, if it behaves as an international organisation of the UN according to international procedures adopted by other UN organisations, then we have no problem. In Iraq, currently, there is a large number of international organisations as part of the UN and we are co-operative with them completely and we have no problem with them or their representatives.

Qu: Iraq has said it would never allow inspection of Presidential palaces and now you are allowing these inspections to take place.

TA: First of all you don't know what we have agreed on and don't rush to conclusions.

Qu: What are the consequences if the agreement is broken?

KA: I did not come here with ultimatums as the Secretary-General of the United Nations...

Qu: How reliable do you judge ... Government of Iraq?

KA: I think I have answered that question already. I have indicated to you that given the kinds of understanding agreement and the atmosphere in which we reached that agreement. If we implement the things we have agreed to, I am sure we will not have any difficulties. I think your concern is, the import of your question is are we going to be back at this same situation in a similar crisis three months, six months from now. We went through all this and I genuinely believe we will co-operate and do the kinds of things we have agreed to do. We will not see that kind of crisis. That is the answer I will give you. We in the UN are determined to work constructively and respectively with the Iraqis and the Government of Iraq. They on their side have the same undertaking and are now determined to work with us in implementing all relevant Security Council resolutions. I think that that is a very good outcome ...

TA: ... In the history of the Arab world since the First World War it has been established for history that the successive British governments did not commit themselves to the promises they made to the Arab nations. There were the main government in this world who has backed down against the commitments it made to the Arabs including the Iraqis. They changed their policies, they did not respect their commitments. This is history.

KA: Before we break I want to thank those governments around the world who have really contributed to the success of this event. There are many leaders who made strenuous efforts to make this happen in this region and in Europe there were millions also out there who were praying for a diplomatic solution. We thank those all who wished us well, we thank those who prayed for us. You can never underestimate the power of prayer...

Appendix VII

Security Council Resolution 1154 (2 March 1998)

RESOLUTION 1154 (1998)

Adopted by the Security Council at its 3858th meeting on 2 March 1998

The Security Council

Recalling all its previous relevant resolutions, which constitute the governing standard of Iraqi compliance.

Determined to ensure immediate and full compliance by Iraq without conditions or restrictions with its obligations under resolution 687 (1991) and the other relevant resolutions.

Reaffirming the commitment of all Member States to the sovereignty, territorial integrity and political independence of Iraq, Kuwait and the neighbouring States,

Acting under Chapter VII of the Charter of the United Nations,

1. *Commends* the initiative by the Secretary-General to secure commitments from the Government of Iraq on compliance with its obligations under the relevant resolutions, and in this regard *endorses* the memorandum of understanding signed by the Deputy Prime Minister of Iraq and the Secretary-General on 23 February 1998 (S/1998/166), and *looks forward* to its early and full implementation;

2. *Requests* the Secretary-General to report to the Council as soon as possible with regard to the finalization of procedures for Presidential sites in consultation with the Executive Chairman of the United Nations Special Commission and the Director General of the International Atomic Energy Agency (IAEA);

3. *Stresses* that compliance by the Government of Iraq with its obligations, repeated again in the memorandum of understanding, to accord immediate, unconditional and unrestricted access to the Special Commission and the IAEA in conformity with the relevant resolutions, is necessary for the implementation of resolution 687 (1991), but that any violation would have severest consequences for Iraq;

4. *Reaffirms* its intention to act in accordance with the relevant provisions of resolution 687 (1991) on the duration of the prohibitions referred to in that resolution, and *notes* that by its failure so far to comply with its relevant obligations Iraq has delayed the moment when the Council can do so;

5. *Decides*, in accordance with its responsibility under the Charter, to remain actively seized of the matter, in order to ensure implementation of this resolution, and to secure peace and security in the area.

Appendix VIII

Procedures under paragraph 4(b) of the Memorandum of Understanding between the United Nations and the Republic of Iraq of 23 February 1998

Introduction

1. On 23 February 1998 a Memorandum of Understanding was signed between the United Nations and the Republic of Iraq. In this memorandum, the Government of Iraq, *inter alia*, reconfirms its acceptance of all relevant resolutions of the Security Council, including resolutions 687 (1991) and 715 (1991). The Government of Iraq further reiterates its undertaking to co-operate fully with the United Nations Special Commission (UNSCOM) and the International Atomic Energy Agency (IAEA). The Government of Iraq also undertakes to accord to UNSCOM and the IAEA immediate, unconditional and unrestricted access in conformity with all relevant resolutions.

2. For its part, the United Nations reiterates the commitment of all Member States to respect the sovereignty and territorial integrity of Iraq. In the performance of its mandate under the Security Council resolutions, UNSCOM undertakes to respect Iraq's legitimate concerns relating to national security, sovereignty and dignity.

3. The Memorandum of Understanding contains specific provisions with respect to the eight Presidential Sites in Iraq. Special procedures shall apply to the initial and subsequent entries into these Sites for the performance of mandated tasks. A Special Group shall be established by the Secretary-General of the United Nations in consultation with the Executive Chairman of UNSCOM and the Director General of the IAEA. The Special Group shall comprise senior diplomats appointed by the Secretary-General and experts drawn from UNSCOM and the IAEA. The Special Group shall be headed by a Commissioner appointed by the Secretary-General.

4. In carrying out its work, the Special Group shall, according to the Memorandum of Understanding, operate under the established procedures of UNSCOM and the IAEA together with specific detailed procedures given the special nature of the Presidential Sites, in accordance with the relevant resolutions of the Security Council.

5. The present text constitutes these specific detailed procedures. They are drawn by the Secretary-General under the authority of the Memorandum of Understanding.

Appendix VIII

Composition of the Special Group

6. The Special Group shall comprise senior diplomats, in the capacity of observers, appointed by the Secretary-General of the United Nations and experts drawn from UNSCOM and the IAEA in the number deemed appropriate by the Executive Chairman of UNSCOM and the Director General of IAEA.

Teams of the Special Group

7. When it is determined in accordance with paragraph 13 below that there is a need to carry out mandated tasks* at a Presidential Site, a team shall be constituted from the Special Group.

8. The expert members of the team shall be designated by the Executive Chairman of UNSCOM and/or the Director General of the IAEA having regard to the nature of the tasks to be performed. The Commissioner shall designate the senior diplomatic representatives, from among those appointed by the Secretary-General, in no case less than two, to accompany the team.

9. The Executive Chairman of UNSCOM and/or the Director General of the IAEA shall designate the Head of the team.

10. The team may be divided into sub-teams for the performance of specific tasks, if the Head of the team so decides.

Functions of senior diplomats

11. The functions of the senior diplomats shall be:

    (*a*) To observe that the provisions of the Memorandum of Understanding and the present specific detailed procedures are being implemented in good faith;

    (*b*) To report on any matter they deem appropriate to the functions of the diplomatic observers, in accordance with paragraphs 19 and 20 below.

Functions of UNSCOM/IAEA experts

12. The functions of the experts drawn from UNSCOM and the IAEA who participate in any team constituted from the Special Group shall be as already established under their respective procedures.

Determination of the need for entry into a Presidential site

13. The Executive Chairman of UNSCOM and/or the Director General of the IAEA shall determine the need, in each instance, for the performance of mandated tasks within a Presidential Site.

---

* Mandated tasks under the Security Council resolutions include those in section C of Security Council resolution 687 (1991); paragraph 3 of Security Council resolution 707 (1991); the Plans for Ongoing Monitoring and Verification approved by Security Council resolution 715 (1991); and the export/import regime approved by Security Council resolution 1051 (1996).

Determination of the time and date for entry into a Presidential site

14. The Executive Chairman of UNSCOM and/or the Director General of the IAEA shall determine the date and time for entry and shall so advise the Commissioner.

15. At a time determined by the Executive Chairman of UNSCOM and/or the Director General of the IAEA, the Government of Iraq shall receive a notification from the Commissioner, or his designee, of the intention to undertake mandated tasks within a Presidential Site. This notification shall indicate the number of persons comprising the team who will participate, including the number of diplomatic representatives accompanying the team.

The rights of the Special Group

16. The rights of the Special Group and its teams in the conduct of their work shall be those provided for in the relevant resolutions of the Security Council; in the exchange of letters of May 1991 between the Secretary-General of the United Nations and the Minister for Foreign Affairs of Iraq regarding the status, privileges and immunities of the Special Commission, applicable *mutatis mutandis* to the IAEA; and in the plans for ongoing monitoring and verification (OMV) approved under Security Council resolution 715 (1991).

Special considerations

17. Upon entry into a Presidential Site, the team shall conduct itself in a manner consonant with the nature of the Site. It shall take into consideration any observations the Iraqi representative may wish to make regarding entry into a particular structure and then decide upon the appropriate course of action. This shall not, however, impede the ability of the team to fulfil its tasks as mandated under the relevant Security Council resolutions.

Reporting

18. The report called for under paragraph 4(c) of the Memorandum of Understanding, prepared by the Commissioner appointed by the Secretary-General shall be submitted by the Executive Chairman of UNSCOM to the Security Council through the Secretary-General.

19. The senior diplomats may report directly to the Commissioner on any matter relevant to their functions.

20. The Commissioner will discuss with the Executive Chairman of UNSCOM and/or the Director General of the IAEA any observations made by the senior diplomats, including any matters arising from such observations that should be conveyed to the competent Iraqi authorities. If he deems it necessary, the Commissioner may also report any matter arising out of the work of the senior diplomats to the Secretary-General and advise the Executive Chairman of UNSCOM and the Director General of the IAEA accordingly.

Revisions

21. These specific detailed procedures may be revised from time to time in the light of experience in their implementation.

Notes

Introduction

1. Geoff Simons, *Iraq: From Sumer to Saddam* (London: Macmillan, 2nd edition, 1996), pp. 345–51.
2. William Blum, *The CIA: A Forgotten History: US Global Interventions since World War 2* (London and New Jersey: Zed Books, 1991).
3. Richard Dowden, 'US soldiers massacred 1000 Somalis in panic', *The Observer*, London, 22 March 1998; Richard Dowden, 'Chaos, panic, then murder', *The Observer*, London, 22 March 1998.
4. Penny Lernoux, *Cry of the People* (New York: Doubleday, 1980); Noam Chomsky, *Deterring Democracy* (London: Verso, 1991); Phil Gunson, 'US trained Mexican "torture squad"', *The Guardian*, London, 1 April 1998.
5. Robert Fisk, 'Israel faces new massacre probe', *The Independent on Sunday*, London, 19 April 1998.
6. Christopher Lockwood, 'US drops China human rights resolution', *The Daily Telegraph*, London, 16 March 1998; 'Chinese man "kept caged like animal"', *Reuters, The Daily Telegraph*, London, 30 March 1998.
7. Stephen Grey, 'They call this religion', *The Sunday Times*, London, 22 February 1998.
8. In Geoff Simons, *Vietnam Syndrome: Impact on US Foreign Policy* (Basingstoke: Macmillan, 1998). I have listed (pp. 299–302) more than two dozen US violations of international law.
9. David Sapsted, 'UN court seeks to block US execution', *The Daily Telegraph*, London, 11 April 1998; Mark Tran, 'US singled out as death penalty is condemned', *The Guardian*, London, 4 April 1998.
10. Patrick Cockburn, 'Iraq's weapons not effective, America admits', *The Independent*, London, 7 March 1998.
11. Kenneth R. Timmerman, *The Death Lobby: How the West Armed Iraq* (London: Fourth Estate, 1992); Michael White, 'UK anthrax strains "sold to Iraq"', *The Guardian*, London, 3 March 1998.
12. Peter Williams and David Wallace, *Unit 713* (London: Hodder and Stoughton, 1989), chapter 17.
13. Sheldon H. Harris, *Factories of Death* (London and New York: Routledge 1994), p. xi.
14. Peter Pringle, 'Retarded boys used in US test on radioactivity', *The Independent*, London, 30 December 1993.
15. Simon Tisdall, 'US admits years of atomic radiation tests on people', *The Guardian*, London, 30 December 1993; Tim Cornwell, 'Life under the cloud of America's "Nazi" tests', *The Observer*, London, 2 January 1994.
16. Jonathan Leake, 'MoD admits 40 years of human radiation tests', *The Sunday Times*, London, 24 November 1996.
17. Paul Lashmar and Tom McCarthy, 'How Britain cast plague on paradise', *The Observer*, London, 15 December 1996.
18. Andrew Gilligan and Rob Evans, 'City dwellers exposed to biological warfare tests', *The Sunday Telegraph*, London, 22 February 1997.

19. Associated Press, 'UK's "secret mustard gas test"', *The Guardian*, London, 18 April 1998.
20. Geoff Simons, *The Scourging of Iraq: Sanctions, Law and Natural Justice* (Basingstoke: Macmillan, 2nd edition, 1998), Preface, p. xiii.
21. *Ibid.*

Chapter 1: Who is to Judge?

1. Patrick Cockburn, 'Iraq's weapons not effective, America admits', *The Independent*, London, 7 March 1998.
2. See, for example, John R. MacArthur, *Second Front: Censorship and Propaganda in the Gulf War* (New York: Hill and Wang 1992); Philip M. Taylor, *War and the Media: Propaganda and Persuasion in the Gulf War* (Manchester, United Kingdom: Manchester University Press, 1992).
3. Louis Dumont, *Homo Hierarchicus: The Caste System and its Implications* (Chicago/London, 1980).
4. Hyam Maccoby, *A Pariah People: The Anthropology of Antisemitism* (London: Constable, 1996).
5. I describe in detail the effects of economic sanctions on the Iraqi civilian population in Geoff Simons, *The Scourging of Iraq: Sanctions, Law and Natural Justice* (Basingstoke, United Kingdom: Macmillan, 2nd edition, 1998).
6. Countries charged by the US State Department with responsibility for 'state-sponsored terrorism' are routinely listed in the annual *Patterns of Global Terrorism*. Typically these countries include: Cuba, Iran, Iraq, Libya, North Korea, Sudan and Syria. These are of course countries that refuse to accept American hegemony. Many other states (for example, Saudi Arabia, Israel and the United States itself) that sponsor terrorism are of course excluded from the list (see pp. 33–8, 191 of the present book).

Chapter 2: US – The Arrogance of Hegemony

1. For substantiation of these various charges see Geoff Simons, *The United Nations: A Chronology of Conflict* (Basingstoke: Macmillan, 1994); Geoff Simons, *UN Malaise: Power, Problems and Realpolitik* (Basingstoke: Macmillan, 1995); and my other Macmillan titles.
2. Consider Lord John Acton's much quoted observation: 'Power tends to corrupt and absolute power corrupts absolutely' (letter in *Life and Letters of Mandel Creighton*, 1904). (We may speculate about what this says of the alleged *absolutely powerful* deity presiding over a pain-racked world.) Acton added: 'Great men are also bad men, even when they exercise influence and not authority.' Compare Anthony Trollope: 'We know that power does corrupt, and that we cannot trust kings to have loving hearts' (*Prime Minister IV*, viii, 1876); and William Pitt, Earl of Chatham: 'Unlimited power is apt to corrupt the minds of those who possess it' (House of Lords, 9 January 1770).
3. James Walsh, 'America the Brazen', *Time*, 4 August 1997, pp. 23–7.
4. Robert W. Tucker and David C. Hendrickson, *The Imperial Temptation: The New World Order and America's Purpose* (New York: Council on Foreign Relations Press, 1992), pp. 14–15.

5. *Ibid.*
6. Martin Walker, 'American Caesar's dream', *The Guardian*, London, 21 January 1991.
7. Noam Chomsky, 'The weak shall inherit nothing', *The Guardian*, London, 25 March 1991.
8. Abdelrahman Munif, 'The war against a civilisation', *The Guardian*, London, 1 April 1991.
9. Patrick Brogan, 'Unrivalled Bush set to police the planet', *The Observer*, London, 25 August 1991.
10. This reached such a pitch that at least one legal expert, Marc Weller, a research fellow at Cambridge University, England, suggested that the deplorable behaviour of Washington in intimidating members of the Security Council should be investigated by the World Court.
11. James Adams, 'US missiles target Third World', *The Sunday Times*, London, 9 February 1992; Paul Rogers, 'A bomb to blast the bullies', *The Guardian*, London, 2 July 1992.
12. Adams, *op. cit.*
13. John Lichfield, 'Sabre-rattling by Stealth: the gunboat diplomacy of our time', *The Independent*, London, 13 September 1996.
14. Bailey Morris, 'World shaker emerges at IMF', *Independent on Sunday*, London, 2 May 1993.
15. Sarah Ryle, 'IMF calls for painful cuts in public services', *The Guardian*, London, 18 April 1996.
16. Kevin Watkins, 'IMF holds a gold key for Third World' (*'The fund must stop grinding the faces of the poor'*), *The Guardian*, London, 10 June 1996; Sarah Ryle, 'World Bank to admit flaws in policies for poor nations' (*'Countries like Uganda may be meeting the Structural Adjustment Programme Conditioning but its poorer people are getting poorer'*), *The Guardian*, London, 23 September 1996.
17. For a listing of more than two dozen US violations of international law see Geoff Simons, *Vietnam Syndrome: Impact on US Foreign Policy* (Basingstoke: Macmillan, 1998), pp. 299–302.
18. Martin Walker, 'Master of the universe', *The Guardian*, London, 7 August 1996.
19. Allan Philps, 'Pentagon shows its reach', *The Daily Telegraph*, London, 16 September 1997.
20. William Waldegrave, 'Britain's eternal interests', *The Daily Telegraph*, London, 16 February 1998. Waldegrave immediately clouds the issue by admitting that the support should not be 'blind' since the United States has made 'bad mistakes' in the past. The implied proposition that it is right to support the United States when it is right is so tautologically banal as to be useless as any guide to policy.
21. Andrew Higgins, 'Uncle Sam disturbs Asia's dreams', *The Observer*, London, 18 January 1998.
22. *Ibid.*
23. Quoted in Jonathan Freedland, 'Child victims of the American Dream', *The Guardian*, London, 4 June 1996.
24. Lewis H. Lapham, *Money and Class in America: Notes on the Civil Religion* (London: Pan, 1989), p. 37.
25. *Ibid.*, p. 46.
26. Lewis H. Lapham, 'Goths are at the gate of Emperor Clinton', *The Guardian*, London, 27 December 1997; extract from *Waiting for the Barbarians* (London: Verso, 1998).

27. *Ibid.*
28. *United States of America: Allegations of Police Torture in Chicago, Illinois*, Amnesty International, AMB 51/42/90, December 1990.
29. *Ibid.*
30. *United States of America: Torture, Ill-Treatment and Excessive Force by Police in Los Angeles, California*, Amnesty International, AMR 51/76/92, June 1992.
31. Report of the Chief Legislative Analyst to the Budget and Finance Committee of the City Council, 25 March 1991.
32. *USA: Torture, Ill-Treatment*, June 1992, *op. cit.*, p. 33.
33. *United States of America: Human Rights Violations: A Summary of Amnesty International's Concerns*, Amnesty International, AMR 51/25/95, March 1995.
34. 'Life and death behind bars: Death row USA', *Amnesty*, Amnesty International, March/April 1998, p. 22.
35. *United States of America: Police Brutality and Excessive Force in the New York City Police Department*, Amnesty International, AMR 51/36/96, June 1996.
36. *United States of America: Use of Electro-Shock Stun Belts*, Amnesty International, AMR 51/45/96, 12 June 1996.
37. *USA: Police Brutality*, June 1996, *op. cit.*
38. *USA: Use of Stun Belts*, 12 June 1996, *op. cit.*
39. M. N. Robinson, C. G. Brooks and G. D. Renshaw, 'Electric shock devices and their effects on the human body', *Medical Science and Law* (1990), Volume 30, Number 4.
40. *United States of America: Ill-Treatment of Inmates in Maricopa County Jails – Arizona*, Amnesty International, AMR 51/51/97, August 1997; cited cases involved Scott Norberg dying of asphyxia after being shackled in a restraint chair with a towel over his face; Eric Johnson who suffered a broken arm; David Hoyle who sustained broken teeth, knee injuries and damage to his spine; David Dalbec who suffered a broken nose; Bart Davis whose eye was seriously damaged during an assault by prison staff. It was also reported that juvenile offenders were being shackled in chain gangs.
41. See also *United States of America – The Death Penalty in Georgia: Racist, Arbitrary and Unfair*, Amnesty International, AMR 51/25/96, June 1996; *United States of America: Death Penalty Developments in 1996*, Amnesty International, AMR 51/01/97, March 1997.
42. Geoff Simons, *Vietnam Syndrome: Impact on US Foreign Policy, op. cit.*
43. See, for example, such publications as *The Link*, published by Americans for Middle East Understanding (AMEU), New York; and *ADC News Release*, published by the American-Arab Anti-Discrimination Committee (ADC), Washington.
44. *ADC News Release*, American-Arab Anti-Discrimination Committee, Washington, 24 September 1990.
45. The ADC reports are supplemented by other press reports: in, for example, *The Wall Street Journal*, 21 January 1990; *The New York Times*, 7 February 1991; *USA Today*, 23 January 1991; and *The Los Angeles Times*, 23 December 1990.
46. *1995 Report on Anti-Arab Racism* ADC, Washington, DC.
47. Olga Craig, 'If you need a heart, kidneys, unlined skin ... we will shoot a prisoner to order', *The Sunday Telegraph*, London, 1 March 1998.
48. *Ibid.*
49. In various Macmillan publications I have described the US-led sanctions against Libya, Iraq, North Korea and Cuba.
50. 'Security Council to hold open session on Libya', J.A.N.A., Jamahiriya News Agency, London, 13 March 1998.

51. Jean P. Sasson, *Princess* (London: Bantam, 1993), pp. 264–5.
52. I have profiled the Saudi human-rights record in Geoff Simons, *Saudi Arabia: The Shape of a Client Feudalism* (Basingstoke: Macmillan, 1998), chapter 1.
53. See *Torture in Saudi Arabia: No Protection, No Redress*, Redress and the Parliamentary Human Rights Group, London, November 1977.
54. John Sweeney, 'One man's agony on the cross', *The Observer*, London, 21 December 1997.
55. *Ibid.*
56. Letter dated 24 August 1997 from the Chargé d'Affaires A.I. of the Permanent Mission of Iraq to the United Nations, addressed to the Secretary-General, S/1997/664, 25 August 1997.
57. See, for example, Robert Fisk, 'Brutal equations of Israel's torture prison', *The Independent*, London, 16 August 1991; Shyam Bhatia, 'Tortured Mustafa left to die in a freezing Israeli jail', *The Observer*, London, 9 February 1992; Sarah Helm, 'Palestinians demand end to deaths in jail', *The Independent*, London, 7 August 1992.
58. Derek Brown, 'Israel "making torture legal"', *The Guardian*, London, 23 October 1995.
59. *Ibid.*
60. See, for example, Jane Hunter, 'The Israeli nuclear threat', *Arab Affairs* (Autumn 1989), Number 10, pp. 41–57.
61. Martin Walker, 'Thin line between might and right', *The Guardian*, London, 19 June 1993.
62. *Denial of Food and Medicine: The Impact of the US Embargo on Health and Nutrition in Cuba*, American Association for World Health (AAWH), Washington, DC, March 1997.
63. David Blundy and Andrew Lycett, *Qaddafi and the Libyan Revolution* (London: Weidenfeld and Nicolson, 1987), p. 10.
64. Robert Fisk, *The Times*, London, 15–17 April 1986.
65. *Ibid.*
66. *Patterns of Global Terrorism 1996*, State Department, Washington, DC, 30 April 1997.
67. Michael T. Klare and Peter Kornbluh (eds), *Low Intensity Warfare: How the US Fights Wars Without Declaring Them* (London: Methuen, 1989).
68. Quoted in Patrick Cockburn, 'Clinton backed Baghdad bombers', *The Independent*, London, 26 March 1996.
69. *Ibid.*
70. *Ibid.*
71. Letter dated 14 July 1997 from the Permanent Representative of Iraq to the United Nations, addressed to the Secretary-General, S/1997/548, 15 July 1997.
72. *Ibid.*, Annex (letter from Iraqi foreign minister Mohamed Said Al-Sahaf). The Annex also highlights a report in the French newspaper *Libération* (23 October 1991), highly relevant to the dispute over UN arms inspectors (see Parts II and III of present book): 'There were obviously secret agents and CIA operatives who were working for their own organisation rather than for the United Nations. Their job definitely involved gathering information, but it also involved behaving provocatively towards Baghdad in order to justify intervention by the United States Air Force, which would return to complete its mission.'
73. Patrick Cockburn, 'Iraqi officers pay dear', *The Independent*, London, 17 February 1998.
74. David Sharrock, 'Mossad revives Saddam plot', *The Guardian*, London, 1 November 1997.

75. Martin Kettle, 'Covert CIA plan to topple Iraqi president leaked', *The Guardian*, London, 27 February 1998.

76. See, for example, the consensual view expressed in four 'quality' British newspapers: 'A better Saddam solution', *The Sunday Times*, 1 February 1998; 'Strategy for Saddam', *The Times*, 5 February 1998; 'The man himself', *Daily Telegraph*, 6 February 1998; 'Target Saddam', *Daily Telegraph*, 11 February 1998; John Sweeney, 'Job vacancy for a nicer despot', *The Observer*, 8 February 1998.

77. Patrick Cockburn, 'US dreams of ways to get rid of Saddam', *The Independent*, London, 3 March 1998.

78. Chris Blackhurst, 'Britons gear up to fight US tax plans', *Independent on Sunday*, London, 22 November 1992.

79. John Palmer, 'EU prepares sanctions for trade war with US', *The Observer*, London, 28 July 1996; 'EU protests against US anti-trade law', *The Guardian*, London, 9 August 1996; Imre Karacs, 'Germany hits out at US over Iran and Libya', *The Independent*, London, 7 August 1996.

80. Joby Warrick, 'A Pentagon Green Light', *International Herald Tribune*, 2 January 1998.

81. Sheldon H. Harris, *Factories of Death: Japanese Biological Warfare, 1932–45, and the American Cover-Up* (New York: Routledge, 1994), p. x.

82. *Ibid.,* p. xi.

83. *Ibid.,* p. xii.

84. *Ibid.,* p. 157.

85. 'Activities of the United States in the Field of Biological Warfare', a Report to the Secretary of War by George W. Merck, Special Consultant on Biological Warfare, p. 4, Record Group 165, Entry 488, Box 182, National Archives, USA.

86. *'Summary of Major Events and Problems, United States Army Chemical Corps. (U), Fiscal Years 1961–1962,* US Army Chemical Corps Historical Office, Army Chemical Centre, Maryland, 1962, p. 16.

87. *New York Times*, 6 February 1989, II, p. 9.

88. Harris, *Factories of Death, op. cit.,* p. 233.

89. Peter Williams and David Wallace, *Unit 731: The Japanese Army's Secret of Secrets* (London: Hodder and Stoughton, 1989).

90. David Usborne, 'Utah trembles as army prepares to destroy weapons', *Independent on Sunday*, London, 28 January 1996; Ian Katz, 'Nerve gas fears in Utah's desert', *The Observer*, London, 28 January 1996.

91. Ed Vulliamy, 'US law blocks weapons inspectors', *The Guardian*, London, 12 February 1998.

92. *Ibid.*

93. *International peace and security as an essential condition for the enjoyment of human rights, above all the right to life.* The Sub-Committee on Prevention of Discrimination and Protection of Minorities, Economic and Social Council, United Nations, E/CN.4/Sub.2/1997/L.11/Add.4, 1997/36.

94. See, for example, Alexander Garrett, 'Morality play on the markets', *The Observer*, London, 6 March 1994.

95. 'Possible Actions to Provoke, Harass or Disrupt Cuba', US Army memorandum, March 1962; Martin Kettle, 'Kennedy-era papers reveal anti-Castro dirty tricks', *The Guardian*, London, 20 November 1997 ('... Cuba occupied the same role in the US political psyche as Saddam Hussein today').

96. Noam Chomsky, 'A stand on low moral ground', *The Guardian*, London, 10 January 1991; Robert Fisk, 'Iron fists: How the West was one', *The Independent*, London, 29 October 1994.

97.　Caroline Lees, 'Oil barons court Taliban in Texas', *The Sunday Telegraph*, London, 14 December 1997; Ed Vulliamy, 'US women fight Taliban oil deal', *The Guardian*, London, 12 January 1998.

98.　Kevin Pratt, 'Gulf war could pose a threat to share prices', *The Sunday Times*, London, 22 February 1998.

99.　Roland Gribben, 'Deal with Saddam sends oil to 4 year low', *Daily Telegraph*, London, 24 February 1998.

Chapter 3:　Iraq – The Background

1.　Ghassan Attiyah, *Al Quds Al Arabi*, London, 14 February 1996, quoted by Said K. Aburish, *A Brutal Friendship: The West and the Arab Elite* (London: Victor Gollancz, 1997), p. 46.

2.　Aburish, *A Brutal Friendship, op. cit.*, p. 137.

3.　*Ibid.* p. 139.

4.　According to testimony by an anonymous *Time* official cited by Aburish, *A Brutal Friendship, op. cit.*, p. 383.

5.　Ghassan Attiyah cites Heikal in *Al Quds Al Arabi*, 12 November 1994; cited by Aburish, *A Brutal Friendship, op. cit.*, p. 383.

6.　See p. 44; see also Geoff Simons, *Iraq: From Sumer to Saddam* (Basingstoke: Macmillan, 2nd edition, 1996), pp. 338–45.

7.　Mohammad Heikal, *Illusions of Triumph: An Arab View of the Gulf War* (London: Fontana, 1993) p. 273.

8.　See, for example, Pierre Salinger (with Eric Laurent), *Secret Dossier: The Hidden Agenda Behind the Gulf War* (London: Penguin Books, 1991); first published in France as *Guerre de Golfe: Le Dossier Secret* (Paris: Olivier Orban, 1991).

9.　See Simons, *Iraq, op. cit.*, pp. 345–51.

10.　These events are traced in detail in Simons, *Iraq, op. cit.*, pp. 260–83.

11.　See, for example, Samir al-Khalil, *Republic of Fear* (London: Hutchinson Radius, 1990).

12.　Shyam Bhatia, 'Saddam breaks torture taboo', *The Observer*, London, 21 November 1997; 'Ritual terror and squalor in execution factory', *The Observer*, London, 15 February 1998.

13.　Shyam Bhatia, 'Ritual terror …', *op. cit.*

14.　See Geoff Simons, *Saudi Arabia: The Shape of a Client Feudalism* (Basingstoke: Macmillan, 1998).

15.　'Pray and pay', *Independent on Sunday*, London, 28 September 1997. We may reflect that politically targeted demons may not be all bad: Adolf Hitler reportedly disapproved of cruelty to animals, one reason for his vegetarianism (Mark Almond, 'Hitler's strange priorities', *The Daily Telegraph*, London, 17 January 1998).

16.　James Adams, 'US troops to get anthrax jabs', *The Sunday Times*, London, 11 May 1997.

17.　Tim Butcher, 'Deadly arsenal is easily hidden from attackers', *The Daily Telegraph*, London, 5 February 1998; see also David Fairhall, Richard Norton-Taylor and Tim Radford, 'Saddam's deadly armoury', *The Guardian*, London, 11 February 1998: 'A mounting fear *lurks* behind the mounting threats to bomb the remnants of Saddam Hussein's military machine: that a missile *hidden somewhere in the desert* would dump a ton of nerve gas or deadly anthrax spores on the population of Tel Aviv, or a dozen other cities within range. *True it is only a remote possibility...*' (my italics); Philip Sherwell, 'Saddam's biological threat', *The Sunday Telegraph*, London, 15 February 1998: '... But he [Saddam] *could* lash out with his arsenal of chemical and biological weapons' (my italics). What arsenal?

18. Con Coughlin, 'Iraq deployed anthrax during 1991 Gulf war', *The Sunday Telegraph*, London, 15 February 1998.
19. Tim Butcher, 'Britain sent anthrax agent to Saddam', *The Daily Telegraph*, London, 14 February 1998.
20. Tim Butcher, 'Germ warfare "jelly" sold to Iraq until 1996', *The Daily Telegraph*, London, 19 February 1998.
21. Kenneth R. Timmerman, *The Death Lobby: How the West Armed Iraq* (London: Fourth Estate, 1992); see also Sir Richard Scott, *Report of the Inquiry into the Export of Defence Equipment and Dual-Use Goods to Iraq and Related Prosecutions* (the Scott Report) (London: HMSO, 15 February 1996), Appendix A (Part A), Schedule of Export Licence Applications 1984–1990'.
22. The character of the 1991 Gulf War is profiled in Geoff Simons, *The Scourging of Iraq: Sanctions, Law and Natural Justice* (Basingstoke: Macmillan, 2nd edition, 1998), pp. 4–27.
23. For a detailed chronology of sanctions, see *ibid.*, pp. 33–103.
24. *Ibid.*, pp. 105–73.
25. *Ibid.*, pp. 24–5, 109–13.
26. *Ibid.*, pp. 113–22.
27. Umeed Mubarak, Iraqi Health Minister, *Reuters*, 12 May 1997.
28. For a detailed account see Simons, *Scourging ...* (1998), *op. cit.*, pp. 215–27; *Unsanctioned Suffering: A Human Rights Assessment of United Nations Sanctions on Iraq*, Centre for Economic and Social Rights, New York, May 1996.
29. *The Realization of Economic, Social and Cultural Rights*, Note verbale (21 May 1996) from the Permanent Mission of Iraq to the UN Office at Geneva, addressed to the Centre for Human Rights, E/CN.4/Sub.2/1996/33, 7 June 1996.
30. Committee on the Elimination of Racial Discrimination (CERD), International Convention, Summary Record of the 1203rd Meeting, United Nations, Geneva, 11th and 12th periodic reports on Iraq, 14 March 1997, CERD/C/SR.1203, 25 April 1997.
31. Letter (20 May 1997) from the Permanent Representative of Iraq to the United Nations addressed to the Secretary-General, S/1997/382, 20 May 1997.
32. Letter (25 May 1997) from the Minister of Foreign Affairs of Iraq, addressed to the Secretary-General, S/1997/402, 27 May 1997; see also letter (11 June 1997), S/1997/452, 12 June 1997; letter (12 July 1997), S./1997/544, 15 July 1997.
33. Antonio Monteiro, letter (30 May 1997) addressed to the president of the Security Council, S/1997/417, 30 May 1997.
34. Report of the Secretary-General pursuant to Paragraph 11 of Resolution 986 (1995), S/1997/419, 2 June 1997, paragraph 49.
35. *Ibid.*, paragraph 51.
36. Letter (16 September 1997) from the Minister for Foreign Affairs of Iraq, addressed to the Secretary-General and to the President of the Security-Council, S/1997/717.
37. There are many estimates of the number of civilian dead caused by the Hiroshima bomb; none exceed 200,000. One UNICEF estimate of the number of Iraqi children killed by sanctions is *two million*.
38. FAO/WFP Food Supply and Nutrition Assessment Mission to Iraq, Special Report, 3 October 1997 ('Malnutrition still remains a serious problem ... Of

major importance is the severe deterioration of the water and sanitation system').

39. Nutritional Status Survey of Infants in South/Centre in Iraq, 27 October to 2 November 1997, Iraqi Ministry of Health and UNICEF, 14 November 1997.

40. 'Nearly one million children malnourished in Iraq, says UNICEF: Surveys reveal deepening crisis', UNICEF, CF/DOC/PR/1997-60, 26 November 1997; see also letter (28 November 1997) from Permanent Representative of Iraq to the United Nations, addressed to the President of the Security Council, S/1997/934, 28 November 1997.

41. Richard Garfield, Sarah Zaidi and Jean Lennock, 'Medical care in Iraq after six years of sanctions', *British Medical Journal*, 29 November 1997, pp. 1474–5.

42. *Ibid.*, p. 1475.

43. Felicity Arbuthnot (letter), 'Iraqi: Who do sanctions hurt?', *The Guardian*, London, 1 November 1997.

44. Ian Aitken, 'Why do we support starvation', *The Guardian*, London, 3 December 1997.

45. John Simpson, 'Sanctions are not the way to beat Saddam', *The Sunday Telegraph*, London, 16 November 1997.

46. Dominic Evans, 'Food crisis worsening, UN warns', *The Guardian*, London, 4 February 1998.

47. 'Suffer the children: What about sanctions?', *The Guardian*, London, 19 February 1998.

48. Maggie O'Kane, 'Sick and dying in their hospital beds, the pitiful victims of sanctions and Saddam', *The Guardian*, London, 19 February 1998.

49. Evidence for these charges is given in Simons, *Scourging ...* (1998), *op. cit.*, in Ramsey Clark *et al.*, *War Crimes: A Report on United States War Crimes against Iraq* (Washington, DC: Maisonneuve Press, 1992); and many other sources

Chapter 4:   From UN Coalition ... (June to November 1997)

1. Letter (18 June 1997) from the Minister for Foreign Affairs of Iraq, addressed to the President of the Security Council, S/1997/473.

2. Letter (27 August 1997) from the Chairman of the Security Council Committee Established by Resolution 661 (1990) Concerning the Situation between Iraq and Kuwait, addressed to the President of the Security Council, introducing the annual report on the work of the Committee, 27 August 1997, Paragraphs 27 and 28.

3. *Ibid.*, Paragraph 32.

4. 'Turkish tanks head into Iraq', *Reuters*, Diyarbakir, *The Guardian*, London, 25 September 1997.

5. Report submitted by the Executive Chairman of the Special Commission ..., published as a Secretary-General Report, S/1997/774, 6 October 1997.

6. Ian Black, 'Allies clash over Iraq sanctions', *The Guardian*, London, 8 October 1997.

7. Tariq Aziz, letter to Juan Somaria, President of the Security Council, S/1997/829, 29 October 1997 (reference made to Aziz, letter, 15 June 1997, S/1997/456).

8. *Ibid.*

9. *Ibid.*

10. *Ibid.*

11. *Ibid.*
12. David Hirst, 'Saddam has little to lose in show of strength', *The Guardian*, London, 31 October 1997.
13. Patrick Cockburn, 'Iraq holds firm to bar on US arms inspectors', *The Independent*, London, 1 November 1997.
14. 'Baghdad "ready for military response"', *The Daily Telegraph*, London, 1 November 1997.
15. Con Coughlin, 'Saddam sells drugs on black market': 'Saddam's son makes a killing from drugs', *The Sunday Telegraph*, London, 2 November 1997.
16. See, for example, Shyam Bhatia, 'Saddam's doomsday arsenal uncovered', *The Observer*, London, 2 November 1997; Marie Colvin and Uzi Mahnaimi, 'Saddam's doomsday option', *The Sunday Times*, London, 9 November 1997.
17. I witnessed television broadcasts in which earnest members of the public were invited to parade their conviction that Saddam was about to explode atomic bombs.
18. Bhatia, 'Saddam's doomsday arsenal', *op. cit.*
19. Robert Shrimsley, 'Inquiry on "anthrax" exports to Baghdad', *The Daily Telegraph*, London, 3 April 1998.
20. Patrick Cockburn, 'UN to call Saddam's bluff over expulsions', *Independent on Sunday*, London, 2 November 1997.
21. Britain's unquestioning support for Washington was deemed so inconsequential (an assumed premise) that the possibility of US/UK military action was often described in the United States as a *'unilateral'* response.
22. David Hirst, 'US trio turned away by defiant Iraq', *The Guardian*, London, 3 November 1997.
23. *Ibid.*
24. Julian Borger, 'UN talks with Iraq end on "positive note"', *The Guardian*, London, 7 November 1997.
25. Christopher Lockwood and Amberin Zaman, 'Iraq on alert for air strikes amid deadlock at talks', *The Daily Telegraph*, London, 7 November 1997.
26. Julian Borger and Ian Black, 'US and Iraq clear decks for combat', *The Guardian*, London, 8 November 1997.
27. *Ibid.*
28. Marie Colvin and Uzi Mahnaimi, 'Saddam invents germ warfare crop-duster to spray cities', *The Sunday Times*, London, 9 November 1997; 'Saddam's doomsday option', *The Sunday Times*, London, 9 November 1997.
29. Shyam Bhatia, 'Iraqi "suitcase bomb" could kill millions', *The Observer*, London, 9 November 1997.
30. Philip Sherwell, 'Britain plans Tornado strikes against Saddam', *The Sunday Telegraph*, London, 9 November 1997.
31. Hugh Davies, 'Saddam is warned on threats to shoot U-2s', *The Daily Telegraph*, London, 10 November 1997.
32. Letter (11 November 1997) from the Minister of Foreign Affairs of Iraq, addressed to the President of the Security Council, S/1997/873, 11 November 1997.
33. Preamble to Resolution 1137 (1997), S/RES/1137 (1997), 12 November 1997 (see also Appendix IV of present book).
34. 'Iraq: diminishing options: sooner or later military action will be considered' (editorial), *The Guardian*, London, 12 November 1997.
35. Christopher Lockwood, 'Robinson tries soft pedal on human rights', *The Daily Telegraph*, London, 13 November 1997; Ian Black, 'Human rights champion says UN has lost the plot', *The Guardian*, London, 13 November 1997 (*'It is*

part of my job to bring to public consciousness the incredible suffering of the Iraqi people ... I won't be the decider of what will be done, but I will be prepared to be a voice').

36. Hugh Davies and Tim Butcher, 'Britain sends in carrier as Iraq raises the stakes', *The Daily Telegraph*, London, 14 November 1997; Martin Kettle, Ian Black and Julian Borger, 'UN pulls out as Iraq war looms', *The Guardian*, London, 14 November 1997.
37. 'Gulf War allies fall away as US goes to the brink', *The Guardian*, London, 15 November 1997.
38. *Ibid.*
39. Mary Dejevsky, 'Last superpower defied by friends and enemies alike', *The Independent*, London, 15 November 1997.
40. Patrick Cockburn, 'Can America match its mouth with its muscle?', *The Independent*, London, 15 November 1997; 'Saddam may not lose a media war', *Independent on Sunday*, 16 November 1997.
41. *Ibid.*
42. Joan Smith, 'Can six slighted Americans be worth a war?', *Independent on Sunday*, London, 16 November 1997.
43. Ivo Dawnay, 'To bomb or not to bomb?', *The Sunday Telegraph*, London, 16 November 1997.
44. *Ibid.*
45. Marie Colvin, 'Saddam hides secret arsenal behind women and children', *The Sunday Times*, London, 16 November 1997.
46. Jon Swain, 'Iraq making lethal gas in covert Sudan pact', *The Sunday Times*, London, 16 November 1997.
47. Marie Colvin and Michael Prescott, 'Blair and Clinton to "stand tough" on Iraq', *The Sunday Times*, London, 16 November 1997.

Chapter 5: ... To US Military Countdown (November 1997 to February 1998)

1. General H. Norman Schwarzkopf with Peter Petre, *It Doesn't Take a Hero* (London: Bantam press, 1992), p. 488.
2. Robert Fisk, 'Arab nations stay away from talks in snub to Clinton', *The Independent*, London, 14 November 1997.
3. Letter (16 November 1997) from the Minister for Foreign Affairs of Iraq, addressed to the President of the Security Council, S/1997/900.
4. *Ibid.*
5. Chris Morris, 'Clash of Kurdish rivals deepens allies' plight?', *The Guardian*, London, 17 November 1997.
6. Anton La Guardia, 'Saddam savours West's dilemma', *The Daily Telegraph*, London, 18 November 1997.
7. Steve Crawshaw, 'Britain and US fear Saddam will be let off the hook', *The Independent*, London, 18 November 1997.
8. Martin Kettle, 'Diplomacy paving the way in Iraq crisis', *The Guardian*, London, 18 November 1997.
9. Ian Black, James Meek and Martin Kettle, 'West offers sweeteners to head off Iraqi clash', *The Guardian*, London, 10 November 1997.
10. Hugh Davies, 'Clinton builds up air power as US edges towards deal on Iraq', *The Daily Telegraph*, London, 19 November 1997.

11. Letter (20 November 1997) from the Permanent Representative of Iraq to the United Nations, addressed to the President of the Security Council, S/1997/908, 20 November 1997.
12. The Joint Russian–Iraqi Declaration is appended to the letter (20 November 1997), *ibid.*, as Enclosure II.
13. Enclosure II, letter (20 November 1997), S/1997/908, *op. cit.*
14. David Usborne, 'Was one man to blame for Iraq crisis?', *The Independent*, London, 20 November 1997.
15. *Ibid.*
16. *Ibid.*
17. Felicity Arbuthnot, 'Iraqi convents searched by UN officials', *Catholic Herald*, 21 November 1997.
18. *Ibid.*
19. *Ibid.*
20. Christopher Lockwood, 'Overnight gain may prove costly in the long run', *The Daily Telegraph*, London, 21 November 1997.
21. Letter (22 November 1997) from the Executive Chairman of the Special Commission Established by the Secretary-General Pursuant to Paragraph 9(b)(i) of Security Council Resolution 687 (1991), addressed to the President of the Security Council, S/1997/922, 24 November 1997.
22. *Ibid.*
23. *Ibid.*
24. Letters (24 November 1997) from the Permanent Representative of Iraq to the United Nations, addressed to the Secretary-General and to the President of the Security Council, S/1997/924, 24 November 1997.
25. Letter (24 November 1997) from the Permanent Representative of Iraq to the United Nations, addressed to the President of the Security Council, S/1997/925, 24 November 1997.
26. Hugo Gurdon, 'Clinton tries to cool Russia's warmth for Iraq', *The Daily Telegraph*, London, 25 November 1997.
27. Maggie O'Kane, *The Guardian Weekend*, London, 16 December 1995.
28. Gurdon, 'Clinton tries to cool Russia's warmth', *op. cit.*
29. Letters (29 November 1997) from the Permanent Representative of Iraq to the United Nations, addressed to the Secretary-General and to the President of the Security Council, S/1997/933, 26 November 1997.
30. Report of the Secretary-General Pursuant to Paragraph 3 of Resolution 1111 (1997), S/1997/935, 28 November 1997.
31. *Ibid.*
32. *Ibid.*
33. *Ibid.*
34. *Ibid.*
35. Sheldon H. Harris, *Factories of Death* (New York: Routledge 1994), pp. xi, 232–3.
36. Letter (3 December 1997) from the Secretary-General, addressed to the President of the Security Council, S/1997/950, 3 December 1997, Appendix, Paragraph 20.
37. *Jordan Times*, 6 December 1997, p. 1.
38. *Ibid.*, p. 2.
39. Richard Norton-Taylor, 'Iraq in fresh clash with UN', *The Guardian*, London, 11 December 1997.
40. Michael Theodoulou and Michael Binyon, 'Saddam executes hundreds in new terror campaign', *The Times*, London, 12 December 1997. King Hussein

described the execution of the four Jordanians as a 'heinous crime... The blood of Jordanians is not cheap' (*Jordan Times*, 13 December 1997).

41. Tom Baldwin, 'PM's secret talks with Thatcher', *The Sunday Telegraph*, London, 14 December 1997.
42. Hugo Gurdon, 'UN finds palace clue to Saddam weapons', *The Daily Telegraph*, London, 20 December 1997.
43. *Ibid.*
44. *Ibid.*
45. Letter (20 December 1997) from the Minister of Foreign Affairs of Iraq, to the Secretary-General and to the President of the Security Council, S/1997/1025, 30 December 1997.
46. Ian Black, 'Iraq "making Libyan arms"', *The Guardian*, London, 8 January 1998. The report later concedes, after the provocative headline and the leading paragraphs: '... evidence is hard to find and there have been misinterpretations of intelligence and Libyan accusations of black propaganda'.
47. Martin Kettle, 'US addresses nightmare of chemical attack', *The Guardian*, London, 10 January 1998.
48. The United States is known to have tested biological, chemical and nuclear agents on unsuspecting human beings (Harris, *Factories of Death, op. cit.*, pp. xi, 232–3).
49. Marie Colvin and Uzi Mahnaimi, 'Iraq tested anthrax on PoWs', *The Sunday Times*, London, 18 January 1998; Mark Tran, 'Iraqis deny human tests', *The Guardian*, London, 16 January 1998; James Burnett, 'Iraq attacks germ test "lies"', *The Scotsman*, 15 January 1998. On 17 January 1998 UNSCOM officials revealed that Iraqi scientists had carried out tests on animals (as if animal experimentation were totally unknown in the United States and Britain) (*The Guardian*, London, 18 January 1998).
50. Hugo Gurdon, 'Iraq faces countdown to attack', *The Daily Telegraph*, London, 19 January 1998.
51. *Ibid.*
52. William Shawcross, 'Deadly games in the desert', *The Sunday Times*, London, 25 January 1998.
53. *Ibid.*
54. Shyam Bhatia, 'Iraqis given anthrax secrets by Porton Down scientists', *The Observer*, London, 25 January 1998.
55. *Ibid.*
56. Jon Swain, 'US poised for strike against Baghdad', *The Sunday Times*, London, 25 January 1998.
57. *Hansard*, House of Commons, London, 26 January 1998.
58. *Ibid.*
59. Michael Evans, 'Royal Navy braced for Iraqi attack', *The Times*, London, 27 January 1998.
60. Michael Theodoulou and Robin Lodge, 'Saddam faces three-day US air offensive', *The Times*, London, 27 January 1998.
61. Christopher Walker and Michael Theodoulou, 'Israel "threatens nuclear reply" to Iraq germ attack', *The Times*, London, 29 January 1998.
62. *Ibid.*
63. Letter (28 January 1998) from Minister for Foreign Affairs of Iraq, addressed to the President of the Security Council, S/1998/89, 28 January 1998. Al-Sahaf makes reference to 127 other letters on this subject that Iraq has addressed to the UN Secretary-General.
64. Ian Brodie, 'Pentagon tests "bunker buster" for Iraq raids', *The Times*, London, 30 January 1998.

65. Hugh Davies, 'American envoys lay the ground for an attack to topple Saddam', *The Daily Telegraph*, London, 31 January 1998.
66. Report of the Secretary-General Pursuant to Paragraph 7 of Resolution 1143 (1997), S/1998/90, 1 January 1998.
67. *Ibid.*, paragraph 29.
68. *Ibid.*, paragraph 67.
69. Paul Rogers, 'Fuse burns to Gulf War II', *The Observer*, London, 1 January 1998.
70. Philip Sherwell, 'One last chance for diplomacy as air strikes are planned on Iraq', *The Sunday Telegraph*, London, 1 February 1998.
71. Marie Colvin, 'Iraqis braced for airstrike', *The Sunday Times*, London, 1 February 1998.
72. Kofi Annan, press conference, United Nations, New York, 2 February 1998.
73. Ian Brodie and Christopher Walker, '"Wider war" risk as Israelis win right to hit back', *The Times*, London, 2 February 1998.
74. *Hansard*, House of Commons, London, 2 February 1998.
75. Robert Fisk, 'Britain and America march towards a battle the Arabs do not want', *The Independent*, London, 2 February 1998.
76. Julian Borger and Ian Black, 'Iraq warned as talks go on', *The Guardian*, London, 2 February 1998.
77. Anton La Guardia, Robert Shrimsley and Tim Butcher, 'West set for air strikes on Iraq', *The Daily Telegraph*, London, 2 February 1998.
78. Michael Binyon, 'Washington seeks to keep Saddam guessing over choice of targets', *The Times*, London, 2 February 1998.
79. David Hirst, 'Ranting lord of the joyful martyrs', *The Guardian*, London, 4 February 1998.
80. Tony Blair, 'We will stop Saddam', *The Daily Telegraph*, London, 5 February 1998.
81. Philip Webster and Michael Dynes, 'We are ready to use force, says Blair', *The Times*, London, 5 February 1998.
82. Peter de la Billière, 'Bombs won't beat him', *The Daily Telegraph*, London, 6 February 1998.
83. Ed Vulliamy and Patrick Wintour, 'We'll shoot them but it won't really be war', *The Observer*, London, 8 February 1998; Patrick Wintour, 'Allied strike at Saddam will end UN inspections', *The Observer*, London, 8 February 1998.
84. Patrick Cockburn, 'So, just how much of a war would you like, Mr President?', *The Independent on Sunday*, London, 8 February 1998.
85. Tim Butcher, 'Republican Guard will be prime target', *The Daily Telegraph*, London, 9 February 1998.
86. Amberin Zaman, 'Turks pour troops over border to curb Kurds', *The Daily Telegraph*, London, 10 February 1998; Chris Morris, 'Ankara acts to block exodus of refugees', *The Guardian*, London, 10 February 1998.
87. Tim Butcher, 'Super-weapons hidden in tissue of lies', *The Daily Telegraph*, London, 12 February 1998.
88. 'Double standard for inspection' (editorial), *The Guardian*, London, 12 February 1998 (see also p. 41 of present book).
89. Julian Borger, 'Amman faces rising anger', *The Guardian*, London, 13 February 1998.
90. Tony Blair, 'For once, there is no third way', *The Observer*, London, 15 February 1998.
91. Matthew Campbell and Andrew Alderson, 'Desert Thunder ready to strike', *The Sunday Times*, London, 15 February 1998.

92. Hugh Davies, 'Pentagon chief says strikes may kill 1500 Iraqis', *The Daily Telegraph*, London, 16 February 1998.
93. *Ibid.*
94. David Fairhall, 'Hunt for the hidden assets: the risks', *The Guardian*, London, 16 February 1998.
95. Richard Norton-Taylor, 'MI5 lists "suspect" Arabs in UK', *The Guardian*, London, 18 February 1998.
96. Martin Kettle, 'White House scores a PR own goal', *The Guardian*, London, 19 February 1998.
97. Michael White and Ian Black, 'Whitehall in spin over lack of public support', *The Guardian*, London, 20 February 1998.
98. Julian Borger, 'Moment of truth dawns for Saddam', *The Guardian*, London, 21 February 1998.
99. David Wastell and Ivo Dawnay, 'The cracks begin to show', *The Sunday Telegraph*, London, 22 February 1998.
100. Jon Swain, Matthew Campbell, Andy Goldberg, Andrew Alderson and Michael Prescott, 'The day of reckoning', *The Sunday Times*, London, 22 February 1998.
101. Tom Baldwin and David Wastell, 'Cook warns Blair over backing for Iraq raids', *The Sunday Telegraph*, London, 22 February 1998.
102. Bruce W. Nelan, 'How the attack on Iraq is planned', *Time*, 23 February 1998, p. 26.

Chapter 6: The Annan Deal

1. David Usborne, 'How Britain came top of the class', *The Independent on Sunday*, London, 15 December 1996.
2. Jonathan Steele, 'Global warning', *The Observer*, London, 22 December 1996.
3. Jonathan Steele, 'A peace of the action', *The Guardian*, London, 30 December 1996.
4. *Ibid.*
5. Martin Walker, 'Red carpet, no greenbacks', *The Guardian*, London, 24 January 1997.
6. *Ibid.*
7. *Ibid.*
8. David Sapsted, 'America wants crackdown on "deadbeat dads"', *The Daily Telegraph*, London, 11 June 1997.
9. Mark Tran, 'Reformer rewrites UN hymn sheet', *The Guardian*, London, 27 December 1997.
10. *Ibid.*
11. Letter (29 December 1997) from the Deputy Prime Minister of Iraq, addressed to the Executive Chairman of the Special Commission ...; Letter (8 January 1998) from the Executive Chairman of the Special Commission ... addressed to the Deputy Prime Minister of Iraq, S/1998/26 (*'It is not the practice of UNSCOM to provide to the members of the Security Council ... materials...'*).
12. Letter (22 January 1998) from the Executive Chairman of the Special Commission ... addressed to the President of the Security Council, S/1998/58.
13. *Ibid.*, paragraphs 59 and 60.
14. *Ibid.*, paragraph 83.
15. Julian Borger 'Pentagon begins countdown against Iraq', *The Guardian*, London, 26 January 1998.

16. Letter (22 January 1998), *op. cit.*
17. Observations of the Government of the Republic of Iraq on the Report of the Secretary-General of the United Nations, issued on 1 February 1998 as documents S/1998/90, S/1998/104.
18. *Ibid.*, page 7.
19. Letter (6 February 1998) from the Minister for Foreign Affairs of Costa Rica, addressed to the Secretary-General, S/1998/118.
20. See, for example, letter (15 February 1998) from the Iraqi UN ambassador to the Secretary-General, S/1998/125.
21. Letter (15 February 1998) from the Permanent Representative of Iraq, addressed to the Secretary-General, S/1998/126. Here 20 'Turkish attacks', on Iraqi territory (23 October to 25 December 1997) are listed.
22. Mark Tran, 'A decent man who carries a polite ultimatum to Saddam', *The Guardian*, London, 19 February 1998.
23. Hugh Davies and Ambrose Evans-Pritchard, 'Anthrax terror plot failed in US', *The Daily Telegraph*, London, 20 February 1998.
24. Emma Daly, 'Armada of doom lies in wait for Saddam', *The Independent*, London, 21 February 1998.
25. Francesca Ciriaci, 'Crown Prince, Annan expect success of Baghdad mission', *Jordan Times*, 21 February 1998.
26. *Ibid.*
27. David Millward and Christopher Lockwood, 'Britain's ports on terror alert as extremists face expulsion', *The Daily Telegraph*, London, 21 February 1998.
28. John Carlin and Robert Fisk, 'Sanctions are true weapons of mass destruction – better to be bombed', *The Independent on Sunday*, London, 22 February 1998.
29. Ed Vulliamy and Patrick Wintour, 'They both blinked at the brink of war', *The Observer*, London, 22 February 1998.
30. 'A breakthrough', *The Daily Telegraph*, London, 23 February 1998.
31. *Ibid.*
32. Hugo Gurdon, 'America's hawks rule the roost', *The Daily Telegraph*, London, 23 February 1998.
33. Christopher Lockwood, 'Saddam again finds victory in defeat', *The Daily Telegraph*, London, 23 February 1998.
34. Anton La Guardia, 'US is losing battle after winning war', *The Daily Telegraph*, London, 23 February 1998.
35. Hugo Gurdon, 'Americans angered by UN "pact with the devil"', *The Daily Telegraph*, London, 24 February 1998.
36. *Ibid.*
37. Tim Butcher and Hugo Gurdon, 'Iraqis begin to unpick UN deal', *The Daily Telegraph*, London, 26 February 1998; Hugo Gurdon and Tim Butcher, 'Deal "threatens arms checks" on Iraq', *The Daily Telegraph*, London, 26 February 1998.
38. See, for example, David Fairhall, 'Russia "continues to develop new germ weapons"', *The Guardian*, London, 26 February 1998.
39. Letter (19 February 1998) from the Executive Chairman ..., plus enclosures, S/1998/176, 27 February 1998.
40. See, for example, *ibid.*, pp. 17–20, 35–40.
41. *Jordan Times*, 28 February 1998.
42. Jon Swain, 'Annan guns for UN's top arms hunter', *The Sunday Times*, London, 1 March 1998.
43. *Ibid.*
44. Robert Fisk, 'Deadly legacies of war', *The Independent*, London, 5 March 1998.

45. Robert Fisk, 'Inside Baghdad's "ward of death"', *The Independent*, London, 5 March 1998; Robert Fisk, 'Iraq's children cling on for a grim life', *The Independent*, London, 6 March 1998; Jon Swain, 'Allied shells linked to Iraqi child cancers', *The Sunday Times*, London, 8 March 1998; Robert Fisk, 'Children starve, Saddam survives', *The Independent on Sunday*, London, 8 March 1998.
46. Letter (6 March 1998) from the Minister for Foreign Affairs of Iraq, addressed to the Secretary-General, S/1998/207, 8 March 1998.
47. *Ibid.*
48. Ian Black, 'Iraq passes first UNSCOM test as searches resume', *The Guardian*, London, 7 March 1998.
49. The evidence for this statement is a CBS *60 Minutes* interview (12 May 1996) of Madeleine Albright by Lesley Stahl:

> *Lesley Stahl*: 'We have heard that half a million children have died [as a result of sanctions against Iraq]. I mean, that is more children than died in Hiroshima ... is the price worth it?'
> *Madeleine Albright* (then US ambassador to the United Nations, now Secretary of State): '... we think the price is worth it'.

50. Hugo Gurdon, 'CIA agents "were on Saddam's payroll"', *The Daily Telegraph*, London, 12 March 1998.
51. Matthew Brace, 'Sailors in Royal Navy's Gulf flotilla turn to harming themselves', *The Independent*, London, 14 March 1998.
52. Ian Black, 'UN's plain speaker back in Iraq', *The Guardian*, London, 21 March 1998.
53. Ian Black, 'Baghdad spies bugging Unscom members', *The Guardian*, London, 21 March 1998.
54. Anthony Bevins, 'All-ports alert over Saddam "plot" to smuggle anthrax into Britain', *The Independent*, London, 24 March 1998; Lucy Ward, 'Saddam anthrax plot warning', *The Guardian*, London, 24 March 1998.
55. Ed Vulliamy, 'Anthrax follies', *The Guardian*, London, 25 March 1998; Richard Norton-Taylor and Ian Black, 'Ministers sound retreat on anthrax warning', *The Guardian*, London, 25 March 1998.
56. Vulliamy, 'Anthrax folies', *op. cit.*; see also Auberon Waugh, 'Sniffing the air for anthrax', *The Sunday Telegraph*, London, 29 March 1998.
57. Richard Norton-Taylor and Ian Black, 'Propaganda drive against Iraq', *The Guardian*, London, 25 March 1998.
58. David Fairhall, 'Gulf heat on "jump" jets forces carrier to abandon Iraq patrol', *The Guardian*, London, 26 March 1998.
59. Letter (27 March 1998) from the Executive Chairman of the Special Commission ... addressed to the President of the Security Council, S/1998/278, 27 March 1998.
60. Waugh, 'Sniffing the air', *op. cit.*
61. Toby Moore, 'Anthrax is found at King's Cross', *The Daily Express*, London, 4 April 1998.
62. Anton La Guardia, 'Annan praises Iraq for opening palace gates', *The Daily Telegraph*, London, 31 March 1998.
63. Report of the UNSCOM team to the technical evaluation meeting on the prescribed biological warfare programme, submitted by Richard Butler, S/1998/308, 1 April 1998.

64. Richard Savill, 'Cancer flight MP denies helping Saddam', *The Daily Telegraph*, London, 15 April 1998; Lawrence Donegan, 'Row over mercy mission for Iraqi', *The Guardian*, London, 15 April 1998; Stephen Farrell, 'Iraqi leukaemia girl reaches UK on mercy flight', *The Times* London, 16 April 1998; Susie Steiner, 'MP denies leukaemia girl is Baghdad's pawn', *The Daily Telegraph*, London, 16 April 1998.
65. Farrell, 'Iraqi leukaemia girl', *op. cit.*
66. Felicity Arbuthnot, 'On the wards of despair', *The Independent*, London, 16 April 1998.
67. Report of the Special Group established for entries into Iraqi presidential sites, submitted by the Secretary-General to the President of the Security Council, S/1998/326, 15 April 1998.
68. *Ibid.*, paragraph 23.
69. 'Doubts over Iraq inspections', *Reuters*, *The Guardian*, London, 16 April 1998; Hugo Gurdon, 'Saddam will break Annan agreement, says UN inspector', *The Daily Telegraph*, London, 16 April 1998.
70. Letter (17 April 1998) from the Permanent Representative of Iraq to the United Nations, addressed to the Secretary-General, S/1998/334, 17 April 1998.
71. *Ibid.*
72. Hugo Gurdon, 'Saddam's palaces "stripped bare" before UN visits', *The Daily Telegraph*, London, 18 April 1998.
73. Patrick Cockburn, 'Iraqi economy has gone to the dogs', *The Independent*, London, 18 April 1998.
74. This aspect is explored in detail in Geoff Simons, *The Scourging of Iraq: Sanctions, Law and Natural Justice* (Basingstoke: Macmillan, 2nd edition, 1998); Ian Black, 'Britain leads move to ease Iraqi misery', *The Guardian*, London, 21 April 1998.
75. Simons, *Scourging of Iraq, op. cit.*, p. 241.
76. Letter (22 April 1998) from the Deputy Prime Minister of Iraq, addressed to the President of the Security Council, S/1998/342.
77. The accumulating evidence on the effects of sanctions is now copious (much is presented in Simons, *Scourging of Iraq, op. cit.*). See, for example, Simon Faulkner, 'Sanctions on Iraq' (letter), *The Independent*, London, 23 April 1998; Patrick Cockburn, 'Children die as sanctions crush Iraq', *The Independent*, London, 21 April 1998; Patrick Cockburn, 'Poisoned Tigris spreads tide of death in Iraq', *The Independent*, London, 25 April 1998.
78. Ian Black, 'Countdown to confrontation begins as UN enrages Iraq', *The Guardian*, London, 29 April 1998.
79. Press briefings by UNSCOM Executive Chairman, 28 April 1998.
80. Press briefings by Foreign and Oil Ministers of Iraq, 28 April 1998.
81. Ian Black (29 April 1998), *op. cit.*

Bibliography

Blum, William, *The CIA: A Forgotten History: US Global Intervention since World War 2* (London and New Jersey: Zed Books, 1986).

Carter, Barry E., *International Economic Sanctions* (New York: Cambridge University Press, 1988).

Clark, Ramsey and others, *War Crimes: A Report on United States War Crimes against Iraq* (Washington, DC: Maisonneuve Press, 1992).

Doxey, Margaret P., *Economic Sanctions and International Enforcement* (London: Macmillan for the Royal Institute of Economic Affairs, 1980).

—— *International Sanctions in Contemporary Perspective* (London: Macmillan, 1987).

George, Alexander (ed.), *Western State Terrorism* (Cambridge: Polity Press, 1991).

Hiro, Dilip, *Desert Shield to Desert Storm: The Second Gulf War* (London: Paladin, 1992).

Leyton-Brown, David (ed.), *The Utility of International Economic Sanctions* (London: Croom Helm, 1987).

MacArthur, John R., *Second Front: Censorship and Propaganda in the Gulf War* (New York, 1992).

Salinger, Pierre, and Laurent, Eric, *Secret Dossier: The Hidden Agenda Behind the Gulf War* (London: Penguin, 1991).

Simons, Geoff, *Iraq: From Sumer to Saddam* (Basingstoke: Macmillan, 2nd edition, 1996).

—— *Libya: The Struggle for Survival* (Basingstoke: Macmillan, 2nd edition, 1996).

—— *Saudi Arabia: The Shape of a Client Feudalism* (Basingstoke: Macmillan, 1998).

—— *The Scourging of Iraq: Sanctions, Law and Natural Justice* (Basingstoke: Macmillan, 2nd edition, 1998).

—— *UN Malaise: Power, Problems and Realpolitik* (Basingstoke: Macmillan, 1995).

Taylor, Philip M., *War and the Media: Propaganda and Persuasion in the Gulf War* (Manchester and New York: Manchester University Press, 1992).

Timmerman, Kenneth R., *The Death Lobby: How the West Armed Iraq* (London: Fourth Estate, 1992).

Woodward, Bob, *The Commanders* (New York: Simon and Schuster, 1991).

Index